This book assesses the efforts of successive British government policies to promote the vocational education, training and employment of young people. Based on extensive field research, it presents a comprehensive survey of this important and developing branch of labour economics. The author looks at the subject both historically and analytically, using an examination of human capital theory and the economic theory of training to provide a context for his research. He relates demographic, educational, economic and technological developments to the effects of successive government training and employment schemes on young people, on employers and on the national economy. He looks at the relationship between the attainment of skills by young people on official training schemes and the demand for skills, and goes on to examine the views of critics of government policies and the reactions of the trade unions. Through a comparison with the alternative, no-policy position, Mr Deakin detects an erratic policy-learning process which has important implications for future government policy in this area.

University of Cambridge
Department of Applied Economics

Occasional paper 62

The youth labour market in Britain: the role of intervention

DAE Occasional papers

Earlier titles in this series and in the DAE Papers in Industrial Relations and Labour Series may be obtained from:
The Publications Secretary, Department of Applied Economics, Sidgwick Avenue, Cambridge CB3 9DE

The youth labour market in Britain: the role of intervention

B. M. DEAKIN

CAMBRIDGE
UNIVERSITY PRESS

Published by the Press Syndicate of the University of Cambridge
The Pitt Building, Trumpington Street, Cambridge CB2 1RP
40 West 20th Street, New York, NY 10011-4211, USA
10 Stamford Road, Oakleigh, Melbourne 3166, Australia

Printed in Great Britain at the University Press, Cambridge

A catalogue record for this book is available from the British Library

Library of Congress cataloguing in publication data

Deakin, B. M. (Brian Measures)
  The youth labour market in Britain: the role of intervention /
B. M. Deakin.
      p.   cm. — (Occasional paper / University of Cambridge.
Department of Applied Economics : 62)
  Includes bibliographical references and index.
  ISBN 0 521 55328 8 (hc)
  1. Youth — Employment — Government policy — Great Britain.
2. Occupational training — Government policy — Great Britain.
I. Title.   II. Series: Occasional papers (University of Cambridge.
Dept. of Applied Economics) : 62.
HD6276.G7D4   1996
331.3'4'0941 — dc20   95–35113   CIP

ISBN 0 521 55328 8 hardback

Contents

Tables

Preface and acknowledgements

Preface

The purpose of this study is to examine and assess the role of intervention by government in the youth labour market in Britain. The economic context of that intervention is drawn in broad terms and the subject is treated historically and analytically.

In recent years the results of a large amount of specialised academic and policy-oriented research have been published on various aspects of this subject. In the present study a broader treatment is offered. This is because, over time, demographic, educational and economic factors have changed greatly and have influenced conditions in the youth labour market. A study of these factors is seen as necessary to the assessments of the impact of government intervention which are made here. The chief aim of these assessments is to estimate the effects of policies upon the youth labour market and upon the employability of young people compared with the alternative, no-policy position. With the future in mind, an attempt is also made to detect the existence of a policy-learning process.

Acknowledgements

This book has been made possible by the award to me of an Emeritus Fellowship by the Leverhulme Trust, which I most gratefully acknowledge.

Some of the data on which analyses in this book are based, and some of the methodology used, come from three policy research studies which I undertook at the Department of Applied Economics between 1985 and 1990 jointly with the following colleagues, to whom I acknowledge my debt: I. G. Begg, A. P. Blake, J. P. Dunne and C. F. Pratten. The results of these three studies are in unpublished, 'mimeo' form. References are made to them in the text and their titles are given in the Bibliography. They were sponsored by the Department of Employment (1985), the Manpower

Services Commission (1987) and the Training Agency (1989), and I gratefully acknowledge the financial support for these studies from these sources.

I have been enabled, by the financial support from the Leverhulme Trust's Fellowship, to engage two Research Assistants, and I wish to thank Stephen Purdom and Moira Wilson for their meticulous work and helpful comments and suggestions.

My colleagues Iain Begg and Paul Ryan read and made valuable comments on early drafts. I am grateful to them, and also to an anonymous reader who greatly helped me to improve and extend my treatment of the subject.

I am indebted to Ann Newton for her care in editing the whole text, and to Anne Mason, Suzanne Fletcher and Shani Douglas, who prepared the typescript with exemplary efficiency and patience through the hazards of many drafts.

My wife Leila greatly helped me by reading numerous drafts and making valuable editorial comments and suggestions.

All of those named above are of course entirely innocent of any errors of fact or analysis which may remain in the text and for which I am solely responsible.

B.M.D.

April 1995

1 Introduction

The processes of vocational education and training greatly influence the character and value of both the supply of and the demand for the labour of young people, and therefore the functioning of the youth labour market. It is a commonly held view that these processes are important both for the economic welfare of young people and for the economic prosperity of the country, but the underlying reasons for that view are rarely examined. It is one of the purposes of this introduction to make such an examination before going on to a study of the youth labour market in Britain and the role that government intervention plays in it.

This chapter is divided into five sections. The *first* is concerned with the concept of investment in human capital, and with the results of empirical work which have shown the yield of such investment in terms of its contribution to economic output and productivity. The *second* provides a concise treatment of the economics of training, which is concerned with the process of investment in young people and the return upon it. The *third* contains an introduction to the features of the youth labour market. The *fourth* introduces certain broad macroeconomic considerations which are influential in the training and vocational processes, and the *fifth* provides an outline of the study.

Investment in human capital

The processes of general education, vocational education and training for skilled work are regarded by many economists as investment in human capital. In modern times (the second half of the twentieth century, say), the landmark study is the work of G. S. Becker, *Human Capital: A Theoretical and Empirical Analysis, with Special Reference to Education* (first edition 1964, second edition 1975). The concept of human capital is a very old one. Its historical roots are explored by Kiker (1966, 1971), who has noted the contributions made by Sir William Petty (1691), Adam Smith (1776), J. B.

1

Say (1803), N. W. Senior (1836), J. H. Von Thünen (1875), L. Walras (1877), E. Engel (1883), and I. Fisher (1906), among others, all of whom regarded human beings or their skills as capital. Economists who have used the human capital concept have done so for various purposes, including that of awakening the public to the need for life and health conservation and, of particular relevance to any economic theory of training, to determine the economic effects of investment in education and training.

If the concept of human capital is accepted, one logical development of economic thought is the assessment, in theoretical and empirical terms, of its contribution to the process of economic growth and wealth creation.

The mechanisms of economic growth occupy a broad band of economic theory, and some economists have attempted to isolate and assess the contribution of human capital to the growth process. An early attempt was made by J. S. Nicholson (1891). In his article in the *Economic Journal* for March 1891 he argues that labour, which he describes as 'living capital', is responsible for the large majority of the nation's income and wealth: 'It is plain that the value of the greater part of moveable property (dead capital) would indeed be dead but for the acquired abilities of the inhabitants (living capital).' He values the total capitalised wealth of the United Kingdom at £55 billion, of which living capital is estimated at £47 billion, 85%.

In more recent times, other economists who have studied this aspect are O. Aukrust (1959) and E. F. Denison (1967, 1974, 1985). R. M. Solow (1957, 1959) argues for at least a partial return to the view that investment in other forms of capital is relatively more important, but he acknowledges the strength of Aukrust's case for the role of investment in labour, differing mainly on the degree of contribution to economic growth by each factor of production.

Aukrust's attempt to explain the component contributions to economic growth was made for the Norwegian economy over the period 1948–55. He finds that the recorded growth rate of 3.4% per annum is divided as to 0.46% p.a. due to increased labour input, 1.12% p.a. due to increased capital input, and 1.81% p.a. to 'better organisation'. Further analysis leads him to conclude:

The rate of growth which can be attained in a modern industrial economy is not strongly influenced by the investment policy which is applied. Whether investments (in physical assets) are high or low, within reasonable limits, national product will increase by 2–3% a year, if the volume of employment remains constant. This is mainly because the human factor alone is sufficient to ensure a growth of 1.5% a year.

Many others, including Solow (1957), Colin Clark (1961), Deakin (1962), have emphasised the *increasing* importance over time of the technological or organisational factor in the production function. This factor is variously described; it clearly includes Alfred Marshall's 'organisation' as a factor of production (Marshall 1890, Book IV, ch. 1, pp. 138–9), and also involves general and vocational education and human skills, as well as applied technical and organisational knowledge arising from the results of technical progress and operational research, all of which arise from investment in human capital.

Labour contributes to output in both quantitative and qualitative terms. The production function approach includes both these aspects. The qualitative aspect, and the contribution to output which stems from it, is included in productivity measures of output per labour hour or, more usefully, per unit of total factor input. That type of measure is considered next.

The sources of economic growth have been intensively and extensively studied by E. F. Denison (1967, 1974 and 1985). In his extensive and seminal comparative study *Why Growth Rates Differ* (1967), Denison compares the relative importance of the various sources of economic growth in the United States and in eight European countries, including the United Kingdom. His analyses for the United States and the United Kingdom have been adapted to match the form of the present analysis, while maintaining comparability, to show (Table 1.1) the relative importance in the growth of productivity (measured here in terms of output per unit of total factor input) of increases in the input of 'education and knowledge' (Denison's terms, the meanings of which are expanded in the notes to Table 1.1).

In the period 1950–62, studied by Denison (1967), the United States economy expanded rather faster than that of the United Kingdom. In both countries the rate of increase in the *quantity* of labour input was small (due in part to hours of work declining) in relation to capital input and in relation to the *qualitative* factors of education and knowledge, which should be regarded as the yield of prior investments in human capital. The input of these *qualitative* factors is measured (in Table 1.1) against increases in output per unit of total factor input in *quantitative* terms. *Changes* in education and in the application of knowledge to the production processes of the whole economy accounted for 67% of the total productivity increase in the United States and 71% in the United Kingdom. (The sum of rows 3a and 3b as a percentage of row 3 in Table 1.1.)

Later studies by Denison (1985) of the sources of long-term economic growth have confirmed earlier conclusions, and have further specified some other influences, such as the negative contributions from pollution abatement, worker safety and health regulations, dishonesty and crime, and labour disputes (Denison 1985, Table 8.1). Over the long-run period 1929–82, Denison finds that, for the United States economy, labour quality

Table 1.1 *Sources of economic growth of total national income in the United States and the United Kingdom, 1950–62 (average cumulative rates of change p.a. at factor cost and constant prices)*

	United States	United Kingdom
1 National income	3.32	2.29
2 Total factor input (excluding labour quality) of which due to changes in:	1.46	0.82
a labour quantity	0.63	0.31
b capital	0.83	0.51
c land	0.00	0.00
3 Output per unit of total factor input of which due to changes in: a labour quality, due to	1.86	1.47
education[a]	0.49 (26%)	0.29 (20%)
b knowledge[b]	0.76 (41%)	0.76 (51%)
	1.25 (67%)	1.05 (71%)
c improved resource allocation	0.29	0.12
d scale economies	0.36	0.36
e other factors[c]	−0.04	−0.06
	1.86	1.47

Notes:
[a]Full-time education in schools and colleges.
[b]Includes all part-time vocational education and training as well as applications of technical change and improved organisation.
[c]Irregularities in the pressure of demand, changes in the lag in the application of knowledge, general efficiency, and errors and omissions.
Source: Adapted from Denison (1967), Tables 21.1, and 21.17.

from education contributed 28% of the increase in total factor productivity, and knowledge 47%, a total contribution of 75%. The negative contributions, which have been specified, reduced total factor productivity. If they are disregarded, the greater resultant increase in total factor productivity would have made the contributions from labour quality due to education, and from the application of knowledge, relatively smaller at 73%.

Later studies and developments in growth theory have also emphasised the important role of labour skills and abilities in the economic growth process.

R. Dornbusch and S. Fischer (1990, p. 718) review empirical work on the sources of economic growth, including the valuable contributions from Solow and Denison.

Their conclusions, which are supported by the adapted results from Denison which are given above, are as follows:

Advances in knowledge and efficiency stand out as the major sources [of economic growth] *and point to the roles of research, education and training as important sources of growth.* (Italics in the original.)

Maddison (1972, pp. 31, 32) has suggested that Denison underestimated the contribution of both education and training to the increase in total factor productivity, and Mincer (1962) estimated that on-the-job training and work experience combined were about as important as general education.

In a recent study Oulton and O'Mahony (1994) find that growth in British industry (chiefly manufacturing industry) over the period 1954–85 owes less than previously thought to increases in productivity due to largely exogenous factors such as disembodied technical progress, and more to the quantity and quality of factor inputs (Oulton and O'Mahony, p. 117). In more detail, they attempt to find an explanation for Fabricant's Law (which is that there is a positive correlation between output growth and productivity growth). In doing so they examine the hypothesis that causation runs from (exogenous) technical progress via changes in relative prices to output growth. They find that hypothesis unsupported by the evidence (Oulton and O'Mahony, p. 180). These authors do not disaggregate the qualitative factors in economic growth as Denison does. However, their finding that movements in factor inputs are the major influence upon growth of output leads to emphasis upon the quality of those inputs. From that it may be inferred (by others) that there is a need for a high level of general and vocational education and of training to ensure the optimal use of human resources, which are employed directly as labour input and also indirectly as capital input, in order to maximise economic growth.

The influence upon economic growth of the yield from various modes of investment in human capital is clearly very great. Investment in vocational education and training is one of these modes. That type of investment is considered next.

The economics of training

The economics of training is a recent and not yet well-developed branch of the general body of economic theory. Contributions made by G. S. Becker (1962, 1964, 1975), J. Mincer (1962), D. Lees and B. Chiplin (1970), P. G. Chapman and M. J. Tooze (1987), E. Katz and A. Ziderman (1990), P. G.

Chapman (1993) and M. Stevens (1994a, b) provide some theory and empirical evidence which sheds light on what has now become an essentially tripartite process of investment in human skills by the trainee, the employer and the government.

Investment in human skills may be analysed and evaluated in a way which is similar to that used for investment in building, plant or equipment. Production of the asset and its improvement are comparable processes in both cases. The decision to invest in people, as in other assets, should depend upon a comparison of the cost of the investment with the expected future returns upon it discounted back to the present at a rate which is at least equal to the current rate of interest.[1]

Becker (1975, p. 26) makes the useful but rather limited distinction between phases of training which he sees as a two-stage process:

Completely *general* training increases the marginal productivity of trainees by exactly the same amount in firms providing the training as in other firms . . . Completely *specific* training can be defined as training that has no effect on the productivity of trainees that would be useful in other firms.

For the first stage, that of general training, trainees invest in themselves by accepting low, sometimes very low pay. They cannot normally raise capital for further investment (e.g. for training fees) at this first stage, nor indeed for the second stage. Other first-stage investment in training is in the form of supervisory costs, training materials and the overhead costs of training at an employer's premises. The employer is likely to be reluctant to undertake this first-stage investment, because the labour mobility conferred upon the basically-trained workers may lead to their recruitment ('poaching') by other employers who do not undertake general training and who thereby benefit from the first employer's investment.

Under conditions of perfect competition, assumed to begin with by Becker, the employer will not invest *any* capital in the basic, general training of school leavers, because the productivity so gained by the trainee would be available to other employers under completely free market conditions. Under such conditions, the trainee would have to meet all the costs of such training by accepting very low pay, or none at all, or pay the employer for his training, depending upon his ability to produce saleable output for the training employer during the first phase of general training.

There are two market externalities here which influence the decision to undertake general training and they contribute to a failure to invest in

---

[1] Support for the concept of training as an investment process is provided by an empirical model constructed by Stevens (1994b). She has shown that the decline in apprentice training in the British engineering industry, 1966–88, was due to high real interest rates, among other explanatory variables.

training under free market conditions. The first is the capital market's failure to provide credit for investment in his or her own training by the typically young prospective trainee. The trainee is unlikely to be able to provide collateral for a loan, and the risk may be seen as high. This is the so-called 'individual externality'. The second barrier to training and a cause of market failure is the externality between firms. This influences the decision to undertake general training by creating uncertainty in both the training firm, about whether 'poaching' will occur and to what extent, and in the 'poaching' firm about whether the training firm will continue to train when 'poaching' occurs and if so for how long, and thus whether the 'poacher' should train. These considerations, which are analysed by Chapman (1993, pp. 96–9), inhibit the decision to undertake general training.

Under more realistic conditions of imperfect competition there must be some doubt as to whether the increased productivity which the trainee gains from the first stage of basic training does confer mobility to an extent which deters the investment in basic training by the employer. Imperfections in youth labour markets, including young people's imperfect knowledge of job opportunities, and the local monopsonist position which some employers possess, is likely to limit mobility to some extent. Furthermore, it has been argued by Katz and Ziderman (1990) that recruiters in firms which do no training ('the poachers') 'do not possess much information on the extent and type of workers' on-the-job training. Workers taken on as trained [in the general sense] may turn out to possess no, or very little, general training'. Hence, asymmetry of information will cause the value of a worker with general training to be highest in his training firm, and therefore investment in general training will tend to be shared by the trainee and the training employer. If accepted, this somewhat modifies Becker's basic thesis. However, these authors also argue that a process of certification of training (which is now more usual than it was in the past) will tend to overcome the asymmetry of information and so return us to Becker's thesis, where this informational point fits with Becker's first assumption of perfect competition.

The second phase of training is investment in higher skills. In so far as these are specific and closely related to the employer's business, the return upon his investment in them may be more secure. The trained person is more likely to remain in the business in which he was trained, particularly so if the employer is either a local or national monopsonist in the labour market for the skills concerned. This aspect is developed by Oatey (1970), who shows how the mobility of young workers trained in specific (and general) skills is restricted under conditions of monopsony in the youth labour market. There is the additional consideration here that only the employer can judge the changing market for his product and accordingly the labour services he needs to meet that demand. It follows that he is in the best position to judge the return upon his investment in specific training, whether he has a fair chance of receiving the returns from it (the risk involved), and thus whether he will undertake it. The trainee will benefit from such investment and will share in it with the employer by accepting wages which at the start of the higher training process are relatively low compared with the earnings of a fully-trained worker, but which rise as training progresses, reflecting rising productivity, and approximately conforming to the productivity–earnings equilibrium of (marginalist) wage theory. The apprenticeship system puts this process into practice, but it is also seen in other forms of training for higher skills. However, a further externality may enter here, one between the firm and the individual trainee. It concerns their relative shares in the cost of specific training. Under a rigid wage system, possibly due to union intervention, uncertainty will arise as to how productivity will increase under training and therefore how the *net* benefits to both parties will be distributed. A mutually beneficial training opportunity may be foregone owing to this externality.

Not all the higher skills achieved through apprenticeships, or similar training schemes, are necessarily unique to the training employer's business, and there is not in all cases a clear-cut distinction between general and specific training. Some engineering and computer skills, for example, are transferable, and 'poaching' by other employers can and does occur during training and after its completion.

The social returns from investment in human capital, and particularly from the training of young people, are likely to exceed the private returns at times of economic recession. The private returns will include those estimated by the employers. Such estimates will vary widely with the business cycle, and the private return upon investment in training may be very low at times of economic recession. In addition, there are the externalities which have been noted and which contribute to market disequilibrium.

The trainee also must be expected to consider the return upon his investment in himself. He is investing by accepting low pay during training, and he may judge that the present and expected future return to him in the form of earnings is better with another employer. The optimum social rate of return will involve the best that is obtainable in relation to the talents of the individual and the benefits to society, and should include the benefit to the trainee of realising and employing his or her full capabilities. These benefits should be contrasted with the wastage of unemployment, and also the under-development of potential talent leading to monotonous unskilled employment without prospects.

Given the risk and uncertainty involved, the amount of investment in training may, over the long term, be inadequate if the whole process is left to private employers and individual trainees. To demonstrate this, an attempt is now made to apply an economic theory of training to the first and second stages of the training process, as defined by Becker (1975). More recently Chapman (1993) has developed Becker's earlier contribution to provide some guidelines on the relationships between the *private* costs and benefits of training and the employer's equilibrium. But he enters a useful early warning: 'a full unification of theory and practice [of training] is not practicable in the present state of knowledge' (Chapman 1993, p. 1).

The following two-stage model is adapted from Chapman, and a social dimension with government intervention is added.

In the first stage, when general training is given, the employer's equilibrium may be written:

$$W_A + T_A = MP_A + TI_A$$

where:

W_A is the trainee's wage during general training.
T_A is the actual cost of general training.
MP_A is the marginal product of the trainee during general training.
TI_A is the employer's investment in general training.

This equation does not show how total costs and benefits are distributed. But if it is assumed that the trainee is paid a wage (W_A) which is equal to his or her marginal product (MP_A), then $T_A = TI_A$ which involves the employer making the total investment in general training. The employer will then look to the increased marginal product of the ex-trainee when, in the post-training period, the ex-trainee is employed in work which matches the general skill acquired in the training period in order to obtain, over a period of time, an adequate return upon the employer's investment in general training (TI_A). That will involve holding the skilled wage of the ex-trainee (W_S) below the level of his marginal product (MP_S).

However, the acquisition of general skills confers labour market mobility upon the ex-trainee, and a post-training wage equal to marginal product can be obtained from another employer. That situation provides the opportunity for employers who do no general training to 'poach' ex-trainees from those who do. If 'poaching' is prevalent and therefore expected, the training employer is likely to ensure that $MP_A - W_A = T_A$. That implies that under a 'poaching' regime the trainee pays the cost of general training and reaps the whole benefit of it.

The results of this process are likely to be: (i) the low training wage will discourage young people from undertaking basic training because their prospective wage in unskilled employment will be greater, and (ii) employers will be discouraged from offering training places because their gain from training is reduced to zero, or below zero if the employer fails, through insufficient anticipation of 'poaching', to transfer all general training costs to the trainee.

In the second stage, training is in skills which are specific to the training employer's business and, it is assumed, are in demand only in that business. In these circumstances the employer will seek an equilibrium during the training period where the gain from specific training (G) is equal to the cost of that training (T_B), so that $MP_B - W_B = G = T_B$, where MP_B and W_B are respectively the marginal product and the wage of the second-stage trainee.

Becker has suggested that in practice G will be shared with the trainee in the proportion α to the trainee. So that $G = (1 - \alpha) T_B$, and $W_B = MP_B - \alpha T_B$. But he gives no guidance on how the value of α is determined, so the only conclusion is that there is a sharing of the total investment in second-stage training between employer and trainee. It may also be shown that these shares are influenced by the post-training situation with regard to the productivity of the newly-trained worker and his or her wage. That is not pursued here because uncertainty regarding shares remains (Chapman 1993, p. 42).

Social costs and benefits are clearly involved in both stages of training youth labour. By way of illustration only: as regards social costs there are those which arise from the unemployment of school leavers who are so placed owing to lack of training. To these costs must be added those due in the longer term to loss of welfare: these are the social costs to the individual and to the economy as a whole due to the underdevelopment of talent and ability, the effects of which may endure in whole or part for a lifetime. The social benefits of training lie in the prevention of these social losses, and also in the gains to the individual and whole economy of trained, rather than untrained, manpower and the higher level of welfare which may be expected to arise from successful training processes.

Both private and social losses occur when youth labour market failure is brought about by a failure to train for the reasons which have been demonstrated. The reduction of such losses by government intervention may be considered. If it is now assumed that a government subsidy to general training (S_A) is provided and made equal to the cost of general training (T_A) then:

$$W_A + T_A = MP_A + S_A$$

There is now no requirement for investment in general training by the training employer. Therefore $W_A = MP_A$, and the trainee does not have to bear the cost of investment in general training, nor the risks involved in that process. These circumstances are likely to encourage both trainees and employers to engage in general training.

After the successful completion of their general training, trainees are assured, by youth labour market competition, of obtaining their marginal product whether or not their employment is with the training employer or another one. Trainees gain the benefit of training, as they did without subsidy (provided they were 'poached'), but in the subsidy case they do not have to bear the cost of their general training either during the training period or afterwards, even if they stay with the training employer.

A subsidy (S_B) to the second stage of training, which is specific to the training employer's business, reduces the cost of investment in training so that:

$$G = (1 - \alpha)(T_B - S_B)$$

and

$$W_B = MP_B - \alpha(T_B - S_B)$$

As previously noted, it is not known how the value of α is distributed, and it now applies to the value of $T_B - S_B$. So the gain, which is equal to the cost of training *net* of the training subsidy is shared between training employer and trainee in a proportion governed by the value of α. This provides minimal guidance only. If $S_B = T_B$, trainees will get wages equal to their marginal product. G will be zero, and the gain from training will be with the trainees under free labour market conditions, but in so far as training is specific to the training employer's business there is some monopsony power in the hands of the employer which may or may not be used. Whether or not that is so is examined in relation to the evidence given in Chapters 9 and 10.

Governments have in fact invested in vocational education and training in partnership with trainees and with employers who have provided on-the-job training. Because the risk of loss of the employer's investment in training is greater in the first phase of general, basic training, the government's share of investment in that phase may need to be a large proportion of the total. In the second phase of training, that for higher skills, the vocational educational element may be seen as forming part of the government's share on grounds similar to those which support the application of public funds for general education. The social costs of not training in the second phase should inform government decisions concerning further investment in that period, and such a consideration will be particularly relevant during downswings in the business cycle, when the private sector is likely to under-invest in training.

The rate of return upon investment in training has been shown by Mincer (1962) to be high, though his estimates are tentative and only broad indications in relation to the rate of return on investment in general education are given. Mincer concludes from an empirical study of United States data that: (i) 'Investment in on-the-job training is a very large component of total investment in education. Measured by cost it is as important as formal education for the male labour force and amounts to more than half of total expenditure (for both males and females) on school education.' And, (ii) 'The rate of return on selected investments in on-the-job training, such as apprentices . . . was not different from the rate of return on total costs of college education.'

Features of the youth labour market

A precise, somewhat legalistic definition of youth labour would be young people included in the group bounded by the statutory school leaving age of 16 and the attainment of adult legal status at age 18. But some vocational education and training processes can start at school as early as age 14 and some can continue to the end of a full apprenticeship of four years at age 20. The present treatment will cover the age range 14–20, with a narrower specification as necessary at particular junctures.

The youth labour market may be taken as being the market for trainees, trained young people and others seeking training places or jobs ex-school who fall within the age range 16–20, but precise definitions have not been laid down by others, and that is not done here.

The broad characteristics of the youth labour market, its institutional features and some of the special aspects which arise from the process of training and skill acquisition, are briefly described below for their contextual and introductory values in advance of the market analyses and treatments which are contained in later chapters.

The national youth labour market is no more coherent conceptually than the national labour market. The segmentation of the national market due to the immobility of labour and the non-competitiveness between skilled occupations is common to both, although inter-skill mobility among trainees is somewhat greater in the youth market, and is in fact facilitated by the main government training scheme, Youth Training, which allows switches between training programmes for different skills.

The institutionalist approach to labour market economics has application to the youth market in the broad segmentation which divides young people who receive the more formal training leading to acquisition of higher skills, and thence to so-called *primary* employment associated with relatively high wages, from those who receive no more than general, basic training which provides at best *secondary* employment which requires little skill and attracts relatively low pay.

Further market divisions occur between trained young people. There are those who are trained, usually in larger firms, and who then enter the *internal* youth labour market (ILM), that is, they obtain employment in the firms in which they were trained; and those who move after training into the *occupational* labour market (OLM), that is the youth labour market which is external to the training firm.

These divisions or segmentations are relevant to a study of government intervention in the training process.

Other institutional elements are also influential in the operation of the youth market: in particular, the influence of trade unions upon the terms, conditions and pay of trainees, and also of trained young workers in that market. In this regard, Garonna and Ryan (1991) have shown that the transition of youth from school to employment may cause problems to the existing labour force by offering competition through their acceptance of relatively low rates of pay which, despite the lower productivity of young workers, may pose a threat to adult jobs. Trade unions have entered here to raise youth pay and control entry, and their influence is examined in Chapter 14 of the present study. It may be noted here that in so far as employers are reluctant to train because of the high cost of youth pay and additionally, as already noted, because of the risk of loss of those recently trained to a general level, the government's intervention process has a higher hurdle to overcome in order to induce extra training places.

The youth labour market is more prone than the national market to large fluctuation and to periods of massive disequilibrium. That is due to a number of factors which are studied later: the chief of these are the swings in supply which are large relative to the size of the youth market and which are due chiefly to demographic influences, and also to changes in the number of young people who continue their academic or vocational education on a full-time basis. Changes in the educational attainment of school leavers are also influential in market disequilibrium, as are broad movements in the demand for all labour and changes in technology and in youth labour market structure.

The causes of the long-term upward trend in youth unemployment in Britain, which began in the early 1970s, have been analysed by Hart (1988), who found supply, demand and structural causes. That trend is examined in the present study in relation to the interventionist policies of governments which were brought about by the economic and social losses which such unemployment was causing.

Broader macroeconomic considerations

The broader, macroeconomic context of vocational education and training is examined under two aspects. The *first* of these is concerned with labour as a natural resource endowment in relation to the other natural resource endowments, particularly land and energy resources. (Capital is a man-made factor of production and its quantity and quality depend basically upon the factor labour and upon management.)

The *second* aspect is concerned with movements in the national supply of labour. Since a very large proportion of total investment in human resources takes place when people are less than 21 years of age, the size of the vehicle for the whole process of such investment clearly depends upon the number of young people, and therefore upon the demographic influences which stem from changes in the birth rate and upon the factors which influence that rate.

As regards the first aspect, the relative economic importance of labour as a factor of production is likely to vary between countries. Some countries, for example Canada, are generously endowed with other natural resources, particularly land, energy and other mineral resources, while other countries such as Japan and the United Kingdom have relatively few non-labour natural resource endowments. The potential for economic growth and welfare is likely to vary for this reason, among many others. The *relative* importance of labour will also be a factor in the competitive advantage of a country, and a country's dependence upon external trade is likely to be inversely related to its non-labour resource endowment. So the relative importance of labour, and of investment in labour, needs to be gauged from a consideration of these factors.

As regards the second aspect, a country's labour force will vary in size over time with such factors as its age structure and changes in the economic activity rates for men and women, but in the long run it is maintained and reinforced chiefly by the flow of young people moving from general and vocational educational institutions into the labour force. They are the foundation upon which the labour force rests. They are in effect the vehicle for the process of investment in vocational education and training which has been shown earlier in this chapter to contribute very largely to the rate of economic growth, which will therefore be influenced both by the size of the youth cohort and by the quality of investment in their skills. Given the age and sex structures of the population, the number of young people coming forward for vocational education and training is determined by the birth rate some 16 years earlier. That lagged effect will influence the size of cohorts of young people, and account has to be taken of fluctuations in their size, which can be of considerable magnitude, in any study of the youth labour market and of the vocational educational and training processes which so greatly influence its character.

Outline

The Group of Seven, the chief industrialised countries of the world (the United States, Japan, Germany, the United Kingdom,[2] France, Italy and Canada) are the subject in *Chapter 2* of a number of comparative reviews of demographic structure. The *quantity* of labour available for economic activity is governed in the first place by the size and structure of the human population. Secondly, that available quantity varies as the rate of economic activity for adults varies, and as the number of young people seeking initial entry to the labour force varies. The Group of Seven countries are in keen product market competition with each other, and with all other producers in the world economy. It is pertinent to ask how well each country in this group is endowed in terms of labour resources and, additionally, how fully those resources are employed, or are available for employment. Forecasts of total population are also provided for each of the Group of Seven countries, for the Group as a whole, and for the European Economic Community (EEC) (now the European Union, EU) as a whole for the years 2000 and 2020. The ranking of the United Kingdom in respect of these forecasts is shown. The supply to the youth labour market comes from the so-called 'late schooling and training age cohorts'. Forecasts are given of the size of these cohorts for each main European country (United Kingdom, West Germany, France and Italy) and for the EEC (12) as a whole for the years 2000 and 2020. Answers which indicate the relative position of the United Kingdom in these respects are given.

The demographic factors which govern the likely future size of the supply to the youth labour market in Great Britain are studied in *Chapter 3*. Fluctuations in the number of births in the past and the likely future changes in that variable are used to forecast the number of young people who will seek to enter the labour market in future. Supply to the youth labour market is put into context with total labour supply. An analysis, including forecasts to the year 2010, is made of the youth cohort aged 16–19. The rising proportions of the cohort of 16, 17 and 18 year olds who continue their general education and/or undertake full-time vocational education

---

[2] The geographical scope of this study is Great Britain. That choice is made because nearly all government interventions which have been made in the youth labour market have been uniformly applied to England, Scotland and Wales. Separate arrangements have normally been made for Northern Ireland. In the analyses made in Chapter 2, and in a few other specified instances, the United Kingdom rather than Great Britain is considered because of the coverage of international, and some national, statistics.

are shown. The magnitude and incidence of the so-called 'demographic time bomb' are analysed. Thus the two main influences upon youth labour supply are brought together: the demographic effect due to the decline in the total number of births in the 1970s, and the continuing full-time education factor.

The most important element in youth labour supply is undoubtedly *quality*. Post-school vocational education and training before full entry into the labour force has been the subject of very great attention and at times intensive study as a basis for action for more than 150 years – it is not a recent problem. For that reason the subject is set out first in its historical context in *Chapter 4*. The first aspect considered is early government interventions to promote vocational training. This begins with the early statutory system of apprenticeships which was started under Elizabeth I in 1563, when the *Statute of Artificers* was enacted. Included are the views of Adam Smith on its shortcomings. Vocational education and training in the nineteenth century is studied in greater detail. The government's interventions at that time and in the first two decades of the twentieth century, are considered for their contemporary influence, and more importantly for the longer-run effects upon vocational education and training in the inter-war period, which are also studied. The national training policies which were pursued in the conditions of near full employment from 1945 to 1970, including the establishment of the Industrial Training Boards in 1964, are traced and set in context with the results of many official studies and reports on vocational education and training. The impact of demographic changes pon the youth labour market in the early 1960s, due to the higher birth rate in the years immediately after the Second World War, is examined.

The long period of full employment in post-war Britain ended in 1975. The implications of that for labour market policy are examined in *Chapter 5*. The sharp increase in unemployment, and particularly in youth unemployment, led to the government's first interventions in the labour market. The causes of the increase in supply and the reduction in demand for youth labour in this period are examined. The early interventions by government to support youth employment via the Manpower Services Commission (MSC) are studied in respect of their scale and impact, and conclusions are reached on their success or failure, and on the policy-learning process involved.

The background to the development of the modern system of youth training is the subject of *Chapter 6*. Youth unemployment reached a peak of 25% of 16–19 year olds in 1983. The policies of the new Conservative Government, elected in 1979, brought substantial changes to interventionist policy in the youth labour market. *Laissez-faire*, which informed much government policy, did not operate here. The background and thinking behind a new, tripartite system of training is examined. That system consisted of the Technical and Vocational Education Initiative (TVEI) 1982, which introduced some vocational education into secondary schools from age 14; the Youth Training Scheme (YTS) 1983, which provided government-sponsored on- and off-the-job training for school leavers aged 16, and the Young Workers Scheme (YWS) 1982, which subsidised the employment of young workers aged 17.

For many young people, the first encounter with the new tripartite intervention by government came with the TVEI. That change in the teaching of vocational subjects in schools is studied in *Chapter 7*. The origin and aims of the TVEI are examined first, and are followed by a description of the interactive processes between it and the National Curriculum, which was established by the *Education Reform Act* 1988. Criticisms of the TVEI have been severe. These are studied alongside the changes which have been made to the original initiative, together with such evidence as there is of the effects of TVEI upon the later experiences of pupils who have taken its courses at schools and at colleges of further education.

In preparation for the analyses in subsequent chapters of government interventions in the youth labour market, particularly the YTS, an account is given in *Chapter 8* of the methodology which has been developed and used for the assessment of the microeconomic and macroeconomic effects of such interventions. By making such assessments, the role of government intervention in the youth labour market may be evaluated, and the basis for establishing the existence or absence of a policy-learning process can be strengthened.

The main plank in the government's new training-oriented policy was the YTS. An assessment of that scheme's effects upon employment and employers is given in *Chapter 9*. The size and relative scale of YTS is set out first, and is followed by an application of the methods of assessment of the employment effects of government interventions in the youth labour market which are given in Chapter 8. The chief mode of assessment used here is to compare the number of training places actually created by YTS with the number which would have been created in a 'no-policy' situation. That is the 'induced training effect'. The employment effect of YTS, in terms of jobs obtained post-YTS training, is also estimated on the same terms, as are the costs and benefits to employers who participated in the scheme.

The macroeconomic effects of YTS upon the government, business, personal and overseas sections of the economy are estimated in *Chapter 10*. The first round macroeconomic effects are analysed in detail. The net cost of the scheme to the government is shown, as are the net benefits to the business sector. A balanced budget hypothesis is used and broad indications are given of the direction of the principal second-round effects of expenditure on YTS. The Cambridge Economic Growth Model is used to trace further macroeconomic influences of YTS. The skill attainments of YTS trainees are examined in *Chapter 11*, against the background of their educational attainments, or lack of them, at school. A youth labour market analysis of the supply and demand by occupation for ex-YTS trainees is also made in this chapter in order to determine the degree of match between supply and demand, and in particular whether supply via YTS met demand in trades which required a relatively high level of skill. Likely future changes in the structure of demand for labour by occupational group are also considered for their implications for government policy on youth training.

The devolution of the management of YTS, and of its successor Youth Training (YT), and the implications for local youth labour market operation, are considered in *Chapter 12*. This involves a study of the role of the Training and Enterprise Councils (TECs). Under this system the government remains the major financer of training services, while the function of provider of these services is devolved upon local labour market agencies – the TECs. This establishes a *quasi*-market structure. That development is examined for the types of gain and loss which may be expected from it.

A review is undertaken in *Chapter 13* of the critics of YTS. These form four groups. The first comprises those who point out the poor educational and training system in Britain compared with many competitor countries, and the failure of YTS and YT to produce qualified skilled workers for the external, or occupational, labour markets, as distinct from the internal labour markets. The second group are those who criticise the emphasis which they see as being placed upon free market forces in the training and employment of youth labour which, it is alleged, leads to the wrong type of training for those who leave school without obtaining employment. The third group are those who are concerned with the priority of policies, particularly the priority which is seen to be given to training policy over manpower policy. The danger, which is a major one in the view of this group, is that young people are trained and are then left without employment because of a failure of manpower policy. The fourth group comprises those who are critical of the organisational structure and of the management, at both central and local levels, of the government's devolved system of youth labour market intervention which includes the TECs.

An assessment of the trade unions' collaboration with and, in some cases, opposition to the government-sponsored training policy is given in *Chapter 14*. That policy, and in particular the YTS and YT programmes, has been opposed by some, but by no means all trade unions. The actions of the General Council of the TUC in relation to the government's intervention in the youth labour market are examined, as is the extent to which the General

Council led the TUC into successful collaboration with the MSC, of which it was an active member, in order to modify the government's interventions over the period 1978–88. The TUC policy of collaboration broke down in 1988, and the reasons for that are given. The actions of individual trade unions which adopted either a collaborative or oppositional approach to the government's intervention are studied, and an estimate is made of the scale of that aspect of their opposition to YTS which took the form of boycotts or strikes.

The final chapter, *Chapter 15*, contains a summary of conclusions on resources and policies in the British youth labour market, and these are followed by conclusions on government intervention in that market.

2 Demographic structure, capacity and economic activity

This study of the youth labour market in Britain is concerned with supply and demand in that market, and particularly with the skills, training for skills and government policies which relate to the training and employment of young people.

In the longer term the factor labour, which is principally involved in the production and in the management of production of all capital and consumer goods and services, is chiefly replenished and sustained by the flow of young people moving into employment from the education system, and from training and vocational courses.

It has been shown in Chapter 1 that labour is of undoubted *absolute* importance in the economy. So that the *relative* importance of the factor labour may also be seen, the other natural resources of the country may be broadly compared with those of the main industrialised countries which are this country's chief competitors in world markets. The results of that study are given in the Appendix. There the United Kingdom's natural endowments in land and primary energy are measured against those of the Group of Seven countries individually as a group, and with the European Economic Community (EEC) as a group. The UK is shown to be relatively poorly endowed in agricultural land. It is at present relatively well endowed with sources of primary energy, but that advantageous position is likely to be short term.

As an international trader and world exporter the UK is relatively large. It also has a relatively high standard of living to maintain and improve. So for future economic growth and national prosperity it must depend largely, in the absence of other resource endowments, upon the factor labour. That dependence is even greater for Japan and West Germany, whose peoples have shown, particularly over the past two decades, that a relative lack of natural resource endowment has not hampered their economic growth at home nor their substantial progress in selling in world markets. So it can be done largely by labour alone, and that must imply that skilled labour is all-important in the creation of economic wealth and in economic growth.

The focus of this chapter is upon demographic factors which influence the total supply of labour in Britain. That provides the essential context for the study of supply to the youth labour market which is given in Chapter 3. Supply to the youth labour market is subject to wide fluctuations which are shown later (Chapters 5 and 6) to be a major factor in the destabilisation of the youth labour market in the 1970s and 1980s, with consequences which form the basis for many of the interventionist policies of government which are the central theme of this book. Hence the importance attached to the demographic context which is treated in this chapter. The approach is by way of a comparative international analysis of demographic structure.

Structure of populations

The demographic structure of a country has a crucial influence upon its economy. It determines the number of people of working age (16–64 for males and 16–59 for females in the UK), the number of young people (under 16 years of age) who are dependents but who are also the source of the factor labour in terms of replacements for those who retire from the labour force, and finally the number of dependents who are over the age of retirement.

The demographic structure itself is chiefly determined by the birth and death rates which prevailed over past decades, and the sharp changes which can and do occur in birth rates have structural, and therefore economic, consequences which will last for 60 years or more.

The demographic structure of the UK in 1990 is shown in Table 2.1, and is set in comparison with that of each country's chief competitors in the Group of Seven, and with the averages of the EEC (12) and the Group of Seven.[1]

In the UK, the 'baby boom', the relatively high birth rates in the 1960s, was over by 1987 in the sense that the cohort of young people born in that decade (1960–70) had passed into higher or further education or into the labour force by 1987.

The UK ranks fourth of the Group of Seven countries in the proportion of young people under age 15 of the total population. The UK proportions, for both males and females, in this age group are below the Group of Seven averages, which are substantially boosted by the USA, but they are higher than the averages for the EEC(12).

In respect of the relative size of the youth cohort, the UK has no great potential advantage over its competitors, nor has it a marked disadvantage – it is close to the average position on the evidence of these data.

---

[1] The form of the EEC statistics is such that young people are in the age bracket 15 and under, and the population of working age is in the bracket 15–64 for both men and women.

Table 2.1 *The demographic structure of individual countries in the Group of Seven and in the EEC(12) as a whole. Population by age and sex, 1990 (percentages of total population)*

Countries in rank order of percentages in the under 15 age group	Under 15		Age 15–64		Age 65 and over	
	M	F	M	F	M	F
USA	11.1	10.6	32.6	33.2	5.0	7.4
Canada (1991)	10.7	10.2	33.7	33.7	4.8	6.7
France	10.3	9.8	32.9	33.0	5.5	8.5
UK	**9.8**	**9.3**	**32.8**	**32.6**	**6.3**	**9.4**
Japan[a]	9.5	9.0	35.0	34.8	4.7	7.0
Italy	8.5	8.0	34.2	34.6	5.9	8.8
Germany	8.3	7.8	34.9	34.0	5.0	9.9
(West Germany 1989)	(7.7)	(7.3)	(35.3)	(34.4)	(5.2)	(10.1)
Group of Seven[b]	10.0	9.5	33.6	33.7	5.2	8.0
EEC(12) (1991)[c]	9.3	8.8	33.8	33.6	5.6	8.9

Notes:
[a]The percentage figures for Japan are based upon estimates made by Eurostat.
[b]Includes Canada (1991) and estimates for Japan (see note a). Includes Germany.
[c]EEC average for 1990 is not available.
Source: *Basic Statistics of the Community* (1993), Tables 3.10 and 3.11.

It may be noted that Germany, owing to very low birth rates since 1972, has a marked disadvantage in the proportion of its male and female population under 15, which is 2.0 percentage points (out of 18) below the EEC(12) average, and even further below the Group of Seven average. Its population structure is weighted towards the working age range 15–64, and its labour force has been substantially reinforced by the union of West with East Germany. That union has also moved the country's demographic structure closer to the EEC average. The UK is well below the EEC(12) and the Group of Seven for this working age range.

The UK and German populations are both heavy in the age range 65 and over. Taking males and females in this range together, the UK figure is 15.7% and that for Germany 14.9%, compared with the EEC(12) average of 14.5%, and the Group of Seven average which is as low as 13.2%.

Thus the UK is in a comparatively disadvantageous structural position in respect of the proportion of its population in the working age range (15–64 years), and in the dependent age range of 65 or over. Its position in the under 15 age range suggests a brighter future for its demographic structure and the economic implications which stem from it. The future is considered further when demographic forecasts are made in a later section of this chapter, but it is already clear that there is an essential need to make good economic use of its young people by the provision of the best possible education and training.

What has been shown so far is a comparative view of demographic structure which has an influence on present and future demographic capacity (the working population). How far that capacity is used in broad economic terms of total employment is considered next.

Demographic capacity, economic activity and participation

The extent to which men and women are in employment or seeking employment is the recognised measure of their economic activity, and is indicative of the extent to which use is made of a country's demographic capacity. The economic activity rate of the UK (the percentage of all those in employment or self-employment and those involuntarily unemployed expressed as a percentage of all persons of working age) was 74.4% on average in the period 1980–90. This may be compared with the average for the same period of 71.3% for the Group of Seven countries, and 65.7% for the EEC(12).[2]

The actual use of labour resources is measured by the economic participation rate (the number of those in employment or self-employment expressed as a percentage of all persons of working age). Although those seeking employment but not finding it are in a sense a reserve asset, they cannot be counted as contributors to current output – rather the contrary as they have to be supported by those in work. For the same period, 1980–90, the average participation rate for the UK was 67.6%, which may be compared with the averages for the Group of Seven of 66.5%, and the EEC(12) of 59.5%.[3]

So, in the *quantitative* terms which are the concern in this chapter, the UK's degree of capacity utilisation of its labour resources (as measured by its average economic participation rate 1980–90) was 8.1 percentage points above the average for the EEC(12), and 1.1 percentage points above the average for the Group of Seven countries.

Population forecasts

Forecasts of population are notoriously hazardous, depending as they do on future changes in birth and death rates which are necessarily based on

---

[2] *Historical Statistics 1960–1990* 1992, Table 2.6.
[3] *Historical Statistics 1960–1990* 1992, Table 2.14.

Table 2.2 *Population forecasts for individual countries in the Group of Seven, and for the EEC (12) as a whole, 1992, 2000 and 2020 (000s, and average cumulative % change p.a. in brackets)*

Countries in rank order of population changes, 1992–2020	1992 (at 1 Jan.)	2000 (1992–2000)	2020 (1992–2020)
USA	253,887	266,096 (0.59)	294,750 (0.53)
Canada	27,243[a,b]	28,488 (0.56)	31,491 (0.52)
France	57,206	59,659 (0.53)	63,915[c] (0.40)
UK	**57,749**	**59,218 (0.31)**	**61,350 (0.22)**
Italy	56,757[b]	59,065 (0.50)	58,688 (0.12)
Japan	123,921[d]	128,470 (0.40)	129,029 (0.09)
Germany	80,275	82,269 (0.31)	81,880 (0.07)
Group of Seven	657,038[e]	683,265 (0.49)	721,103 (0.33)
EEC (12)	345,383	357,326 (0.43)	368,011 (0.23)

Notes:
[a]At 1 December 1991.
[b]Provisional.
[c]This forecast for 2020 for France was revised upwards in 1993 by 9.0% (5.3 million) compared with that made in 1992.
[d]1991 estimate.
[e]Includes Japan 1991 estimate.
Source: *Basic Statistics of the Community* (1993), Table 3.1.

past evidence. The former are particularly erratic. Since 1960 birth rates in the UK have varied from 18.8 per thousand population in 1964 to 12.0 per thousand in 1976.

Demographic forecasters have made their projections, which are frequently revised, and these are given in Table 2.2 for the individual countries in the Group of Seven, for that group as a whole, and for the EEC(12). Total populations are projected to the year 2020, with an intermediate projection to 2000.

For the period to 1992–2020, and for the industrialised countries considered here, the faster population growth, by a wide margin, is expected to take place in North America. France and the UK rank third and fourth respectively.

Population growth is expected to continue up to the year 2000 in all the countries and groups examined. Thereafter to 2020 slower growth rates are forecast for the two North American countries, and for the UK, Japan and France. Population is expected to decline in Germany and Italy between 2000 and 2020.

Population changes reflect changes during the period reviewed in birth and death rates, which are influenced by changes in the age structure of the population, which in turn reflect changes in birth and death rates in earlier periods. The chief factor in the moderate but steady growth in the UK population must be, in the light of the relatively high proportion of persons in the 65 + age group (shown in Table 2.1), a relatively high birth rate. In 1991 the UK birth rate, 13.8 per thousand of population, was well above the EEC(12) average of 11.6 per thousand;[4] and in 1988 the total fertility rate (TFR) for the UK was 1.84 and for the EEC(12) 1.60.[5]

Changes in demographic structure

Forecasts of changes in the age structure of the populations of the four main European countries and of the EEC(12) as a group are given in Table 2.3 for the years 1995, 2000, 2010 and 2020.

Substantial changes in demographic structure are forecast, and broadly they are such as would be expected from the various divergent growth rates for whole populations which are predicted and shown in Table 2.2.

The United Kingdom ranks first in terms of the average proportion of young dependents in the population in the years which are forecast. Italy and, particularly, West Germany (forecasts for the whole of Germany are not yet available) are expected to have much lower average proportions of young dependents and much higher proportions of those aged 65 and over, and in West Germany in 2020 the proportion for young people aged 0–14, at 11.7%, is barely half the proportion of old dependents, at 22.4%. This structural change, which arises from a decline in total population due to falling birth rates, has important implications for economic and fiscal policy and also, as the number and proportion of young people decline, there are inevitable consequences for the supply of youth labour and for policy on vocational education and training.

The position of the United Kingdom on these comparisons is relatively

---

[4] *Basic Statistics of the Community* 1993, Table 3.12.
[5] *Demographic Statistics 1990* 1990.

Table 2.3 *Forecasts of changes in demographic structure. Proportions of total population of persons of working age (15–64), young dependents (0–14), and old dependents (65 +). Major EEC countries and the EEC (12) as a whole, 1995, 2000, 2010 and 2020 (percentages)*

Countries in rank order of average proportion of young dependents	1995	2000	2010	2020	Average proportions for the four years forecast
United Kingdom					
Working population	64.4	64.1	65.1	63.9	64.4
Young dependents	**19.9**	**20.4**	**19.0**	**18.3**	**19.4**
Old dependents	15.7	15.5	15.9	17.8	16.2
France					
Working population	65.4	65.3	66.0	63.5	65.0
Young dependents	19.7	19.0	17.7	16.8	18.3
Old dependents	14.9	15.7	16.3	19.7	16.7
Italy					
Working population	68.8	67.7	65.9	65.4	66.9
Young dependents	13.7	14.8	13.9	11.8	13.6
Old dependents	17.5	17.5	20.2	22.8	19.5
West Germany					
Working population	68.0	71.0	67.0	65.9	67.9
Young dependents	15.4	11.5	12.5	11.7	12.8
Old dependents	16.6	17.5	20.5	22.4	19.3
EEC (12)					
Working population	66.7	66.2	66.2	65.1	66.1
Young dependents	17.8	17.7	16.3	15.2	16.7
Old dependents	15.5	16.1	17.5	19.7	17.2

Source: Based on Demographic Statistics 1990 (1990) pp. 220, 221 and for the assumptions on which the projections are based, pp. 230, 231.

favourable in terms of both the young people and the old. Despite some dire predictions which have been given for the UK when seen outside its European context, the forecast average proportion for its old dependents is lower than that for any other country shown here and lower than that for the EEC(12) as a whole in the period to 2020.

The broader demographic context has now been drawn and forecasts have been given to 2020. It seems useful to be able to see and examine this context in order to set in perspective the likely future trend in the supply to

Table 2.4 *Forecasts of the late schooling and training age cohort (15–19) expressed as a percentage of the population of working age (15–64). Major European countries and the EEC(12) as a whole, 1995, 2000, 2010 and 2020 (000s, and % in brackets)*

Countries in rank order of average percentage size of 15–19 cohort	1995	2000	2010	2020	Average percentages for the four years forecast
United Kingdom	**3,437**	**3,633**	**4,153**	**3,758**	
	(9.2)	**(9.7)**	**(10.6)**	**(9.7)**	**(9.8)**
France	3,698	3,866	3,666	3,439	
	(9.9)	(10.2)	(9.5)	(9.2)	(9.7)
Italy	3,715	3,052	2,875	2,617	
	(9.4)	(7.8)	(7.8)	(7.5)	(8.1)
West Germany	2,974	3,095	3,289	2,361	
	(7.1)	(7.2)	(8.4)	(6.6)	(7.3)
EEC (12)	20,634	19,655	19,975	17,931	
	(9.4)	(8.9)	(9.2)	(8.5)	(9.0)

Source: Demographic Statistics, 1990 (1990) pp. 220, 221, 230 and 231.

the youth labour market in the UK, and to view that trend against those in the main European countries.

In Table 2.4 are set out forecasts of what is named 'the late schooling and training cohort' of young people of both sexes aged between 15 and 19. This cohort will comprise last-year-at-school pupils, further and higher education students, young people undergoing apprenticeships or other forms of on- and off-the-job training, and also some who are unemployed.

The UK has the strongest trend over the period 1995 to 2020 in terms of growth of the absolute number of young people in the late schooling and training cohort. By 2020 the UK is expected to have the largest cohort of young people in terms of absolute number in this age group of the four European countries examined, and also the highest percentage of this age group of the total population of working age. The French position is close to that of the UK, but Italy and West Germany are far below the UK level and are expected to suffer a decline in the number of young people in this age group, and also a fall in this group as a percentage of their total populations of working age.

It is from this group of young people that the workforce, which includes those who are seeking work, is largely replaced and reinforced. Other sources of labour input are adult women entering the labour force for the first time, or re-entering after a lapse of time, and immigrant labour.

Table 2.5 *Actual figures and projections of UK population at age 16, for each year 1985 to 2000, and for 2010 and 2020, 1991-based (000s)*

1985	897[a]	1994	663
1986	869[a]	1995	719
1987	852[a]	1996	747
1988	827[a]	1997	743
1989	778[a]	1998	732
1990	728[a]	1999	732
1991	709[b]	2000	729
1992	681	2010	804
1993	652	2020	728

Notes:
[a] Actual figures, OPCS.
[b] Provisional.
Source: National Population Projections 1991-based (1993) Series PP2, No. 18.

Immigrant labour has been particularly important in maintaining and building up the population of working age and the labour force in West Germany, and that is reflected in its relatively large proportion of population of working age (see Table 2.3). Immigration is not currently a large factor in the growth of the UK labour force, and is not expected to be in the future period considered here. In more precise terms, the actual annual supply of young people into further academic education, vocational education, training and availability for employment is shown in the projection of the UK population at age 16 (Table 2.5).

The population at age 16 has fallen sharply since 1985 to reach a low point in 1993. Thereafter to 2010 an increase is predicted. A further decline is expected to occur between 2010 and 2020.

An analysis of the supply to the youth labour market in Britain and its relationship with the stock of labour is given in Chapter 3.

3   Supply to the youth labour market

It has been shown in Chapter 2 that there will be a buoyant flow towards the British labour market from the all-important youth labour cohort (15–19 years), particularly for the 25 years from the mid 1990s. Although in the 1980s there was a decline in the number of 16 year olds entering higher education or the labour market directly from school, that trend has now reversed, and numbers will increase strongly in the second half of the 1990s.

A further perspective is now needed in the form of past and future time-series analyses of the flows of labour in Britain, particularly youth labour, into employment; and the relationship between that flow and the stock of labour (the total working population) which is supported and reinforced by it.

The other main source of new labour is the increased economic activity of women, which was particularly strong in the 1980s. That also needs to be considered as part of the context of youth labour market conditions.

An understanding of these conditions in the wider labour market is a necessary precondition for the analyses which are presented in later chapters, and which are concerned with government legislation and interventions in the youth labour market which first began on a large scale in 1978 and which have continued since then. These interventions aim to provide, or encourage others to provide, work experience, vocational education and training for young people with the objective of ensuring that best use is made of that important part of the labour factor of production by raising skill accomplishments, and thereby enhancing their employment and earnings prospects.

In Table 3.1 the youth cohort, which for this analysis of national trends recognises the British school leaving age of 16 and is the group aged 16–19, is shown in absolute numbers and as a percentage of the total civilian working population (the workforce) of Great Britain for 1971, 1978 and for the continuous period 1980–92. This comparison is made in this form to show the total *potential* supply of youth labour to the total civilian labour

Table 3.1 *Resident population age 16–19 compared with the total civilian labour force, 1971, 1978 and 1980–1992, with projections to 2006, GB*

	Population aged 16–19: the youth labour cohort[a] (000s)	Total civilian labour force[a] (000s)	The youth population cohort as a percentage of the total civilian labour force (%)
Estimates			
1971	2,975	23,604	12.6
1978	3,425	25,031	13.6
1980	3,613	25,369	14.2
1981	3,679	25,366	14.5
1982	3,715	25,229	14.7
1983	3,717	25,155	14.8
1984	3,640	25,827	14.1
1985	3,572	26,085	13.7
1986	3,496	26,239	13.3
1987	3,442	26,568	13.0
1988	3,362	26,877	12.5
1989	3,245	27,309	11.9
1990	3,114	27,483	11.3
1991	2,956	27,313	10.8
1992	2,804	27,190	10.3
Projections			
1995	2,628	27,234	9.6
2000	2,844	27,884	10.2
2006	3,039	28,532	10.7

Note: [a]GB labour force definitions up to 1983. ILO definitions from 1984. 'The difference between the two measures is small' (*Employment Gazette* (1994) April, Technical Note, p. 117). Working age population is of men aged 16–64 and women aged 16–59.
Source: *Employment Gazette* (1994) *April, pp.* 111–21.

force. The degrees by which that potential is subject to delayed entry due to engagement in further education, and underused due to unemployment, are analysed later.

The absolute size of the youth cohort was lower in 1992 than it was in 1971. But a large increase did occur in the late 1970s and early 1980s as the result of the marked increase in the birth rate which occurred in the 1960s.

That boosted the total civilian workforce, which for that reason among others increased by 15% from 1971 to 1992.

The youth cohort, of which only a part are actually in the workforce at any time while the remainder are staying on at school or are on further full-time general or vocational education courses, increased in size from 1971 to 1982. Since then the decline which has occurred in the relative size of this cohort is only partly due to the decline in the absolute size of 16-19 age group. Another factor is that the total workforce has increased, for a reason which is now explained.

Over the 21 years from 1971 to 1992 the increase of 3,586,000 in the total civilian workforce in Britain has been very largely due to an increase of 3,099,000 in the number of women in the workforce. That accounts for 86% of the total increase.

The chief reason for this change in the proportions of men and women in the total civilian workforce shown in Table 3.2 is the large increase in the economic activity rate for women, which increased from 56.7 in 1971 to 70.9 in 1992, while the corresponding rate for men fell from 90.7 to 85.7 over the same period. There is also a small 'population effect' in these changes, but the chief influence is the 'economic activity rate effect'. As regards the future, it is expected that the economic activity rate for men will decline further to 82.1 by 2006 and that the rate for women will continue to increase, to 75.4 by that year, but more slowly than in the period 1971–92. A further factor which influences these comparisons is variation in the proportions of workers who leave the workforce owing to retirement and other causes, but the central point is that the input of youth labour has declined since 1982 in both absolute and relative terms (Table 3.1). That decline will be reversed in the first half of the 1990s and thereafter a recovery is expected. The *net* effect of these and other factors upon the size of the total civilian labour force is to produce a growth rate of 0.35% per annum over the period 1992–2006. The rate over the period 1971–92 was 0.68% per annum. Movements in the size of the youth cohort are now considered in greater detail.

In Table 3.3 forecasts to 2010 are shown of movements in the youth cohort (aged 16–19) and in the cohort aged 16. The trend in the size of the youth cohort is downwards from 1985 to 1995 when a low point is expected to occur. In that year the total number of 16–19 year olds will be 26% lower than in 1985. A recovery in numbers is expected over the 15-year period 1995–2010. By then the cohort is expected to be about 19% above the low point in 1995.

The much discussed 'demographic time bomb', by which is meant the particularly low number of youth entrants to the labour force in the early 1990s, arises from low birth rates in the period 1973–77. A low point of 11.8 births per thousand of population occurred in 1977. From 1978 there was a

Table 3.2 *The civilian labour force of working age*[a] *analysed by sex, 1971, 1978 and 1980–92, with projections to 2006, GB*

	Men (000s)	Women (000s)	Proportion of women in total civilian labour force (%)
Estimates			
1971	15,034	8,571	36.3
1978	15,199	9,832	39.3
1980	15,310	10,058	39.6
1981	15,310	10,056	39.6
1982	15,176	10,053	39.8
1983	15,093	10,062	40.0
1984	15,282	10,545	40.8
1985	15,363	10,722	41.1
1986	15,355	10,885	41.5
1987	15,447	11,122	41.9
1988	15,575	11,302	42.1
1989	15,681	11,628	42.6
1990	15,751	11,732	42.7
1991	15,650	11,663	42.7
1992	15,520	11,670	42.9
Projections			
1995	15,359	11,874	43.6
2000	15,491	12,393	44.4
2006	15,681	12,851	45.0

Notes: [a]GB labour force definitions up to 1983. ILO definitions from 1984. 'The difference between the two measures is small' (*Employment Gazette* (1994) April, Technical Note, p. 117). Working age population is of men aged 16–64 and women aged 16–59.
Source: *Employment Gazette* (1994) April, pp. 111–21.

recovery in the crude birth rate, which rose in most years of the 1980s reaching 13.9 per thousand of population in 1990. But to set this in context, in the 'baby boom' of the 1960s the birth rate reached 18.8 per thousand of population in 1964, and that may be compared with the rate of 23.1, which was the average in 1920–22.

It is shown in Table 3.3 that the youth cohort aged 16 is expected to recover in number over the 17 years to 2010, but beyond that date the supply will start to decline again. It has been shown earlier that the increase

Table 3.3 *Trends in the size of youth cohorts in Britain aged 16–19 and aged 16, 1981 and 1985–92, with projections to 2010, GB (000s, and index 1981 = 100 in brackets)*

	Youth cohort aged 16–19		Youth cohort aged 16	
1981	3679	(100)	936	(100)
1985	3572	(97.1)	869	(92.8)
1986	3496	(95.0)	840	(89.7)
1987	3442	(93.6)	852	(91.0)
1988	3362	(91.4)	800	(85.5)
1989	3245	(88.2)	751	(80.2)
1990	3114	(84.6)	702	(75.0)
1991	2956	(80.3)	684	(73.1)
1992	2804	(76.2)	657	(70.2)
Projections				
1995	2628	(71.4)	693	(74.0)
2000	2844	(77.3)	703	(75.1)
2005	3017	(82.0)	756	(80.8)
2010	3118	(84.8)	779	(83.2)

Sources: (1) For figures of youth cohort aged 16–19: 'Revised population estimates for 1981–1990' *OPCS Monitor*, PP1, 94/1, 1994. For later figures and projections: *OPCS Monitor*, PP2, 94/2, 1994. (2) For figures of youth cohort aged 16: *National Population Projections 1991-based* (1993). Series PP2, No. 18. The figures for 1981–1990 are 1989 Census-based. Those from 1991 are 1991 Census-based.

in the average economic activity rate for women is slowing, and that makes the supply of youth labour relatively more important.

The figures for the youth cohorts given in Table 3.3 are gross, and account now has to be taken of the number of young people staying on at school or entering full-time further education. Changes in these figures and in their shares of the total population of the age groups concerned have been changing rapidly in the direction of a higher proportion of the total entering full-time or part-time education. That trend is shown, for England only, in Table 3.4.

Throughout the 1980s there was, as has been shown earlier, a decline in the total population of young people. There was also a modest rise in the proportion entering full-time or part-time further education, so that the number of those available to enter the labour market directly from school declined rather faster than the total youth population. Since 1989/90 there has been a dramatic increase in the proportion entering full-time further

Table 3.4 *The participation of 16, 17 and 18 year olds in full-time and part-time education 1982/83, 1985/86 and 1988/89–1992/93, England, all persons (000s, and % in brackets)*

	Population aged 16, 17 and 18	In full-time education[a]	In part-time education[a]	Not in education[b]
1982/83	2381	781 (32.8)	314 (13.2)	1286 (54.0)
1985/86	2240	717 (32.0)	345 (15.4)	1178 (52.6)
1988/89	2115	738 (34.9)	338 (16.0)	1039 (49.1)
1989/90	2035	767 (37.7)	317 (15.6)	951 (46.7)
1990/91	1912	792 (41.4)	272 (14.2)	848 (44.4)
1991/92	1816	859 (47.3)	222 (12.2)	735 (40.5)
1992/93[c]	1749	919 (52.6)	185 (10.6)	645 (36.8)

Notes:
[a]Includes those on government youth training schemes if these involve full-time or part-time college courses.
[b]In employment, unemployed, or economically inactive.
[c]Estimated.
Source: Adapted from *Department for Education Statistical Bulletin*, Issue No. 16/93, 1993.

education, and some decline in the proportion entering part-time education. The *net* effect of these changes upon the number of those available for the full-time employment in the labour market, if they choose to seek it, has been a decline of 45% from 1985/86 to 1992/93.

Many of those in part-time education are also in part-time employment, as indeed are some of those in full-time education.[1] So the activities of further education and of work experience and training[2] go together for many young people, including those on government-supported youth training schemes.

[1] It has been shown from Labour Force Surveys that in Winter 1992 out of 913,000 16 and 17 year olds in full-time education, 299,000 (33%) were also in part-time employment (Sly 1993).

[2] In some cases the part-time jobs may be taken only to earn money, rather than to gain meaningful work experience and training.

Those who go on from school to full-time further education enter the labour market at later dates, and by then they should have improved their educational and vocational qualifications. This encouraging trend towards a higher proportion of the youth cohort engaging in further education and aiming for relatively high levels of qualification should be noted.

In the late 1970s and early 1980s there occurred what has been named 'generational crowding'(Freeman and Bloom 1985).[3] That term refers to a demographic 'bulge' in the number of young people who have recently joined the labour force or who are about to enter it from school. A large increase in the supply to the youth labour market for this reason worsens initial job opportunities, and also the longer-term prospects for the earnings of young people. The latter are the so-called long-term 'scarring effects' of early unemployment due to generational crowding, which can endure for many years as an exceptionally large cohort moves up the age scales. This 'scarring effect' had been studied earlier, by Freeman and Wise (1982), who found, for the United States, that 'early unemployment experience has virtually no effect on later employment after controlling for persistent characteristics of individuals, such as education . . . But not working in earlier years has a negative effect on subsequent wages because wage increases are related to experience' (p.15).

There is no doubt that a generational crowding effect did occur in Britain in this period due to the demographic factors which have been explained. Its deleterious influence upon young people would have been particularly great had there been no policy of government intervention in the youth labour market. Furthermore, the generational crowding effect occurred during a period when the average economic activity rate for women was rising very fast, as has been shown (Table 3.2). That trend added an 'age crowding' effect to the generational crowding one. Both these effects were to the disadvantage of young people and their prospects of acquiring skills, jobs and longer-term employment in occupations in which they could exercise their talents to the full.

Since the mid 1980s the generational crowding effect has somewhat diminished as the youth cohort (aged 15–19) has declined in size, but the age crowding effect has continued as the average economic activity rate for women has continued to increase.

As to the future, this problem is expected to return as the size of the youth cohort begins to grow again from the mid 1990s and as the average economic activity rate for women continues, as forecast, to increase, albeit at a slower rate than in the recent past.

[3] Freeman and Bloom's mimeo paper served as the basis for an article in *Employment Outlook* (OECD 1986).

4 Vocational education and training in historical perspective

Past and expected future changes in the absolute and relative supply of young people to the labour market has been considered in *quantitative* terms in Chapters 2 and 3. The important *qualitative* aspects of that supply are studied next, starting with an historical perspective.

The quality of youth labour depends essentially upon vocational education and training, although general education underlies the vocational processes, and that will be alluded to as the major educational reforms occur and exert influence upon the development of vocational education. The large subject of vocational education has generated much attention over the past decade in particular and has been given detailed attention by governments. It might be thought that the subject is new, but that would be wrong.

Over a long period of history the matter of training young people to acquire vocational and occupational skills has been a subject for study, debate, report and action by governments who have at some times intervened and at other times withdrawn and left employers to do the job on their own. The degree of urgency and importance attached to training has swung with cycles of economic activity, with advances in technology and with the incidence of major wars. The persistence of the subject arises in part from the double problem of skill shortages at times of high economic activity and of unemployment of youth labour at times of economic depression and slack demand for labour, particularly youth labour.

Early government interventions to promote vocational training

From medieval times (about the twelfth century) to 1563 the craft guild system of training by trades was basically a private enterprise arrangement under some municipal control (Trevelyan 1948, pp. 191–3). Relations between master, journeyman and apprentice, questions of wages and prices, the right to trade in a locality, and the conditions under which trade should be carried on was decided in each locality by a craft guild which was in effect a municipal authority. In the fourteenth century the *Statute of Labourers 1351* had unsuccessfully aimed to fix a maximum wage for the whole country. Nearly two centuries later, under Elizabeth I, the power of the Crown was greater nationally, the guild system was weaker and economic activity had spread into country districts where there was no kind of municipal authority. A national system of craft training was brought in by the *Statute of Artificers 1563 (5 Elizabeth I)* to replace training by the craft guilds. Under this statute a universal apprenticeship system was established by law. This involved the binding of apprentices in specified trades to a master for a term of seven years. Justices of the Peace were responsible for granting indentures, and were given powers to control local wages and prices as well as relations between master and apprentice. On the whole the system worked well and it endured until dismantled in 1814, when the *Statute of Artificers* was repealed. The advance of technology, changes in the modes of production which occurred as the Industrial Revolution progressed, and the influence of Adam Smith's principles of *laissez-faire*, all contributed to this change. Trevelyan (1948, p. 193) deplores it and makes the following comment which remains true to-day: 'The situation so created has scarcely yet been made good.'

In the early nineteenth century the factory system was developing, and new technologies, new materials and new manufacturing processes were being introduced. Many new skilled, semi-skilled and particularly unskilled jobs were being created which were not covered by the specified apprentice trades of the Elizabethan Statute of Artificers. Adam Smith assessed the restrictive influence of the old statute:

The statute of apprenticeship obstructs the free circulation of labour from one employment to another, even in the same place. The exclusive privileges of corporations obstruct it from one place to another, even in the same employment. (Smith 1976, p. 150.)

Before the industrial revolution most skilled economic activity took place within small workshops. The Elizabethan statutory apprentice system ensured the continuity of what was in modern terms self-employment. The apprentice was generally regarded as a member of the master's family and was likely to succeed the master in due course – it was not an employer/employee relationship. With the rapid increase in population[1] and the coming of the industrial revolution, and with it much technological improvement and the factory system, greater mobility of labour was needed. The introduction of machinery required some labour of

---

[1] The population of the United Kingdom has been estimated at 10.5 million in 1751 and 21.0 million in 1821 (Deane 1967, pp. 6 and 8).

high skill, but also much semi-skilled and unskilled labour. Employer/ employee relationships were established which were much more remote and separate than that which had existed between master and apprentice under the Elizabethan system. One effect of technological advance, coupled with the application of Adam Smith's principle of the division of labour in factory production, was to drive employers and workers apart, and in that process can be seen the beginning of workers' associations and later the Trade Unions, which became legal after the repeal of the *Combination Acts* in 1825.

So despite the increasing demand for skills, many of them new skills associated with the new inventions, particularly steam power, the seven-year apprentice system of long standing was abolished. Freer market conditions for youth labour resulted. These entailed the many abuses which occurred before the *Factory Acts* and the *Education Act 1870* were passed, but freer conditions of employment were demanded by manufacturers as *laissez-faire* capitalism produced strong economic expansion. Parliament acceded to this demand and repealed the Elizabethan *Statute of Artificers* in 1814.

Vocational education and training in the nineteenth century

The process of parliamentary and electoral reform began with the *Electoral Reform Act 1832*, and the franchise was further extended in 1867, 1884 and 1918, but it was not completed until 1967. Although it now seems inevitable that progressively wider enfranchisement would lead to demands from the electorate for better education and training, that process was extremely slow. It was with great reluctance that Parliament interfered with the internal conduct of industry throughout the nineteenth century. However, some action was taken, particularly as regards the education and employment of children. The *Factory Act* of 1833 provided for the compulsory school attendance of employed children between the ages of nine and thirteen for two hours daily, six days a week. Later *Factory Acts* in 1844, 1874, 1891 and 1901 limited children's working hours, raised the minimum age for the employment of children and increased the hours of school attendance. Schools were private, with some financial support from government from 1833. State education was founded then, and it was substantially advanced by the *Education Act 1870*, but there was no Ministry of Education until 1944.

Many charitable foundations provided a skeleton of a public education network. There were two particularly important ones. The first was the Institution for Promoting the British System for the Education of the Labouring and Manufacturing Classes of Society of every Religious

Persuasion. The shorter name for this institution is the British and Foreign Schools Society, founded by the Quakers in 1808. The other was the National Society (for the Education of the Poor in the Principles of the Established Church throughout England and Wales), founded in 1811. Some government support for education was made *via* these societies. In 1833 the government grant to these two societies jointly was £20,000, rising to £837,000 by 1859 (Perry 1976, p. 15).

In 1861, Commissioners were appointed to examine the condition of education amongst the 'poorer classes', and to consider means for extension and improvement. The result was the Newcastle Report (*Report of the Commissioners Appointed to Inquire into the State of Popular Education in England*) which found that government intervention over the previous thirty years had improved standards by the introduction of inspectors and by encouraging voluntary financial support. The Commissioners decided against a compulsory system,[2] after taking evidence in continental European and other countries. Among the recommendations of the Newcastle Report was one of financial and general encouragement for evening classes.[3]

Official inquiries into educational matters continued. In 1864 the revenues and management of nine 'public' schools were examined in the Clarendon Report. Each was considered and recommendations were made (*Report of H. M. Commissioners Appointed to Inquire into the Revenues and Management of Certain Schools and Colleges* 1864, Volume 1, pp. 325–6).

In 1867 the Taunton Report examined the state of England's endowed schools in the context of the national education system as a whole (*Schools Inquiry Commission* 1867). About a quarter of the 3000 or so endowed schools were included in this study. Those chosen were chiefly grammar schools endowed by charitable funds which provided a 'higher education', which was defined as education beyond the age of 12 or 13 years and the inclusion of Latin or Greek in the curriculum. Inter-country comparisons were made, and the conclusion reached that Britain needed more technical and special schools to teach the science-based subjects which were in demand by industry as technology advanced rapidly. The Commissioners accepted that classics should remain the basis upon which technical education should be built, and among their recommendations was one that greater finance from local rates should be directed towards the cost of school building and maintenance.

The conclusions of the Clarendon and Taunton Reports led on to a more

---

[2] Such a system was soon to be adopted in the *Education Act* 1870.
[3] The Newcastle Report (1861) Volume 1, Part I, pp. 542–52. See also the evidence of Professor Stuart of Cambridge University to the Samuelson Commission (1884) referred to later in this chapter.

specialised examination of the teaching of science in both public and endowed schools. This was done by the Devonshire Commission (*Report of the Royal Commission on Scientific Instruction and the Advancement of Science* 1875). The Commissioners found that only 63 out of 128 endowed schools which responded to questions actually taught science, and only 13 of these possessed a laboratory. Only 14 of the 128 schools spent more than four hours per week teaching science subjects. The Commissioners recommended that schools should teach science subjects for not less than six hours per week, and also that in the General School Examination, and in the leaving examination, not less than one-sixth of the total marks should be for science subjects (Sixth Report, pp. 65 and 74).

Meanwhile, in 1870, primary education had been greatly advanced by the *Education Act* of that year, and government funding for education was increased. This major reform dealt only with basic education. The government provided no financial support for vocational education or training. Industry was on its own in that respect for a long period.

The apprentice system continued after 1814, but on a more flexible basis to suit demand in the labour market and the needs of various skilled trades. The Mechanics Institutes, which had been started in the late eighteenth century as a mode of technical education by evening classes, began to provide technical off-the-job education and training on a larger scale. These Institutes were rapidly developed in the 1820s, and by the end of that decade every main town had its Mechanics Institute. They received no financial support from public funds. The Edinburgh School of Arts (founded 1821), the Manchester Institute (1824) and the London Institute (1823) became major centres for technical education. Regional Unions of Mechanics Institutes were formed and the Royal Society of Arts (RSA) became the examining body for these Regional Unions in 1852.

After the *Education Act 1870* (the Foster Act) the movement toward technical education and training gathered fresh impetus. The Livery Companies founded the City and Guilds of London Institute for the Advancement of Technical Education in 1878, and that institute took over the technical examinations from the RSA, which retained an examining role for commercial and clerical subjects. That system, in basic form, continues to-day. In addition, further technological progress and economic growth gave impetus to the foundation of privately-funded polytechnics in the 1880s.

An attempt was made by the Samuelson Commission during the years 1882–84 to investigate the link between economic growth and the progress of educational and vocational training (*Reports of the Royal Commission on Technical Instruction* 1882–84). The Commissioners visited factories and technical colleges and other training institutions in seven continental

European countries and in Britain. Their second and final report, dated 4 April 1884, is a very thorough treatment of the subject. Their conclusions are generally favourable to the British position: 'Great as has been the progress of foreign countries, and keen as is their rivalry with us in many important branches, we have no hesitation in stating our conviction, which we believe is shared by Continental manufacturers themselves, that, taking the state of the arts of construction and staple manufacture as a whole, our people still maintain their position at the head of the industrial world . . . Machinery made in this country is more extensively exported than at any former period'(Second Report, pp. 506 and 507). The age of excessive British pessimism about vocational education and training and the over statement of real or imagined shortcomings, which now prevails, had not yet begun. However, the Commissioners had some improvements to propose. They made specific recommendations and proposals, (*ibid.*, pp. 536–40), which included the following:

1 Recommendations requiring legislative action:

> For public elementary schools: include elementary drawing as a single subject, and geography as an elementary science. [This emphasis on drawing runs throughout the report.] Classes in science and art should be more practical.
>
> Children under 14 should not be allowed in full-time factory work unless the fifth standard had been passed.
>
> Greater facilities should be provided for the training of elementary teachers.
>
> Classes for artisans under the Science and Art Department should contain more practical science and should be subject to greater inspection by qualified persons.
>
> Secondary and technical instruction should be advanced by (i) accelerating the application of private endowments to that purpose, and (ii) by the Charity Commissioners making provision for the establishment of schools for the study of natural science, drawing, mathematics and modern languages, rather than Greek and Latin.
>
> Local authorities should be empowered to establish, if they think fit, and maintain secondary and technical schools and colleges.

2 General recommendations not requiring legislative action:

> That it be made a condition by employers of young persons . . . that such young persons requiring it receive instruction in science or arts, as required, either in schools attached to the works or in such classes as may be available, the employers and trade organisations contributing to the maintenance of such classes.

That the managers of science teachers should arrange the emoluments of teachers so that they aim to retain their pupils for more advanced studies.

That scholarships for technical education be more liberally funded.

That the subscriptions given by the City of London be made adequate to support the work undertaken by the City and Guilds Institute.

These recommendations were concerned primarily with improving those parts of the curricula of schools which dealt with the more practical aspects of science and art, including elementary drawing, so as to make a firmer base for secondary and technical instruction, or what would now be called vocational education, which the Commissioners also wished to see improved and extended.

A point of relevance to modern conditions may be made about off-the-job training. Evidence and opinion is presented, particularly by Professor Stuart of Cambridge University, who was then in the process of establishing the mechanical workshops of the University, that it was essential that trainee artisans and apprentices should 'attach theoretical [engineering] work done in the evenings to the practical work done in the daytime' (*Reports of the Royal Commission on Technical Instruction* 1884, Second Report, p. 422). The Commissioners looked very favourably on the strong trend, then evident, towards evening classes where theoretical subjects were taught.

Yet another Royal Commission which was to some extent concerned with education and training was set up in the 1880s. It examined, exhaustively, the evidence for 'the causes of the severe and prolonged depression in trade and industry' which started about 1875 and extended well into the 1880s. Among the causes identified by the Commissioners was the insufficient technical education of British workers compared with workers employed by Britain's overseas competitors (*Reports of the Royal Commission Appointed to Inquire into the Depression of Trade and Industry* 1886). William Brocklehurst MP, a silk manufacturer, gave evidence and opinion to the effect that the country had suffered very much due to a lack of technical education compared with France and Germany (Second Report, p. 501). The old apprenticeship system had been reduced by the 1880s, and Brocklehurst argued for a substitute in the form of technical schools. An analysis of returns from Chambers of Commerce, who were canvassed for their views, showed that in their opinion remedial measures should include improvements in technical and artistic education (Final Report, p. 712).

A major result of these commissions and reports was a large boost for vocational education. The polytechnic movement, pioneered by Quinton

Hogg, who established the Regent Street Polytechnic in 1882, expanded fast. The new polytechnics drew finances from charitable funds unfrozen by the *City Parochial Charities Act 1883*, and later by public money from local authorities who were enabled by the *Technical Instruction Act 1889*, which empowered the new local authorities to levy rates for the purpose of establishing technical schools for teaching 'the principles of science and arts applicable to industries'. The *Local Taxation Act 1890* provided additional public funds for the same purpose (Perry 1976, p. 24). These two Acts also enabled the local authorities for the counties to tap a further source of revenue by using incomes from licence fees for public houses for the purposes of technical education. This so-called 'whisky money' was used to support technical colleges and polytechnics. These institutions were administered by the school boards, and the two systems were amalgamated in the *Education Act 1902* (the Balfour Act).

The character of the demand for labour was now changing fast as technological progress advanced in the 1890s. The generation and application of electricity followed the main engine of the industrial revolution – steam power. The gas and chemical industries and shipbuilding expanded fast at this time as did the mechanical engineering industry, which moved ahead even faster with the invention of the internal combustion engine at the end of the century. The demand for skilled labour increased rapidly, but a high proportion of the total demand for labour was still for unskilled or semi-skilled labour in many large manufacturing industries, such as textiles and clothing. Here, such skills as were needed were learnt on the job and employers were content with the recruitment of youth labour directly from schools. However, in the technological growth industries higher skills were essential, and the demand for them grew strongly. It was met in part by the apprenticeship system, and by the new technical colleges and polytechnics. But for many young people training took place on the job, supplemented by attendance at evening classes. In some cases such attendance was compulsory.

In the 1890s and up to 1914 there was undoubtedly an increase in the total demand for skills, but also some deskilling as industrial processes became more mechanised. At the same time, there was much need for re-skilling as technological change made some skills redundant and gave rise to demands for new skills.

As technology advanced further, the employers in the industries concerned found that the basic school education was an insufficient foundation for the technical training which was now needed. The pressure for raising the school leaving age came from this group and also from educational reformers. On the other hand, the employers in the industries which depended largely on unskilled labour opposed this reform. They did not see the need for more basic education, or for specialised vocational training beyond what they provided themselves. This latter group carried the day and the raising of the school leaving age from 13 to 14 was delayed for many vital years until 1918.

In the skilled trades, apprenticeships still served a useful purpose to both employers and employees because they enabled both cost and risk to be minimised, but some risk was nevertheless involved. The employer could have no guarantee that the employee would stay once he had completed his training at work and at a technical college where his fees had been paid by the employer, and the employee had to risk failure in an examination and had no guarantee of employment after training (More 1980, p. 219).[4] The modern problem of 'poaching' recently trained skilled workers started about this time.

A further large step forward was made in the general education system by the *Education Act 1902*, which followed the recommendations of the Bryce Commission of 1895, which found that education at all levels was 'unco-ordinated and illogical'(*Reports of the Royal Commission on Secondary Education* 1894–5). The *Education Act 1902* abolished the school boards (which controlled the so-called 'board schools') set up under the *Education Act 1870*, and the local technical instruction committees. All forms of state elementary and secondary education were put under the control of the county and county borough councils. These became Local Education Authorities (LEAs).

By 1900 there were already half a million children in higher grade board schools, organised science schools under local authorities and 'higher tops' of elementary schools. After the 1902 Act the provision of grammar schools (either endowed or provided) increased at a rapid rate (85,000 pupils in 1904–05, 135,000 in 1908–09 and 334,000 in 1925), but competition for secondary school places became keener (quickened by the 25% free place system), and to meet this rapid increase in demand higher elementary schools re-appeared, usually under the name of central or senior schools. (Argles 1964, p. 59).

As regards youth training in technical skills, trade schools were established and later became known as Junior Technical Schools. These schools took in pupils at the elementary school leaving age of 13 and prepared them for artisan or industrial skilled occupations. By 1913 there were 37 such schools with 2,900 pupils (Argles 1964, p. 59).

The large and sustained growth in population and in economic activity strongly stimulated by the fast technological progress which took place in the nineteenth century was supported, after a great deal of study and

---

[4] See More (1980) also for a general treatment of education and training between 1870 and 1914.

examination by Royal Commissions and other official bodies, by fundamental improvements in general and vocational education and training. These improvements did not move forward together. In the 1890s in particular, and until the reforms contained in the *Education Act 1902*, general school education was insufficient to support the vocational and technical education which was needed. After the 1902 Act, however, the two educational processes moved more closely in step with each other.

It may be doubted how far lessons can be learned from history, but the present day system is seen by some to be out of step because the general educational process has failed in recent years to provide an adequate basis for vocational education and training (see Chapter 11). This has been due to failure of the teaching process, but it has had effects similar to the shortage of secondary education caused by financial stringency and ineffective organisation in the late nineteenth century. The lesson from the earlier period is that the two processes should develop in step with each other and should be closely matched and effectively linked together.

An important advance in government measures to improve the operation of the labour market, and in particular the youth labour market, was made in 1909 when, following a recommendation of the Royal Commission on the Poor Laws (set up in 1905), a national system of employment exchanges was established under the *Labour Exchanges Act*. In a number of these exchanges the Board of Trade included special juvenile departments. This process of helping school leavers and other young people under 17 to find suitable employment was carried a stage further the next year when the *Education (Choice of Employment) Act 1910* empowered Local Authorities in England and Wales to provide a career advice service for young people under seventeen in their areas. These arrangements, with some administrative changes, endured until the Ministry of Labour was made responsible for the service in 1927, following the recommendations of the Malcolm Committee 1925 (q.v.) (Parker 1957, pp. 349–350).

Wartime training and employment

The First World War was at first expected to be short, and little planning of manpower resources was done until 1915 when measures were taken to check the indiscriminate enlistment of men in the armed services regardless of their industrial skills. After a long process of trial and error, a system of 'reserved occupations' was worked out and successfully applied so that sufficient resources of skilled manpower were retained for the munitions industries.

Nevertheless, the demand for munitions soon outpaced supply. A Ministry of Munitions was set up in June 1915. A little earlier, in March

1915, a Treasury Agreement had embodied a contract with the Trade Unions for the suspension for the duration of the war of their restrictive job demarcation practices, which provided that only skilled men of a certain grade were permitted to do some jobs. The unions agreed to remove these restrictions. Many practical difficulties then arose, but were resolved by the appointment of a Director of Dilution by the Ministry of Munitions. The process of dilution of labour followed. This entailed the breakdown of many skilled jobs into a number of operations which required only the semi-skilled labour that suited the mass production line modes of manufacture which employers had introduced to meet the demand for munitions. As a result, young people and previously unemployed women were recruited and trained to perform a wide range of semi-skilled jobs on these production lines.

Training was organised by the Ministry of Munitions and took place in technical schools, in instructional factories, and in instructional bays within factories. The technical schools remained formally under the management of the local authorities, but they were re-equipped with modern machinery and financed and inspected by officials of the Ministry of Munitions. By 1918, 100 technical schools had been re-equipped and a dozen large instructional factories, each capable of teaching several hundred trainees at a time, were set up. The aim in nearly all cases was to produce competent machine operators capable of only a few individual operations (Sheldrake and Vickerstaff 1987, pp. 7–8). That was generally sufficient to meet the needs of the employers who were producing munitions. An example of the aims of these wartime training schemes for women is given in the *Dilution of Labour Bulletin* for March 1918: 'In order to render the bulk of women's work productive rapidly, it was no good attempting to teach them a trade but only that part of it which she was going to be employed on – in fact to specialise'.

The strength of the British Army in November 1918 was 3,759,500, compared with 499,100 in August 1914, and between 1914 and 1918 the Army's total battle casualties (killed, wounded, prisoners of war and missing) were 2,526,800. In spite of the huge demand for manpower for the Army which these figures imply, to which must be added the demand for manpower for the Royal Navy, the number of workers in the munitions industries (metal industries including engineering, chemicals, government arsenals and dockyards) rose from 1,869,000 males in July 1914 to 2,309,300 in November 1918. Female workers employed in these industries increased over the same period from 212,000 in 1914 to 944,700 in 1918. So a *net* increase in total labour resources of 1,173,000 persons, of whom 732,700 were women, took place in these industries during the First World War – an increase of 56.4% (Parker 1957, p. 6, Tables 1 and 2 and p. 16, Table 4).

This very substantial direction and deployment of labour by the government was the first example of such action in British history. It was not unsuccessful. The lessons learned were used in the Second World War of 1939–45, and some government intervention in labour markets continued in the inter-war period, which is now examined.

The inter-war period: the beginning of the end of *laissez-faire*

This period started promisingly with substantial progress in educational reform. The *Education Act 1918* (the Fisher Act) extended compulsory education to the secondary stage. It abolished half-time academic education, but made provision for compulsory part-time day continuation schools for vocational education on the German model, but that recommendation was not implemented – a casualty of the post-war depression of 1920–21.

The powers of Local Education Authorities were increased under the Fisher Act, and not less than 50% of the cost of education was henceforth met by grants to the LEAs from the Exchequer. The Fisher Act declared Parliament's intention to raise the school leaving age from 14 to 15 years, but that was not done until 1947. It was raised to its present level of 16 years in 1972 following, after considerable delay, a recommendation of the Crowther Report (*Report of the Central Advisory Council for Education, 15–18* 1959–60).

The advance in academic education enabled by the Fisher Act provided an improved basis for vocational education and training. What was also needed, in the early post-1918 period, was parallel improvement in technical education and training. However, there was first an extra task of special importance which involved government intervention in the labour market. This was the training or re-training of ex-Servicemen. The Ministry of Labour began to plan for this task in 1917. An Industrial Training Scheme was established to assist disabled ex-Servicemen in particular, but also non-disabled men who had enlisted in the armed forces before entering or before completing their training for a skilled trade. Employers' associations and trade unions collaborated in the National Trade Advisory Committees which the Ministry of Labour established. Industrial training schemes were set up. They comprised a period of from six to eighteen months at a technical school or Ministry of Labour Instructional Factory followed by eighteen months as an 'improver' at a factory. At the end of this training programme the person concerned would be expected to be fully skilled, and also eligible to become a member of the appropriate trade union.

The depression of 1920/21 intervened, unemployment increased and, as was to happen again in similar economic circumstances in future (see Chapter 14), the trade unions used their power to restrict the number of men admitted for training (Sheldrake and Vickerstaff 1987, p. 9).[5] Between 1919 and 1924, 88,800 ex-Servicemen received training; of these, 82,800 were disabled and only 6,000 were non-disabled. In 1922 the Geddes Report (*Interim Report of the Committee on National Expenditure* 1922), whose recommendations became known as the 'Geddes Axe', recommended large cuts in government expenditure, and an end to government-supported training for able-bodied ex-Servicemen. Even the disabled ex-Servicemen suffered from these economy measures. At the start of 1922, 35,000 disabled ex-Servicemen were awaiting industrial training. Only 9,000 were accepted, and the remainder were offered grants *in lieu* of training under the Civil Liberties Schemes. The Ministry's Instructional Factories were reduced under these economies from 58 to 13, and its other training centres from 252 to 43 (Swann and Turnbull 1978, p. 206).

There were two other rather more successful training schemes for non-disabled ex-Servicemen. The Interrupted Apprenticeship Scheme was for ex-Servicemen who had been prevented by war service from starting or finishing an apprenticeship. Up to 31 December 1924 the number of apprentices accepted under this scheme was 44,718. This scheme was financially supported by employers and by government grants which comprised a maintenance allowance, family allowances for married men, apprentice fees and in some cases fares (Swann and Turnbull 1978, p. 159). 'It is also known that some employers adopted the scheme for their industry, but did not make application for the State allowance. It is estimated that as many men benefited by the scheme in this way as were actually brought under it, and it is probably not an exaggeration to say that nearly 100,000 ex-Servicemen apprentices received the advantages of the Scheme' (*Ministry of Labour Report* 1923 and *Ministry of Labour Report* 1924, p. 109).

The apprentice system itself was disrupted by the war: 'Boys and girls who in normal times would have been apprenticed went from school into factories where they worked long hours for high wages but learned very little' (Swann and Turnbull 1978, p. 112). The Coalition Government, elected in 1918, took action for this section of the youth labour market but it was not fully remedial. Juvenile Unemployment Centres (JUCs) were established, and there were 215 of these by May 1919. But they were short-lived, and the last centre closed in February 1920. Later the JUCs were revived by the Labour Government in 1924, who supported them with 100% grants.

---

[5] The union representatives achieved this through their membership of the Local Technical Advisory Committees which controlled entry to the Industrial Training Scheme.

The *Unemployment Insurance Act 1930*, established the Juvenile Instruction Centres (JICs) for unemployed youths under the age of 18, and 132 of these were set up by December 1931. The JICs were operated by the LEAs. Approved courses of instruction were supplied by the National Advisory Council on Juvenile Employment with the aim of assisting young people into employment in industry. This process was carried forward in the *Unemployment Insurance Act 1934*, which made provision for the establishment of training courses for unemployed juveniles, and day continuation classes were held at existing institutions (Swann and Turnbull 1978, p. 112). Some 200 JICs were in operation by the end of 1936. As economic conditions improved later on the number of JICs declined.

An opinion on the operation of the JICs was given by a contemporary writer:

A serious weakness [of the JICs] lay in the policy of establishing centres on the shifting sands of unemployment. No school [JIC] could be started or maintained unless there were fifty juveniles attending and likely to go on attending. Nowhere was it possible to say how long that condition would last. The brighter boys got employment quickly and the average period of attendance was little over three weeks. Active juvenile transference from the Special Areas played a part. Yet on the whole, the extended movement did splendid service. Many girls and boys were given what amounted to a new start in life. New discoveries were made in the art of blending practical and academic instruction, and in the art of handling these adolescent wage- earners of fifteen or so, who were no longer children. The pity was that the employed could not enjoy the same advantages as the unemployed young people. In other words the success of the JICs, wherever they had a fair chance, added another potent argument in favour of compulsory part-time day continuation schools for all. (Davison 1938, p. 121)

These early government interventions in the youth labour market in Britain were tentative, but in form they foreshadowed later developments in this section of the market and they are notable for that reason.

In 1919, for the first time, the need to consider the vocational education and training of women was recognised. Many women had been engaged in war work between 1914 and 1918. Many of these did not wish to stop working, but neither did they wish to return to or to enter domestic service. There were also many war widows who were seeking employment, and 5,000 of them applied for job training (Swann and Turnbull 1978, p. 160). The government provided a training grant of £150,000, and a further £170,000 was provided from the National Relief Fund, for the purpose of running courses for women 'whose capacities and opportunities have been injuriously affected as a result of conditions arising out of the war' (Ministry of Labour 1925, p. 222). Courses were established on a range of subjects which included nursing, institutional housekeeping, homecrafts, clerical

skills and, a precursor of larger technological changes to come, comp-
tometer operating. The courses ran for between three and twelve months.

The economic depression of the early 1920s (the trough was in 1921) led
to the establishment in 1925 of Government Training Centres (GTCs).
Their objective was to give training in various trades to unemployed
workers in industrially depressed areas. Later some of these were designated Special Areas and received government grants for this and other
purposes under the *Special Areas (Development and Improvement) Act 1934*.
The GTCs were maintained during the more severe unemployment in the
early 1930s. Sixteen of them were still open in 1939, and they were greatly
expanded as centres of training in the Second World War.

In the mid 1920s the government instituted an enquiry into apprenticeship and training, which was undertaken by the Ministry of Labour. In the
tradition established in the nineteenth century, a report in seven volumes
was produced (*Report of an Enquiry into Apprenticeship and Training for
Skilled Occupations in Great Britain and Northern Ireland, 1925–26* 1928).
The first six volumes deal with particular industries in considerable detail.
The seventh volume is a general report with summary and conclusions. It
was considered by the authors of this report that the chief method of
training new entrants to skilled trades in the labour market from school was
via apprenticeships. 'Apprenticeship is still of supreme importance in the
modern industrial system and is still the recognised and by far the most
systematic method of entry into the ranks of skilled men in the most
important industries of the country' (Volume 7, p. 163).

The general conclusion reached by this very thorough enquiry was that
the apprenticeship system was not in decline as a whole. There had been
some changes in 'density' (the ratio of apprentices to journeymen – as
skilled and experienced workers were still called) in some trades between
1909 and 1925. For example, an increase in density in the building trades
was noticed, as was a decline in density in the printing and allied trades. For
all skilled occupations the average density ratio was found to be 4.4: 1,
journeymen to apprentices. In total in the Census of Population year 1921
there were 315,000 boy apprentices and 110,000 boy 'learners'.[6]

The burden of apprentice training fell largely upon smaller firms – large
firms contributed little. This aspect caused concern to the Ministry of
Labour's enquirers, as did the attractions to would-be apprentices of less

---

[6] An apprenticeship is a contractual relationship between employer and trainee, with stated
terms and period (usually 5–7 years at this time). A learner is engaged by an employer for an
agreed period of training and provided with facilities for learning a branch or process of the
industry. An apprenticeship led to 'skilled status', a learnership successfully concluded was
usually limited to operating a single type of machine or process which entailed only
semi-skilled work.

Table 4.1 *Relative weekly pay of apprentices and journeymen fitters in the engineering industry, 1909 and 1925, UK (shillings and pence)*

| | Apprentices | | | | Journeymen | |
| | First year of apprenticeship | | Last year of apprenticeship | | | |
	1909	1925	1909	1925	1909	1925
Pay of engineering fitters	4/10	10/3	12/5	24/10	36/7	56/6
(Apprentice's pay as % of journeyman's pay)	(13.2)	(18.1)	(33.9)	(44.0)		

Source: *Report of an Enquiry into Apprenticeship and Training for Skilled Occupations in Great Britain and Northern Ireland, 1925–26* 1928, p. 116.

skilled occupations which had higher *initial* rates of pay.

On the matter of pay, a trend was noted which recurred in the 1970s and 1980s. An example is given in Table 4.1. There was clearly a substantial upwards drift in the pay of apprentices relative to that of journeymen in this trade between the years shown in Table 4.1.

A view of the relative size and scale of apprentice training and the training of learners in 1925 is given in Table 4.2.

Perhaps the most useful and significant figure is the 28.2% of the male workforce under 21 who were either apprentices or learners with firms in 1925.

Table 4.2 *Relative size of schemes for apprentices and 'learners' in the UK, 1925*

	% of total employers taking male apprentices or learners	% of total male workforce who are apprentices or learners	% of total male workforce under 21 who are apprentices or learners
Apprentices	23.2	3.8	19.5
Learners	7.0	1.6	8.7
Total	30.2	5.4	28.2

Source: *Report of an Enquiry into Apprenticeship and Training for Skilled Occupations in Great Britain and Northern Ireland, 1925–26* 1928, p. 24.

Table 4.3 *Projections (made in 1926) of juveniles at age 16 and 'likely to be occupied'*[a] *each year, 1926–39, GB (000s)*

1926	660	1934	471
27	647	35	479
28	640	36	707
29	646	37	655
30	647	38	641
31	630	39	594
32	579		
33	537		

Note: [a]Based on the ratio between occupied juveniles to total juveniles for 1921, and on the assumption that this ratio would remain unchanged.
Source: Report of an Enquiry into Apprenticeship and Training for Skilled Occupations in Great Britain and Northern Ireland, 1925–26 1928, p. 116, Appendix Table V.

On-the-job training was increasingly allied in the 1920s with off-the-job vocational education, usually at evening classes, but also at part-time day release classes. Most employers encouraged this trend and some made off-the-job class attendance obligatory.

Although, with some good reasons, the Ministry of Labour's Enquiry of 1928 concluded that the processes for the training of apprentices and learners was satisfactory in terms of quality and quantity, doubt and some apprehension was expressed about the decline in the birth rate and the implications of that trend for the supply of juveniles of both sexes at age 16 in the 1930s. The trend in the GB population at age 16 from 1926 to 1939, shows (Table 4.3) similarity with the modern trend (shown in Chapter 2, Table 2.5) for the period 1985–2000.

There was a remarkable but unsustained surge in the birth rate in 1920, which is reflected in the figure for occupied juveniles for 1936, but the main trend is a sharp decline in total number between 1930 and 1935. In this latter respect this governing factor in the supply to the youth labour market has recurred in the 1980s and 1990s.

The already firmly established national practice of setting up commissions and inquiries into education, training and the labour needs of industry was continued in 1928 when the Malcolm Report (*Report of the Committee on Education and Industry (England and Wales)* 1928) was produced, to be followed only a year later by the Balfour Report (*Report of the Committtee on Industry and Trade* 1928–1929, Volume VII).[7]

The first of these reports, on education and industry, was important for its general conclusion that there was an urgent need for education and

---

[7] All quoted page numbers refer to this volume unless otherwise stated.

industry to work together for the common cause in 'close and continuous cooperation', and the Committee noted that a successful education system was a necessary condition for the prosperity of industry and commerce (Malcolm Report, Part II pp. 58 and 59). Among the more specific conclusions and recommendations of the Malcolm Committee are the following:

1 The Board of Education should issue to industrialists a descriptive handbook on the education system (p. 59).
2 There should be a formal system of educational and career advice for leavers from elementary school [the start of the present day careers service] (p. 62).
3 There was seen to be no need for specialised vocational education in elementary schools, and 'great caution' should be exercised when giving any vocational bias to instruction in secondary schools (p. 59).
4 The secondary school leaving age was higher than the age limits on entry to apprenticeship, and there was a need to alter the latter to match (p. 61).
5 Conditions in evening schools should be improved, because of the burden placed upon pupils who came to evening classes after a long working day. It was noted that a large proportion of pupils failed to complete the 2-year courses (p. 62).
6 The Committee recognised that while education and commerce were organised locally, industry was often organised nationally. It was proposed that the Board of Education should develop a role as coordinator of information between schools and industry (p. 64).
7 The LEAs should try to establish standard methods for assessing school leavers in order to decrease confusion amongst employers on standards of certification (p. 60).

If increased contact between school and industry were established following these and other recommendations to the same end, the Committee proposed that the Board of Education and the Ministry of Labour should allow the National Council for Juvenile Employment to be responsible for maintaining this liaison.

The conclusions of the Malcolm Report are given in some detail because of its importance in attempting to improve the efficiency of the youth labour market in Britain, its main method being to promote the flow of information in both directions between the demand and supply sides of this market.

The Balfour Report of 1929 ranged more widely, examining British overseas trade and the country's ability to meet competition and satisfy foreign demand (p. 415). It regarded education and training as of prime importance to industrial efficiency, but avoided overlap with the Malcolm Report by confining its work to stating what industry needed:

Table 4.4 *Rates of unemployment in the United Kingdom, 1928–38*

	Insured unemployed as % of all insured employees	Total unemployed as % of total employees
1928	10.8	8.2
1929	10.4	8.0
1930	16.1	12.3
1931	21.3	16.4
1932	22.1	17.0
1933	19.9	15.4
1934	16.7	12.9
1935	15.5	12.0
1936	13.1	10.2
1937	10.8	8.5
1938	12.9	10.1

Source: Feinstein 1972, Table 58, p. T128.

1 A steady and even flow of recruits to fill vacancies particularly in the 'growing body of semi-skilled workers' (p. 621).
2 Increased co-operation between industry and education authorities [similar to Malcolm] (p. 622).
3 Relationship between school and workshop. New demarcation of school and workshop functions was seen to be needed. A joint board was proposed to organise this (p. 624).
4 Day release for technical instruction, on the grounds, pointed out in the Malcolm Report, that evening classes were poorly attended because they took place after a full day's work (p. 626).

In the long view, perhaps the most important result of the Balfour Committee was its cautious support for a memorandum submitted to it by the Board of Education. This was that 'each industry should establish machinery by which it may examine and formulate its own requirements with regard to industrial training, and co-operate with educational authorities in ensuring that these requirements are suitably met' (Balfour Final Report p. 204). No action was taken on this for 35 years, until 1964 when the *Industrial Training Act* of that year established Industrial Training Boards (ITBs) for each industry.

The 'great depression' of the early 1930s had a marked effect upon unemployment, as shown by two series in Table 4.4. The unemployment insurance system was far from complete in this period. Those who were insured and unemployed were ready claimants and registered at once. In

Table 4.5 *Unemployment rates among insured juveniles and adults in Great Britain, 1927–32 (%)*

	Juveniles (age 14–18)	Adults (age 18 +)
1927	3.5	10.2
1928	3.6	11.4
1929	3.3	10.4
1930	5.7	16.8
1931	7.6	22.7
1932	7.6	23.3

Source: Ministry of Labour Gazette, 1928–1933.

each of these two series the numerator and denominator are different, but the alternative measures of unemployment which they provide show similar trends.

The population of working age was rising fast at this period, from 20,740,000 in 1928 to 23,582,000 in 1938. So labour supply rose steeply while labour demand (total employment) fell from 19,204,000 in 1928 to a low point of 18,665,000 in 1931, rising to 21,418,000 in 1938. This of course led to a massive imbalance in the labour market. One method which the authorities attempted to use to improve labour market efficiency and to reduce unemployment was to transfer unemployed workers, including 80,000 juveniles, from the depressed areas (some were designated Special Areas in 1934) of the country to the relatively more prosperous areas which were largely in the South East. In the period 1928–38, the Ministry of Labour encouraged and arranged the transfer of 250,000 workers (Davison 1938, p. 27). Later policies adhered to the principle of 'taking the work to the workers', rather than the other way round, and that change was due to the relative failure of the first policy and the social problems associated with the transfers of workers in this period.

So far as figures (for Great Britain) are available, the youth section of the labour market fared better than the adult section, as is shown in Table 4.5. However, it must be recorded that many unemployed juveniles in particular were uninsured. For what these figures are worth the *trend of* increase in unemployment for both juveniles and adults was similar: a two-and-a-quarter-fold increase between 1929 and 1932. Comparisons between the two series for any one year are likely to be unreliable. It was noted earlier, from figures given in Table 4.3, that owing to wide fluctuations in the birth rate during and after the world war of 1914–18, the number of juveniles seeking employment in the years 1930–35 was rather lower than for earlier and later years. So the problem of youth unemployment was less in the worst years of the 1930s' depression than it might otherwise have been. This position is in marked contrast to that shown in Chapters 5 and 6, where in the 1970s and early 1980s the cohort of juveniles was exceptionally large owing to high birth rates in earlier years, and their unemployment rates were much higher than the corresponding rates for adults.

Training in the Second World War

Sixteen Government Training Centres (GTCs), established in 1925, remained in operation in 1939. They were then greatly expanded to meet the massive increase in the demand for skilled and semi-skilled labour, chiefly for the engineering industries, during the Second World War (*Report of the Committee on Manpower Needs* 1940, the Wolfe Report). During the war 350,000 men and women were admitted to GTCs and of these, 270,000 successfully completed their training and were placed in appropriate employment (Parker 1957, p. 389).

Upon the change of government in May 1940, the new Minister of Labour, Ernest Bevin, who was a convinced believer in both the short-term and longer-term benefits of good industrial training, acted fast to increase the number of GTCs to 35 by the end of 1940. The prospects for employment and the financial allowances, and later (from May 1941) the wages paid at the GTCs, were such as to attract a strong flow of recruits from among the unemployed.

Women did not at first enter the GTCs in large numbers, but there was a rapid increase in their numbers in 1942 (Table 4.6). During 1943, the demand for trained workers in engineering began to decline. Demand from the aircraft industry continued to be strong until early 1944, but from then onwards the labour needs of the engineering group of industries were satisfied.

Many employers criticised the GTC courses as being too long, and too general and theoretical to meet their needs for the semi-skilled work involved in setting up and operating one type of machine tool – an urgent labour demand at that time. The Ministry of Labour accepted these criticisms and shortened the courses at the GTCs. The number of GTC places was cut down sharply in 1942, and more on-the-job training was carried out at industrial premises.

The Ministry of Labour also urged employers to undertake the training of their own workers, starting with general instruction, so as to fit them for transfer to such other employment as might be necessary, before undertaking the more specialised training to suit them for work in the employer's own business. The larger firms, who were able to provide the necessary

Table 4.6 *Engineering courses completed at Government Training Centres, 1941–44 (000s)*

	Men	Women	Total
1941	65.5	9.3	74.8
1942	32.2	39.3	71.5
1943	28.7	32.9	61.6
1944	19.5	11.0	30.5

Source: Parker 1957, p. 382.

instructors, did organise training on these recommended lines. There were, however, many smaller firms which did not have the resources to do so. Hence the need for the GTCs.

As in the First World War, some schemes for the dilution of labour were introduced. The supply of apprentice-trained labour in engineering, where the skills required five or six years of training to acquire, soon became very scarce. So dilution, the breaking down of production processes into several operations each of which required only semi-skilled abilities, took place. But this was done less extensively than in 1914–18 owing to the 'reserved occupation' scheme which was in operation in the Second World War.

The shift in the pattern of juvenile employment towards the war-time industries of general engineering, and aircraft and motor manufacture was marked. Between 1938 and the peak in 1942 the general engineering industry increased its employment of boys by 26,000 and of girls by about the same number, and in aircraft and motors, where the peak was in 1943, 23,000 more boys and 22,000 more girls were recruited (Parker 1957, p. 355).

Towards the end of the war the Ministry of Labour introduced the 'Training within Industry scheme for Supervisors' (TWI). The aim of TWI was to develop the skills of supervisors at all levels in industry. In particular, skills in instruction, in handling workers, and in improving methods. Courses were held in working time to teach these supervisory skills. Initially, the Ministry provided trainers, but soon the larger firms provided trainee trainers at courses run by the Ministry.

A large amount of training was done at employers' premises during the war and, largely due to Ministerial advice and help, the principle of training within industry became accepted and was to yield good fruit, particularly for young workers, when peace-time conditions returned (Parker 1957, ch. 22).

The early post-war period, 1945–60

As early as April 1942 the post-war training of young workers was being studied. At that time the Ministers of Labour and Education attended a Joint Consultative Committee meeting to examine the problems of the technical education and industrial training of young workers after the war. They observed that in Britain pre-employment vocational training had not been developed to the same extent as in some other countries, and the system of apprenticeships had not been adjusted to make full use of the increased facilities for technical education (Parker 1957, p. 366). A committee was then set up to seek information and opinion from a range of industries on the training of young workers. The committee sought information on:

1 Their plans for training via apprenticeship and other forms of instruction.
2 The introduction of minimum standards of training for young workers.
3 An increase in the strength of the Juvenile Employment Service.

The committee issued a progress report in December 1944. This contained recommendations on the Juvenile Employment Service, on the distribution of information to young people on industrial employment, and on the training and supervision of young workers.

On the basis of this progress report the Minister of Labour set up the Ince Committee in January 1945 to investigate the Juvenile Employment Service (*Report of the Committee on the Juvenile Employment Service* 1945).

The Ince Committee decided that the main defect of the old, pre-war system of Juvenile Employment Committees was its voluntary nature. Limited use had been made of that system because schools did not co-operate fully. So the Committee opted for a compulsory system of vocational guidance for school leavers. This was to take the form of more information on careers being made available to school leavers, combined with interviews with Juvenile Employment Officers. The Committee rejected compulsory placement of juveniles in those industries experiencing recruitment difficulties 'because it would be wrong and wholly unacceptable to public opinion'(Ince Committee Report 1945, p. 22, paragraph 97). This may be contrasted with the compulsory Juvenile Transfer Scheme of the 1930s, and is an example of how government interventions in the youth labour market vary between times of slack demand (in the early 1930s) and buoyant demand (the early post-war period).

A New National Advisory Council on Juvenile Employment was set up and appointed by the Minister of Labour and National Service.

Most of the Committee's recommendations were accepted, with two important exceptions: (i) vocational guidance was not to be compulsory, and (ii) a limit was placed upon information on school leavers which the school authorities were obliged to place at the disposal of the Juvenile Employment Service. This meant that Juvenile Employment Officers could not command the full co-operation of school teachers.

It is the view of Parker that the new administrative procedures removed the acrimony between the Ministry of Labour and the education authorities which had tended in the past to impede the progress of the Juvenile Employment Service (Parker 1957, p. 370).

The recommendations of the Ince Report were embodied, after the exceptions which have been noted, in the *Employment and Training Act 1948*. Section 3 of the Act empowered the Minister to provide 'such training courses for persons, whether employed or not, who are above the upper limit of the compulsory school age, as he thinks necessary or expedient . . . provided that contributions . . . shall not exceed half a million pounds in any year'. The Youth Employment Service (the re-named Juvenile Employment Service) was reformed by this Act, but the Act had little effect on vocational training in industry and commerce (Perry 1976, p. 51).

The Second World War produced many significant developments of a scientific and technical nature. The need in the post-war period for an expansion of technological education was seen as early as 1944. The Percy Committee was appointed in that year and reported in 1945 (*Higher Technological Education: Report of a Special Committee* 1945). It examined higher technological education with regard to the needs of industry and assessed the contributions of the Universities and the Colleges of Technology. The Committee's principal recommendations were as follows.

1 A limited number of technical colleges should develop courses of a university standard.
2 Regional Advisory Councils, similar to some already existing, should be set up to co-ordinate technological studies in Universities and Colleges of Technology.
3 A single national institution, a National Council of Technology, be established as the centre for the post-graduate study of industrial administration. The students would normally be graduates with a few years' experience in industry.
4 All students of technology at Universities or Colleges of Technology should be introduced to industrial organisation and management methods in the final one or two years of their courses.
5 Industry should release some of its specialists as part-time teachers.

The Committee, and in particular Lord Percy himself, attempted 'to lay the foundations for a single national policy of technological education' (Percy

Committee Report, p. 25). This led on to discussion as to whether, and how, to extend degree-granting powers to Colleges of Technology. Percy himself argued for a BTech (equivalent to a BSc) degree to be granted where appropriate by the proposed 'Royal College of Technology'. The issue was controversial, but is of interest as a forerunner of later debates on the so-called 'binary divide'. It was recommended that the idea of a technological BSc be developed. This took a long time. It was ten years before the Diploma (not a BSc) in Technology came into being.

The Barlow Committee reported on scientific manpower in 1946 (*Scientific Manpower* 1946). Prospective changes in the demand for and supply of qualified scientists were examined. The Committee noted that even if the total post-school student population in scientific subjects was doubled immediately, Britain would still compare unfavourably with the USA and with some European countries. It therefore supported the recommendation of the Percy Committee that a full-time university-status technology course ought to be developed, and in addition the status of technical colleges should be strengthened so that we could 'raise the currency of technical qualifications'. This proposal was not acted upon, and was to arise again in the 1980s and 1990s.

Recommendations were also made for the expansion of universities and the establishment of new ones, but little action was taken on this until the large expansion in the early 1960s.

The government produced a White Paper on Technical Education in 1956 (*Technical Education* 1956). This reviewed the state of technical education in Britain. It noted that although it was satisfactory that the number of university students in science and technology had doubled between 1938 and 1955, this rate of increase did not compare well with the United States, some European countries and the Soviet Union. Much more needed to be done to 'strengthen the foundations of the economy'.

As regards technical college students, their number had also increased, particularly part-time day students on release from their jobs (Table 4.7).

The White Paper proposed, among other action to the same end, that the output of advanced courses should be increased by 50%, and the number of day-release places should be doubled. Once again a call was made for closer liaison between schools and industry. It noted that employers had done some good work, for example the establishment of vocational training schools on site. But more needed to be done to 'bring technical education within the reach of all in this country.'

Throughout the 1950s the economy was fully stretched, and unemployment was at an exceptionally low rate (Table 4.8).

The Ministry of Labour maintained a watching brief on apprenticeship schemes, but its main policy with regard to training was to allow industry to

Table 4.7 *Number of technical college students in England and Wales, 1937–38 and 1954–55 (000s)*

	1937/38	1954/55
Full-time	20	64
Part-time day	89	402
Evening students	1094	1575
Total	1203	2041

Source: Technical Education 1956.

Table 4.8 *Rates of unemployment in the United Kingdom, 1948–61[a] (annual average % unemployed)*

1948	1.5[b]	1955	1.2
49	1.6	56	1.3
50	1.6	57	1.6
51	1.3	58	2.2
52	2.2	59	2.3
53	1.8	60	1.7
54	1.5	61	1.6

Notes:
[a]Registered unemployed capable of and available for work. Percentage figure is the number of unemployed expressed as a percentage of total employees in employment and the unemployed as defined.
[b]July figure.
Source: Liesner 1985, Table UK10, p. 26.

make its own arrangements. A voluntarist structure prevailed, with some official help at the margins for the disabled, the hard to place and, under the *Employment and Training Act* 1948, some largely advisory services for school leavers.

Towards the end of the 1950s it was foreseen that there would soon be a substantial increase in the number of school leavers owing to the rise in the number of births in the late 1940s. In 1956 the Carr Committee was set up to examine the training of young people. It reported in 1958 under the title *Training for Skill: Recruitment and Training of Young Workers in Industry*. The 'bulge' which was then foreseen is given now in historical figures in Table 4.9.

As can be seen, from a very stable position in the years 1955–58, this important demographic cohort had increased by 1965 by 28% over the level in 1958, and continued well above the base level for the remainder of

Table 4.9 *The 'late schooling and training' cohort of young people aged 15–19, 1955–70, UK (000s, and Index 1955 = 100 in brackets)*

1955	3336	(100)	1963	4206	(126.1)
1956	3304	(99.0)	1964	4266	(127.9)
1957	3303	(99.0)	1965	4287	(128.5)
1958	3357	(100.6)	1966	4278	(128.2)
1959	3459	(103.7)	1967	4081	(122.3)
1960	3585	(107.5)	1968	3951	(118.4)
1961	3770	(113.0)	1969	3883	(116.4)
1962	4058	(121.6)	1970	3839	(115.1)

Source: Annual Abstract of Statistics, various issues.

the 1960s. The Carr Committee had no doubt that British industry could absorb the foreseen increase in the number of young people in this cohort, but commented: 'we are equally certain that it will fail to do so – to its own cost – unless it increases substantially its present intake into apprenticeship ... Therefore we urge each industry most strongly to lose no time in re-assessing its need for skilled workers, and to maintain labour quality in order to enable us to maintain our place as one of the great manufacturing and trading nations of the world' (Carr Report 1958, pp. 32–6).

In more specific terms, the Report's findings and recommendations included:

1 Existing facilities for apprenticeship training were inadequate in quantity and, in some cases, also in quality.
2 Training arrangements should be flexible for each industry – no stereotype was applicable to all.
3 Proposed means of increasing training:
     group apprenticeship schemes
     joint training centres
     pre-apprenticeship courses.
     block release schemes for off-the-job vocational courses.
4 'Poaching' of skilled workers by employers who did not undertake any or insufficient training themselves was deplored and considered 'irresponsible'. [The Committee did not suggest any ways in which this practice could be stopped, but it did propose that 'firms which are unable to provide training themselves might make some contribution towards the cost of training the skilled workers their industry requires' (p. 33). This foreshadows the formation of the Industry Training Boards (ITBs), and their associated levy upon employers, which were enabled by the *Industrial Training Act 1964*.]

5 The scope of training by apprenticeship should be widened to meet the challenge of technical change, and industries should regard the need to meet possible change as fundamental.

6 Employers should place someone in charge of training programmes, even if their firm is small, and the qualifications of trainers should be improved.

7 Once again, the need for closer co-operation between industry and educational institutions was recommended.

8 Girls should be encouraged to take up craft apprenticeships.

9 A National Apprenticeship Council should be established to follow up and report on action following the Committee's Report and to disseminate information on the collective problems of training.

The Carr Report offered some cogent advice on training for skill, but basically it endorsed the voluntarist system of leaving training in the hands of industry, and it effectively ratified the divisions between industry and government. There was much concentration on modernising and improving the apprenticeship system, but as the Report itself noted 'a boy who fails to obtain an apprenticeship has usually little chance of obtaining other systematic training in employment'. The Report did nothing for him.

The end of 'voluntarism'

Although the Carr Report recommended no radical structural change in the training system, it did foreshadow many of the changes to training policy which occurred in the 1960s. In particular, its recommendation that training arrangements should not be stereotyped for all industries recognised that each industry had its own labour requirements and methods of training. The Committee was aware of the practice of 'poaching' skilled labour, and it followed that by making proposals (not acted upon at the time) for sharing the cost of training among all firms in an industry. These observations and proposals led on to later consideration of whether training should be more oriented towards an industry-by-industry system, which is discussed later in this chapter.

Meanwhile, the long post-war period of economic growth, with an almost fully employed labour force, continued (Table 4.10). Labour shortages and particularly shortages of skilled workers were becoming much more acute.

Conditions in the labour market were very 'tight' in the late 1950s and early 1960s, and the National Joint Advisory Council (NJAC) of the Ministry of Labour set up a Working Party on the Manpower Situation in 1961.

The Report of this Working Party, which was accepted by the NAJC, included the following conclusions:

1 'Manpower resources are limited and likely to remain so. The real reserve to be found among the unemployed is much smaller than the figures suggest. Large contributions [of labour] from other sources are, on balance, unlikely.

2 It is therefore essential to our future prosperity to use such manpower as we have both economically and efficiently. This needs to be more widely realised. The government, employers and trade unions should frame their policies accordingly.

3 In particular an increase in the skilled labour force is vital. Industry and the government should continue their efforts to ensure that young people are given the opportunity and encouragement to acquire skills by apprenticeships or other means.

4 Apprentice training must remain the main source of the badly needed increase in the skilled labour force. But in some occupations more training of adults will also be needed if skill shortages are to be overcome.

5 While primary responsibility must remain with industry, the government may need in future to play a larger role in industrial training. If this principle is accepted, it will be necessary to examine more closely the form which the government's contribution might take and the conditions under which more training of adults might be undertaken.'

The Working Party's view about the government playing 'a larger role in industrial training' set the tone for the future. That fitted with the changes in the climate of opinion which was then, in the early 1960s, moving towards greater central economic planning. The National Economic Development Council (NEDC) was set up in 1962, together with the related Office, NEDO; and the National Plan was published in 1965.

Meanwhile, the government issued a White Paper on Industrial Training (*Industrial Training: Government Proposals* 1962). A Training Bill was proposed under which the Minister of Labour would be given statutory powers to set up Boards (later named Industrial Training Boards (ITBs)) which would be responsible for all aspects of training in individual industries. The range of functions which these boards might be expected to undertake were given. The chief of these are set out below:

1 Establishing policy for training in the industry, including such questions as admission to training (apprenticeship or otherwise), length of training, registration of trainees, and a provision for appropriate attendance at colleges of further education.

2 Establishing standards of training and syllabuses for different occupa-

Table 4.10 *Rates of unemployment*[a] *in the United Kingdom, 1960–70 (annual average percentages)*[b]

1960	1.7	1966	1.6
1961	1.6	1967	2.5
1962	2.1	1968	2.5
1963	2.6	1969	2.4
1964	1.7	1970	2.6
1965	1.5		

Notes:
[a]Registered unemployed capable of and registered for work.
[b]Percentage unemployed of total employees in employment and the unemployed as defined.
Source: Liesner 1985, Table UK10, p. 26.

tions in the industry, taking into account the associated technical education required.

3 Providing advice and assistance about training to firms in the industry.
4 Devising tests to be taken by apprentices and other trainees on completion of training and, if necessary, at intermediate stages – for example, at the end of the first year.
5 Establishing qualifications and tests for instructors.
6 Establishing and running training courses in the Board's own training centres.
7 Paying grants to firms to reimburse them all or part of the costs incurred in the provision of approved training.
8 Paying allowances to trainees not taken on by firms while being trained in public, or the Board's own, centres.
9 Collecting money from establishments in the industry by means of a levy.
10 Borrowing.

A levy on firms was seen as an essential part of the proposal, since the Boards would incur costs in undertaking the functions described above at paragraphs 6, 7 and 8.

One aspect of the contemporary background situation was described in the White Paper (paragraph 5): 'A serious weakness in our present arrangements is that the amount and quality of industrial training are left to the unco-ordinated decisions of a large number of individual firms. These may lack the necessary economic incentive to invest in training people who, once trained, may leave them for other jobs. While the benefits of training are shared by all, the cost is borne only by those firms which decide to undertake training themselves'.

So the government's main aims, as shown by this White Paper, were to establish and maintain higher standards of training on an industry-by-industry basis; to alleviate the problems posed by the 'poaching' of skilled workers trained by others by spreading training costs fairly, it was thought; and to finance the whole policy very largely by a levy on firms and only in a minor way by grants from public funds.[8]

The Industry Training Act was passed by Parliament in March 1964. A Central Training Council (CTC) was established, whose functions were advisory and consultative only, and Industry Training Boards (ITBs) to manage the levy/grant system were set up. The first ITB was established in June 1964, two more in July, including the important Engineering ITB. By 1969 there were 27 statutory ITBs (Perry 1976, p. 175).

Concurrently, the Government Training Centres (GTCs), much used during the Second World War and somewhat reduced since, were expanded to provide more government-supported training places. They were used, among other purposes, for first-year apprenticeship training for the engineering and construction industries. They also provided training to meet the requirements of some ITBs, particularly the Engineering ITB. Training was provided from government funds, the employees were paid their normal wages, and employers had to undertake to provide employment for their employees who undertook these GTC courses. The expansion of training at GTCs was substantial in the 1960s (Table 4.11). Trainees were paid a tax free allowance by the government. In 1970 these were between £8.5.0 and £14.10.0 per week, according to family circumstances. Courses provided training in basic skills in 50 different trades. Approximately 90% of trainees who completed their courses were placed in jobs in the trade for which they had been trained (Orchard 1970).

There was, as has been mentioned, some collaboration and interaction with the ITB system, but broadly the GTCs operated alongside and in addition to the ITBs.

By March 1969, 26 of the 27 statutory ITBs were in operation, and 15 million employees were within the scope of the Boards. The numbers in training in the manufacturing industries increased by 15% between 1964 (when the *Industrial Training Act* was passed) and 1969, and approximately £120 million was set aside by the ITB's in 1967–68 for training grants to employers ('Review of training levy and grant schemes', *Department of Employment Gazette* 1969, pp. 208–10). There have been several studies of

---

[8] Public money was for certain administrative purposes, not to meet training costs directly.

Table 4.11 *Number of Government Training Centres and the number of training places available at them, 1962–68*

	Number of GTCs	Number of available training places
1962	13	2,500
1964	25	3,900
1966	32	6,500
1967	38	8,000
1968	42	10,000

Sources: Department of Employment Gazette February 1968, p. 104, and October 1970, p. 856.

the working of the ITB system. The one containing the most thorough treatment is Perry 1976, particularly Chapters 19, 22 and 24.

Even as early as the late 1960s criticisms of the system began to build up. In summary form these were as follows.[9]

1 There was no central direction. The Central Training Council (CTC) was only advisory and consultative, it had no power to direct the ITBs.
2 Small firms got very little for their levy and the time they spent dealing with the associated paperwork. They regarded the levy as another tax. They were often unable to take up and use small training grants because of the associated overhead and staff costs. Some paid the levy but received no grants, or grants which were less than the levy they paid. The most benefit some could obtain was from joining group training schemes, and using their small training grants in that way.
3 Large firms continued their apprentice-based training practice much as before the 1964 Act. Although off-the-job training and the use of further education facilities were encouraged by the ITB, there was little emphasis upon training for future needs, and nothing was done to change the short-term approach of most employers. In general, the system was designed to promote quantity rather than quality.
4 There were problems of defining industry boundaries, and not all workers came within the scope of the ITB system.
5 The training arrangements remained essentially employer-based and

[9] Sources of criticism of ITBs: BACIE Conference 1967, comments by Perry (1976); Tavernier 1968, p.18; *Training and Education Bulletin* 1968; Lees and Chiplin 1970; other sources of critical appraisal of the ITB system can be found in Sheldrake and Vickerstaff 1987, ch. 6 and in Perry 1976, chs. 19, 22 and 24.

industry-oriented. There was accordingly no commitment to the training needs of the economy as a whole, and little training for transferable skills.

6 Vocational educational interests were represented on the ITBs but did not have full voting rights on the levy.

The ITB system was a product of the then widely accepted belief in planning. Firms received grants for training provided they trained in a way approved by the relevant ITB. In principle, planning decisions are based on the premise that there is some central source of wisdom and foresight which, when applied, will produce the right solution across a wide range of activities in the real world. The *Industrial Training Act 1964* tried to do that in respect of training through direction by the ITBs. Firms were not thought to be capable of investing in training their youth and adult labour in ways which were most suitable to meet the demands of the product markets they faced.

The ITBs were not abolished but substantial changes were made. In 1972 the Secretary of State for Employment published a paper on 'Training for the Future – A Plan for Discussion'.[10] This paper contains the results of a review of the operation of the ITBs:

i the general grant/levy system provided an essential 'shock treatment' which has led to a major change in the attitude of British industry to systematic training;

ii general grant/levy schemes now need to be phased out at a reasonably early date; they have never been relevant to the needs of small firms, and there is now a serious risk that they are becoming an obstacle to the effective development of the industrial training boards;

iii for many industries the industrial training board system offers a good way of helping firms to recognise and meet their own training needs. It also encourages training activities useful to the industry as a whole but beyond the needs of individual firms;

iv the work of the industrial training boards in providing an advisory service, in setting sound standards of training, in encouraging the establishment of group training schemes, and in developing, in conjunction with the education service, programmes of training and further education, must be maintained and expanded;

v there will still be a need for financial incentives for training of particular importance to the economy, but these incentives should be offered on a selective basis;

vi a central organisation will be needed to make arrangements to fill the gaps left at present by the industrial training board system, and to promote training in occupations which cut across industrial boundaries. (*Department of Employment Gazette* 1972, February, p. 132)

[10] *Department of Employment Gazette* 1972, February, pp. 131–4, gives a fuller summary of this paper.

This puts a brave face on this intervention which had lasted eight years. A new phase of intervention policy was about to start, and that is examined in the next chapter.

The summary of results from the review of the ITBs (given above) shows clearly that a policy-learning process had begun with respect to government intervention in vocational education and training.

5 Direct government interventions: early schemes

The long period of full employment in post-war Britain came to an end in the mid 1970s (Table 5.1). There was also, in the early 1970s, a shift in the structure of demand for skilled workers as technology changed. The Industrial Training Board system, set up in 1964 and based on a grant/levy mechanism without major government funding, was failing to deliver the training which was needed. That system was substantially changed by the *Employment Training Act 1973*, under which a centralised national training body, the Manpower Services Commission (MSC), was set up. The MSC had two executive arms: the Employment Services Agency and the Training Services Agency.

Thus the scene was then set for direct government intervention in the labour market. The amount of training and re-training of adults in order to match the shift in the pattern of demand for skills was increased by the Training Opportunities Programme, which had been started in 1972. But before much more could be done to improve training total unemployment increased greatly.

The government's first major direct intervention in the labour market in peace time, and it is important for that reason, was directed to alleviating total unemployment. The instrument used was the Temporary Employment Subsidy (TES). That scheme was started in August 1975 and continued to 1979. It was a contra-cyclical marginal wage subsidy for employees about to be made redundant, and its aim was to preserve their jobs in the longer term. It was for workers of all ages. Action in the youth labour market came later and is examined in this and in later chapters. The economic influences and consequences of the TES have been assessed elsewhere (Deakin and Pratten 1982) and found to have achieved some success. It was on a large scale and a major step in general labour market intervention. By the end of 1978 the cumulative total of employees who had at any time been supported by TES represented 6.1% of all employees in manufacturing industry, and 2.2% of all employees in Britain. The central

Table 5.1 *Unemployment in Great Britain, 1971–81*

	Number of unemployed persons[a] (000s)	Percentage rate of unemployment
1971	713	3.2
1972	799	3.6
1973	566	2.5
1974	571	2.5
1975	902	3.9
1976	1250	5.4
1977	1345	5.7
1978	1321	5.6
1979	1234	5.2
1980	1591	6.8
1981	2422	10.5

Note: [a]Annual averages. Claimant basis estimated by the Department of Employment.
Source: *Employment Gazette*, December 1982, S26.

outcome of the TES was found to be that jobs attributable to the subsidy after 12 months were 41% of the jobs initially supported, and the macroeconomic effect upon *net* government expenditure was shown to have been £30 million per £100 million expended on the subsidy (Deakin and Pratten 1982, p. 168).

New methods of assessment of the effects of labour subsidies were developed at that time. They have been further developed since and are described in Chapter 8 in relation to the assessments of the Youth Training Scheme (YTS) which are made in Chapter 9.

Other labour market interventions followed TES. Their aim was job preservation by encouraging short-time working. In effect, leisure was subsidised. These were the Short Time Working Compensation Scheme (STWCS) 1978, and later the Temporary Short Time Working Compensation Scheme (TSTWCS) 1979. Redundancies were deferred by offering government-aided short-time working as an alternative. Unemployment was not cured by these measures, but the available work was shared around. Nearly a million workers were involved in these schemes. They were at least as effective in preventing unemployment in the short term as was TES, but the government expenditure on TSTWCS was greater in terms of *net* expenditure per job preserved (Lindley 1986, p. 167).[1]

There were also two smaller schemes at this time. They were of the

---

[1] For further assessments of STWCS and TSTWCS see Metcalf 1982a, b.

Table 5.2 *Number of unemployed school leavers compared with total unemployment, 1955, 1960, 1965 and 1970–80, GB (annual averages, 000s)*

	(1) Unemployed school leavers[a]	(2) All unemployed[a]	(3) % col. 1 of col. 2
1955	4.2	213.2	2.0
1960	8.6	345.8	2.5
1965	8.6	317.0	2.5
1970	9.0	582.2	1.5
1971	14.8	758.4	2.0
1972	19.1	844.1	2.3
1973	7.0	597.9	1.2
1974	13.3	599.7	2.2
1975	45.3	935.6	4.8
1976	81.6	1304.6	6.3
1977	99.8	1422.7	7.0
1978	93.7	1409.7	6.6
1979	78.0	1325.5	5.9
1980	120.1	1715.9	7.0

Notes:
[a]Registered unemployed.
[b]The school leaving age was raised from 15 to 16 years in 1972. This influenced the number of unemployed school leavers in 1973 in particular, as a whole annual cohort of young people aged between 15 and 16 stayed on at school.
[c]The figures for 1974 and 1976 are based on monthly figures for 11 months only, owing to strikes by staff at the Department of Employment.
Source: Department of Employment Gazette and the *Employment Gazette*, various issues.

job-creation type. The Small Firms Employment Subsidy (SFES) 1977–80 aimed to stimulate employment by small firms. The scale was small, but about 40% of supported jobs were induced by the SFES. There was some substitution of employees for hours, involving a reduction in overtime working (*Department of Employment Gazette* 1978, May, p. 549). The Adult Employment Subsidy (AES) 1978–79 was on an even smaller scale, and it was found that most of the employment supported would have occurred in the absence of the scheme (*Review of Services for the Unemployed* 1981, p. 34).

Meanwhile, attention had been turning to the youth labour market which by 1975 had moved into massive disequilibrium.

The number of school leavers who were unemployed increased sixfold from 13,300 in 1974 to 81,600 in 1976. As a proportion of total unemployment, which was also rising fast in this period, unemployed school leavers represented 2.2% of the total in 1974 and 6.3% in 1976 (Table 5.2). The demographic background to this breakdown should be noted. The population youth cohort aged 16–19 increased markedly during the 1970s. The size of this cohort in 1971 was 2.98 million, and by 1981 it was 23.5% larger at 3.68 million, reflecting the much higher birth rates of the 1960s (see Chapter 3, Table 3.1).

When the youth labour market and indeed the whole labour market was tight, as it was in the early post-war years (1946–60), government intervention in the market consisted chiefly of help in terms of information and career advice to young people, and school leavers in particular, on choice of occupation. The strength of labour demand was such that several alternative jobs were then available to most school leavers. That situation continued well into the 1960s, despite an upsurge in the number of school leavers due to high birth rates in the late 1940s, but in the mid 1970s the demand for youth labour weakened at the same time as its supply increased for demographic reasons.

The weakening of demand for youth labour, which was much more marked than that for labour as a whole, was considered to have been due to two main factors: (i) a shift away from demand for the more traditional craft skills which had been mainly provided by apprenticeships (see Chapter 6, especially Table 6.2), and, (ii) the much researched and debated influence upon the demand for youth labour of the well-documented rise in the pay of young people relative to that of adults. That well-covered subject is not pursued here, but a sound analysis and useful further treatments may be found in Wells (1983) and Junankar (1987) respectively. In so far as that thesis is accepted, it is relevant to the design of programmes of government intervention in the youth labour market, since sponsored youth employment and training programmes lower the relative remuneration of the young people involved.

The youth labour market imbalance, due chiefly to these supply and demand influences, posed the major national problem of high youth unemployment in the mid 1970s. The government acted by direct intervention in the youth labour market, starting in 1975, at first on a small scale.

Recruitment Subsidy for School Leavers (RSSL)

This subsidy scheme was introduced in October 1975. In that month there were 65,000 unemployed school leavers. Employers were offered £5 per week for six months per school leaver recruited. By the end of June 1976,

29,000 applications for the subsidy had been approved, but by that time there had been 5,000 early leavers from the scheme. Nevertheless, the number of unemployed school leavers increased steeply in 1975, and further in 1976 (Table 5.2).

The Department of Employment commissioned a survey of participants in the RSSL (*Department of Employment Gazette* 1977, July, p. 696). The results were disappointing. In March 1976, 76% of sample firms stated that they would have recruited as many school leavers since October 1975 without the subsidy. There was also some *substitution* of subsidised school leavers for adult part-time female workers. So the additional recruitment of school leavers due to the RSSL was less than 20% of the total number supported by the subsidy.

The RSSL was terminated in October 1976 and was replaced by the Youth Employment Subsidy.

Youth Employment Subsidy (YES)

This subsidy was aimed at the more disadvantaged among the youth cohort aged 16–20. The experience of the RSSL had appeared to show that the recruitment of recent school leavers would proceed largely unaided, and that it would therefore be best for the government to be more selective and to intervene only to help those who had failed to get employment.

The terms of the YES were a payment to employers of £10 per week for a period of 26 weeks for every recruit under 20 who had been unemployed for six months or more (*Department of Employment Gazette* 1976, August, pp. 827–8). Neither this scheme nor the RSSL placed any obligation upon the subsidised firms to provide training for the young people recruited with the aid of the subsidy. It was required that the work for the subsidised youths must be 'normal full time employment, and the vacancy must not have been created by discharging another worker'. All employers in the private sector and in the nationalised industries were eligible to apply for the YES unless they had already received the TES or a training grant.

The YES was in operation from 1 October 1976 to 28 February 1978. In July 1976 there were approximately 44,000 young people aged under 20 and unemployed for six months or more. By the end of February 1978, 38,497 young people had been supported by YES at a cost to government of £8.7 million (*Department of Employment Gazette* 1978, April, pp. 424–5). Most (80%) of the subsidies were paid for the full 26 weeks. The Research and Planning Division of the Department of Employment surveyed a sample of firms receiving YES in July and August 1977. Employers in the sample reported that 75% of the subsidised young workers would have entered their employment regardless of the subsidy, and that of the remaining 25%

only one half were filling jobs which would not have gone to an adult person in the absence of the subsidy. So the so-called *deadweight* effect of the subsidy was 75%, and the *substitution* effect[2] was a further 12.5%, although the subsidy may be seen as enabling preference over other job seekers to be given to this 12.5% of the total of unemployed young people who benefited from the subsidy. The survey results also indicated that the subsidised workers were not generally employed in unskilled jobs, that they were as productive as other young workers, and that the subsidy had a beneficial effect in launching them into permanent full-time employment. But the effectiveness of the subsidy in improving the operation of the youth labour market was slight.

Interventionist policy concurrently involved a work experience scheme for young people.

Work Experience Programme (WEP)

This programme provided subsidised work experience places in industry for young people aged 16–18. It was started in September 1976 and ended as a separate programme early in 1978, and so was approximately concurrent with the YES. The WEP continued, with the same objectives and criteria, as a part of the Youth Opportunities Programme (YOP), which was started in 1978 and which is described and analysed in the next section of this chapter.

All recruitment of unemployed young people into the WEP was through either the Careers Service or the Employment Service Agency. WEP schemes were designed by employers in collaboration with the MSC and employers were allowed the final decision on entry. Trainees were paid an allowance of £18 per week, which was not liable for income tax or national insurance contributions, for a programme of 26 weeks in most cases (though a maximum of 52 weeks was allowed in some cases).

Employers received no payment for running a WEP. A total of 44,351 WEP places were available at the end of 1977. By then 34,000 young people were on the programme and 13,500 had been on it, making the total number of entrants 47,500 (Lasko 1978). The main objective of WEP was to provide planned and varied work experience at the place of work, but no training was specifically required under the terms of the scheme.

An assessment of the effectiveness of WEP was made by the Department of Employment in terms of the employment position of a sample of participants who had gained work experience on the scheme. The basic result in these terms (given in Table 5.3) was that 61% of all participants obtained a full-time job after completing their work experience under the

---

[2] The methodology of assessment of youth labour subsidies is described in Chapter 8.

Table 5.3 *Employment position after WEP, 1978 (%)*

	All participants	Early leavers	Scheme completers
Full-time job with WEP employer	38	30	47
Full-time job with another employer	23	41	6
Unemployed	35	26	43
Other, including part-time employment, full-time education	4	3	4
	100	100	100

Source: *Department of Employment Gazette* 1978, August, p. 901.

scheme or after leaving before completion. Many of those who left early clearly did so in order to take a job with another employer. Those who completed the scheme had the best chance of obtaining employment with the firm in which they had gained work experience.

These early government interventions in the youth labour market were to promote employment. Training was not directly supported by government funds, and the degree of success was thereby limited. In the case of the RSSL it was also limited because the target group was *all* school leavers and may therefore be seen as being insufficiently marginal. It has been shown that TES was a marginal employment subsidy, available (under certain conditions) only to those about to be made redundant. The YES was more marginal in the sense that it applied to all those aged 16–20 who had been unemployed for six months or more, but it was no more successful than the RSSL in promoting recruitment which would not in its absence have taken place. The WEP was judged by the Department of Employment on different grounds. It had some measure of success as judged by the proportion of its participants who obtained employment after a period of subsidised work experience. No doubt work experience involved some on-the-job training, or at least some 'learning by doing'.

The MSC who, with the Department of Employment, devised and supervised these three schemes, was still at this time concerned to reduce unemployment by promoting employment directly. At first the Commissioners intervened to preserve jobs, chiefly of adults, by the TES, then as youth unemployment increased dramatically they turned their attention to youth employment measures. Not until the New Training Initiative of 1981 (*A New Training Initiative: A Programme for Action 1981*) did they very seriously turn to measures to promote youth training as a means of reducing youth unemployment and the major waste of resources which was thereby being incurred.

Youth Opportunities Programme (YOP)

In 1977, annual average youth unemployment (for school leavers) was still very high at 99,800 (Table 5.2), representing 7.0% of total unemployment, and an unemployment rate of 11.8%. The continuation of very high youth unemployment, and the only moderate success of the direct government intervention measures which had hitherto been adopted to secure a higher level of employment of school leavers and other young people under 18, led early in 1978 to the government asking the MSC to produce a programme of places and recruitment on such a scale that no Easter or Summer school leavers in 1978 would still be unemployed by Easter 1979. The MSC produced the Youth Opportunities Programme, which started in March 1978. In April 1978, 29,300 young people aged between 16 and 18 were in the programme, and by September 58,600.

The YOP was larger than any previous government intervention on behalf of youth labour. The scale of the programme is set out in Table 5.4. In total there were 1,834,700 million entrants to YOP, including 4,100 still on the programme in 1983/84 after it had been replaced by the Youth Training Scheme (YTS) in April 1983.

Table 5.4 *The Youth Opportunities Programme: number of entrants and average numbers in training, 1978/79–1982/83*

Years to 31 March	Entrants to YOP[a]	Annual average number in training[b]
1979	162,000	53,906
1980	216,000	77,900
1981	360,000	127,500
1982	553,000	188,400
1983	543,000	241,700

Sources:
[a]Information supplied by the Statistical Services Division of the Employment Department, Sheffield.
[b]*Manpower Services Commission Report for 1982/83* (1983), pp. 11–13.

There were three basic schemes within the Youth Opportunities Programme:

Table 5.5 *YOP entrants by type of scheme, 1978–79, 1980–81 and 1982–83, years to 31 March (000s, percentages in brackets)*

	1978/79	1980/81	1982/83
Work Experience	128.2	304.5	393.4
	(79.0)	(84.6)	(72.4)
Work Preparation	34.0	55.5	67.8
	(21.0)	(15.4)	(12.5)
New Training	–	–	81.9
			(15.1)
Total YOP entrants	162.2	360.0	543.1

Source: Manpower Services Commission Report for 1982/83 1983, pp. 11 and 12.

1 *Work Experience places.* The large majority of these were at the premises of private sector employers for up to six months (the acronym for these was WEEP: work experience at employers' premises). Others were at training workshops for 6–12 months, or on community projects at the premises of local authority or voluntary community groups.
2 *Work Preparation places.* These were short training courses of about 13 weeks at skill centres, colleges of further education and at employers' premises. Others were 'remedial and preparatory' courses, also of about 13 weeks, at colleges of further education and rehabilitations centres, with the aim of providing remedial education in basic literacy and numeracy. There were also some short, 2–3 week assessment and induction courses to help choice of suitable work and to improve basic social skills.
3 *New Training places.* These were not offered under YOP until 1982. They were instituted as part of the transition to the Youth Training Scheme (YTS), which was started in April 1983. The places were for 12 months with time divided between a sponsor's premises, e.g. training workshops or information technology centres, and colleges of further education.

The take-up of these constituent schemes within the YOP is shown for the first, middle and last years of the programme in Table 5.5.

It may be seen from these data that the YOP was basically a work experience scheme. Over 70% of participants were on that part of the scheme in each of the years shown in Table 5.5. Each entrant was paid £19.50 per week free of income tax and national insurance at the start of the programme in 1978. By 1982 this allowance to participants had been increased to £25 per week. Training for the YOP participants in the Work Experience and Work Preparation schemes was left to employers, and was

Table 5.6 *Subsequent experience of young people six months after leaving YOP work experience schemes, 1980/81–1982/83 (%)*

Activity at time of survey	1980/81	1981/82	1982/83
In employment	52	47	47
In full-time education	3	3	2
On another MSC scheme	7	8	8
Unemployed	33	40	38
Other	5	2	5
	100	100	100

Source: *Manpower Services Commission Report for* 1982/83 (1983) p. 13.

not a condition of those two main constituent parts of the scheme. The New Training places, which were provided in 1982, indicated that the national policy on intervention in the youth labour market was beginning to move towards a greater emphasis upon training as a means of encouraging and promoting employment.

The MSC surveyed leavers from the YOP six months after they had left work experience schemes. Its findings are given in Table 5.6. It should be noted that participants in YOP were to some degree disadvantaged. They were school leavers or other young people aged 16 to 17 years who had previously failed to gain either entry to higher or further education, or permanent employment on their own merits, and some needed remedial teaching in literacy and numeracy. The YOP helped about 60% of entrants either to get employment or to get onto other schemes and courses which might be expected to increase their employability.

There were several other surveys of YOP participants. One of these was concerned, among other aspects, with the qualifications of YOP entrants. The survey took place in April 1982 when the programme had been in operation for four out of its five years,[3] and comparisons were made with a similar survey in 1978/79 (Table 5.7). It can be seen that the school qualifications of YOP entrants improved over the period shown, as did the two background characteristics shown here. Over the same period fewer school leavers were able to obtain employment (Table 5.2), so it is reasonable to infer that the intake to YOP included a larger number of better qualified young people in 1980/81 than it had done in 1978/79.

The YOP had some success in reducing unemployment by providing work experience places in private industry and, on a smaller scale, with

---

[3] Conducted by Social and Community Planning Research for the MSC. Results published in the *Employment Gazette* 1982, October, pp. 440–3.

Table 5.7 *The qualifications and characteristics of YOP entrants, 1978–79 and 1980–81 (%)*

	1978/79	1980/81
0 Level or equivalent or above	29	34
No educational qualifications	42	34
Previous history of school truancy	22	15
Previous unemployment of more than six months	19	12

Source: Bedeman and Courtney (1982), pp. 440–3.

local authorities and public sector employers. The total number supported by YOP was large, 1.8 million over the duration of the programme, March 1978 to April 1983.

A summary is given in Table 5.8 of the four interventions by government in the youth labour market during 1975–83. It should be noted that the assessments of success or failure, which were made by the Department of Employment, were approximations, and indeed some methods were not fully developed until later in order to assess the performance of YTS (see Chapters 8 and 9). The Department of Employment did estimate *dead-weight* and *substitution* effects for first two small schemes, the RSSL and the YES, but for the other two, the WEP and YOP, success or failure is judged simply by recording the outcome of the programmes in terms of jobs obtained.

A policy-learning process can be detected from the record of the interventionist actions of government in the youth labour market in this period, and may be summarised as follows: The RSSL was replaced by a more discriminating subsidy, the YES. The WEP, and the YOP in its early versions, contained no element of training, but they were improvements on the RSSL and the YES in that they provided work experience and did much more for the much larger number of young people concerned than the earlier, small-scale recruitment subsidies. Training came late, but it did arrive. The New Training Places version of the YOP was started in 1982. From that tentative beginning sprang the Youth Training Scheme (YTS). The background to that scheme is examined further in the next chapter.

Table 5.8 *Summary of assessments by the Department of Employment of early direct government interventions in the youth labour market, 1975–83*

Scheme	Period of operation	Total number of participants	Results
Recruitment Subsidy for School Leavers (RSSL)	October 1975 to October 1976	29,000 by June 1976 of which 5,000 were early leavers	*Failure.* Less than 20% of participants would not have been recruited in the absence of the subsidy. 80% *deadweight*
Youth Employment Subsidy (YES)	October 1976 to February 1978	38,497 during period of the scheme	*Failure. Deadweight* 75%, *substitution* 12.5%
Work Experience Programme (WEP)	September 1976 to February 1978	47,500 by the end of 1977	*Some success.* 61% of all participants obtained full-time jobs after completion or after leaving before completion of WEP
Youth Opportunities Programme (YOP)	February 1978 to March 1983	1,834,700 entrants during period of the programme	*Partial success.* Helped many relatively disadvantaged young people aged 16-17 to obtain jobs. 60% obtained jobs or got on to courses which improved their employability. *Partial failure.* Little or no training was required of participating employers

6 The development of the modern system of youth training

Youth unemployment

A new Conservative Government was elected in 1979, and soon adopted a *laissez-faire*, free market approach to economic policy. However, with the youth labour market in massive disequilibrium, supply being far in excess of demand, the interventionist policies adopted by the Labour Government in the late 1970s had to be continued. In fact, soon after 1979, economic conditions worsened and the rates of both total and youth unemployment rose sharply.

The general economic climate had changed in an unfavourable direction since 1979: the gross domestic product (at factor cost and constant prices) fell by 2.1% in 1980, and by a further 1.1% in 1981, before recovering to a growth path in 1982.

The rate of total unemployment in Britain, which had been rising relatively slowly in the late 1970s, surged ahead in the early 1980s (Table 6.1). The rate for school leavers available to the youth labour market, that is those who had not moved onto *full-time* further education, rose to 20% by 1983, and the rate for all young people in the age range 16–19 years was 25% in the same year. That rate is more than twice that for all persons in the labour force (10.6% in 1983).

Although the economy recovered in terms of output from 1982, and increased by an average annual rate of 4.2% in the years 1985 to 1988 inclusive, there was the usual time lag before a reduction in the unemployment rate occurred; also, that rate remained higher than it would otherwise have been because the total labour force was increasing throughout the 1980s, by 6.6% between 1980 and 1990.[1] The relatively more severe impact of adverse movements in the economic cycle upon the employment of youth labour, compared with that of all workers, is seen in Table 6.1, and it also

[1] *Annual Abstract of Statistics* 1992, Table 6.1 and *Employment Gazette* 1992, October, p. 58.

Table 6.1 *Comparative rates of unemployment for all workers, school leavers available to the labour market and young people aged 16–19 years, 1979–83, GB (annual average, %)*

	All workers[a]	School leavers available to the labour market[a,b]	Young people aged 16–19[c]
1979	5.0	9.8[d]	8.9
1980	6.0	15.0[d]	n.a.
1981	9.4	14.8	22.7
1982	9.7	18.4	n.a.
1983	10.6	19.9	25.1

Notes:
[a]Claimant basis except for 1979, registered basis. For adults, claimant unemployed (seasonally adjusted) as percentage of total workforce.
[b]All school leavers aged 16 to 18 *less* those in *full-time* further education.
[c]Labour Force Survey basis.
[d]Based on estimates of school leavers available for employment.
Sources: Employment Gazette, various years. *Education Statistics for the United Kingdom*, various years. *Labour Force Surveys* for 1979, 1981 and 1983.

occurred in the previous economic depression in the 1970s (Chapter 5, Table 5.2). It is a well-established relationship.[2]

On the supply side, the demographic situation facing policy makers in the early 1980s was one of relatively stable numbers of school leavers: there were 887,000 in 1979–80 and 911,000 in 1982–83. These numbers are high compared with those which followed later in the decade when the demographic 'bulge' due to high birth rates in the 1960s had passed (Chapter 3, Table 3.3). A similarly stable situation existed for numbers of school leavers available for direct entry to the labour force – the increase in the proportion of school leavers going on to full-time further education was only just starting to occur in this period (Chapter 3, Table 3.4).

In this stable supply situation the demand for youth labour declined, and unemployment among school leavers available to the labour market rose from 64,600 in 1979 to 117,300 in 1982.[3]

[2] See Hart 1988, ch. 2 and work on youth labour markets carried out by the OECD in the late 1970s, particularly OECD 1980, pp. 16, 17 and Table 2. 'Youth unemployment rates are typically double or treble those of adults' (OECD 1980, p. 16).
[3] *Employment Gazette* 1983, November, S24. These figures are of claimant unemployed. The figures for registered unemployed school leavers (a series which was discontinued in 1982) are 78,000 in 1979 and 159,600 in 1981 (*Employment Gazette* 1982, November, S20).

Table 6.2 *Apprentices in training in Great Britain, 1965, 1970, 1975, 1980–83 and 1984–92 (000s)*

| | Old Series | | New Series[a] | | |
	Manufacturing	Production industries	Service industries	Construction	All industries[b]
1965	243.3				
1970	218.6				
1975	155.3				
1980	149.5				
1981	147.6				
1982	123.7				
1983	102.1				
1984	82.0	132	116	64	332
1985	73.2	130	130	68	357
1986	61.8	119	117	54	318
1987	58.0	101	124	64	314
1988	55.7	94	149	64	329
1989	53.6	111	148	81	367
1990	53.5	116	130	77	352
1991		98	132	74	330
1992		92	136	66	325

Notes:
[a] The new series are of apprentices of all working age groups. In 1991 about 60% were in the age group 16–19.
[b] Includes apprentices not classified by industry.
Sources: The statistics (at March each year) for apprentices in manufacturing industry are estimates from the *Employment Gazette* (1980) September, and various later issues. Apprentices of working age in all British industries, *Labour Force Survey* (1984–92) Spring issues.

The YOP, which had been introduced on a large scale in 1978, had provided work experience only, although in 1982 a training element had been added. The youth labour market performance as regards both school-leavers and the 16–19 age group as a whole indicated that YOP was providing an insufficient preparation for the employment of young people. Since youth unemployment rose faster than total unemployment, the economic depression could not have been the sole determinant of the youth labour market disequilibrium. Furthermore, there was at this time evidence that training for skills by the traditional system of apprenticeship, which was wholly in the private sector, was in decline. The number of apprentices in manufacturing industry was halved between 1965 and 1982 (Table 6.2). That sharp decline, which continued throughout the 1980s, reflects both the decline in employment in that sector, and some falling off in the demand for the craft skills which the traditional apprenticeship system provided. The total number of apprentices in British industry as a whole shows a much steadier trend over the period 1984–91, reflecting some decline in the production industries but an increasing number of apprentices in the service industries, which expanded their employment as the structural shift toward service output, rather than goods production, occurred in Britain and in other developed countries over this period.

A new training initiative

Against the background of economic recession which lasted from 1979 to 1982, the very serious imbalance in the youth labour market which has been described, and the decline in apprenticeships, the MSC issued in May 1981 a consultative paper under the title: 'New Training Initiative'. This set out three major national objectives for future industrial training. These merit quotation in full because they became the basis for much subsequent government policy:

To develop skill training, including apprenticeships, in such a way as to enable young people entering at different ages and with different educational attainments to acquire standards of skill appropriate to the jobs available and to provide them with a basis for progress through further learning.
To move towards a position where all young people under the age of 18 have the opportunity either of continuing in full-time education or of entering a period of planned work experience combined with work-related training and education.
To open widespread opportunities for adults, whether employed or returning to work, to acquire, increase or update their skills and knowledge during the course of their working lives.

These proposals were canvassed among employers, trade unions and educational and training bodies. There was a large measure of support for them, and they formed the basis for the government's White Paper under the title *A New Training Initiative: A Programme for Action*, presented to Parliament in December 1981.

Bearing in mind the conditions in the youth labour market, it is perhaps unsurprising that government intervention in this market continued the actions started by the Labour Government in the mid 1970s, the *laissez-faire* economic philosophy of the new Conservative Government notwithstanding.

However, the type of intervention was greatly changed. In the New Training Initiative the chief policy proposals for youth labour placed the accent upon training in contrast to the earlier policy of alleviating youth unemployment by providing work experience places in industry.

The new proposals for youth training were as follows:

1 A new £1 billion a year Youth Training Scheme, guaranteeing from September 1983 a full year's foundation training for all those leaving school at the minimum age without jobs.
2 Increased incentives for employers to provide better training for young people in jobs.
3 Development of an 'Open Tech' programme to make technical training more accessible to those who have the necessary ability.
4 A working group to report by April 1982 on ways of developing the Youth Training Scheme to cover employed as well as unemployed young people, within available resources.
5 Setting a target date of 1985 for recognised standards for all the main craft, technician and professional skills to replace time-serving and age-restricted apprenticeships.
6 Better preparation for working life in initial full-time education.
7 More opportunities for vocationally relevant courses for those staying on in full-time education.
8 Closer co-ordination of training and vocational education provision nationally and at local level.
9 A £16 million fund for development schemes in particular localities and sectors.
10 Examination of longer-term possibilities for more effective, rational and equitable sharing of the costs of training between trainees themselves, employers of trained people and the general taxpayer.

These proposals were the basis for the training and youth labour market policies of the 1980s, and they underlie much current policy.

The central proposals for the youth labour market which were carried into effect were: (i) the design and implementation of the Youth Training Scheme (YTS): proposals 1 and 4; (ii) the setting up of the Young Workers Scheme (YWS), which aimed to improve the job security and training of young people under 18 by lowering their wage rates relative to those of older workers: proposal 2 (training was not made a condition of the YWS, but participating employers were encouraged to train and many did so: see *Fourth Report of the House of Commons Committee on Public Accounts* 1983/84); (iii) the setting up of more vocationally relevant courses for those still in the educational system by the establishment, among other measures, of the Technical and Vocational Educational Initiative (TVEI): proposals 6,

7 and 8; and (iv) a start on the road to a better understanding of the economics of training and of the financial management of the training process: proposal 10.

The authors of the White Paper saw the problem in the following terms: 'In 1979 nearly 40% of the 700,000 school leavers who found jobs received no training at all. About another 20% were receiving training for only eight weeks or less. Our efforts must therefore be directed not only to creating jobs for young people but also to ensuring that they are properly trained for them'.

The Technical and Vocational Education Initiative (TVEI) was introduced in 1982 to 'provide pupils aged 14 with a four-year course of full-time technical, vocational and general education, including appropriate work experience and leading to recognised qualifications'. It was designed to cater for young people of a wide range of ability, and to operate within national guidelines with full local involvement (including that of industry) in its running.

The general aim was to prepare young people for the world of work before they left school. Looking ahead to 1991, it is interesting to note that under the terms of the new National Curriculum the TVEI is supported, with general, technical and vocational subjects being given equal status with traditional academic subjects (*Education and Training for the 21st Century* 1991). That was the aim, but the outcome was not very successful (see Chapter 7).

The TVEI was the first step in the government's new vocational and educational policy. The next step, in young peoples' career sequence, was the Youth Training Scheme (YTS) for school leavers aged 16 or 17 who were unemployed, and the Young Workers Scheme (YWS) to support young people under 18 in jobs by lowering their pay and encouraging their training.

So the parts of the policy were designed to fit together. The sequence started at school with the TVEI and continued, for those who did not find employment on leaving school, with the YTS and then the YWS, which was designed to support the employment of young people who were moving, either directly from school, from unemployment or from YTS training.

The TVEI is examined next, in Chapter 7, and the YTS and YWS in Chapters 9 and 10.

7 The first stage in the vocational education and training sequence

The government's change of policy in the early 1980s from interventions to relieve youth unemployment by providing work experience placements, chiefly by means of the YOP, to interventions to promote training, led also to consideration of a new curriculum for vocational education in schools which would be designed particularly for school children between the ages of 14 and 16 whose interests were more practical and technical than had previously been recognised and catered for in the education system. The aim of this policy change was to establish a new vocational education system.

Technical and Vocational Education Initiative (TVEI)

The TVEI was announced on 12 November 1982. The MSC was given the task of delivering the programme and of drawing up proposals for its implementation.

The government's aim in making this intervention into the curriculum of state secondary schools was to provide teaching in technical and vocational subjects, in addition to general education, which would lead to recognised vocational qualifications. These courses were to run in parallel with the usual academic courses which led through secondary schools and sixth-form colleges towards 'A' Level qualifications.

Less able pupils were thought to be unable to gain much educational benefit beyond the GCSE level, and there were of course some who failed to gain any qualifications at that level (Sime 1991). The TVEI was to include work experience in addition to class teaching, and the general aim was to provide a smooth transition between school and the 'world of work'.

The announcement of the TVEI was completely unexpected. The Local Education Authorities (LEAs) had not been previously consulted, and at first they regarded it as an 'invasion of their territory' (*NATHFE Journal*, December 1982, p. 3). Later, the LEAs were keener to participate, not least because the TVEI was well funded by the government and their education budgets were subjected to cuts in other areas. Pilot TVEI programmes were launched in 1983 in 14 LEAs and they were followed by further and larger 'rounds' of pilot schemes in other LEAs in 1984, 1985 and 1986 (Helsby 1989, p. 77). In 1987 the TVEI was introduced into all state secondary schools, with transitional three-year preparatory projects in schools that had not run pilots (Luck 1991, p. 543). In 1989, the TVEI Focus Statement (quoted in Luck 1991, p. 544) set out the aims of TVEI in the following terms:

1 To relate learning to the world of work.
2 To improve skills and qualifications, especially in science and technology.
3 To provide work experience.
4 To enable young people to be effective, enterprising, and capable of work through active practical learning methods.
5 To provide counselling, guidance and individual action plans.

The contents of TVEI courses appear to have varied a good deal. There was no set curriculum. Courses with a practical or vocational application were encouraged, such as business studies, technology, agriculture, information technology and catering. In the late 1970s a Craft, Design and Technology syllabus, examinable later as a GCSE subject at age 16, had been introduced and was gradually taken up by schools in the 1980s. The approach to teaching technology contained in this syllabus had a powerful effect upon the content of TVEI courses (Bierhoff and Prais 1993, pp. 25–27), and in turn the developments brought about by the TVEI had an influence upon the National Curriculum (NC).

The NC was established by the *Education Reform Act 1988*. It made the teaching of 'technology' obligatory for all pupils aged 5–16, and it was intended 'to provide the detailed framework of curriculum and assessment within which all schools, including TVEI projects, will operate' (HMI 1991, p. 5).

There have been some severe criticisms of the TVEI. The critics divide broadly into three groups. The first, HM Inspectorate of Schools (HMI), had some criticisms of the organisation and development of the TVEI; the second were those who took the view that the needs of employers dominated the scheme too much; and the third considered that the needs of employers did not sufficiently influence the teaching done under the TVEI.

The criticisms from HMI are contained in a review of the development and progress of the TVEI over the period 1983–90 (HMI 1991). They identified a number of achievements, unintended outcomes, negative features and problems which had hindered success. The achievements noted are referred to later in this chapter. The criticisms, which HMI classified as either negative features or unintended outcomes, include: (i) problems in providing a balance of subjects and a coherent education with a systematic progression in difficulty, (ii) much time spent developing new courses in the early stages of the TVEI was wasted when these developments were overtaken by the introduction of the National Curriculum (NC) in 1988, and (iii) NC specifications curbed some of the more innovative TVEI developments and caused continuity problems as material was switched between courses to fit NC requirements.

The second group of critics took the view that the needs of employers dominated the TVEI too much. The National Association of Teachers in Further and Higher Education (NATFHE) carried motions expressing opposition to the TVEI at its conferences in 1984 and 1987. The main points of opposition in 1984 were sex-role stereotyping, streaming and control of the curriculum by business. In 1987, a more comprehensive oppositional stance was taken:

Conference rejects Government attempts through the MSC to centralise control of the curriculum, to introduce selection and division in comprehensive schooling through the TVEI and establish new institutions, such as the CTCs (City Technology Colleges), in order to transform education into training and transform the bulk of the 14–18 age group into a pool of ill educated labour. (*NATFHE Journal*, Summer 1987, p. 49)

The National Union of Teachers (NUT) do not seem to have opposed the TVEI in the same way, as Helsby (1989, pp. 77–78) explains:

In the event, many teachers found that not only could they accept the aims of TVEI, but also that they could become enthusiastic about developing them in practice. Changing employment patterns had long since made it impossible accurately to predict future needs in the area of vocational skills, and had put a premium upon personal and inter-personal competencies, and upon familiarity with the new technologies and attitudes to work and training. Such wide developmental aims could be seen as being of benefit to all young people, within or outside employment, since either situation is likely to require qualities such as flexibility, initiative and ability to cope with and to solve problems. Thus the aims of those concerned primarily with the future well-being of young people found a degree of convergence with the aims of manpower needs planners. Without this convergence, TVEI might never have taken off in the way that it did . . . but there was a price attached in the form of an implicit contradiction between increased control at the top and the wealth of local initiatives which it [TVEI] spawned at the bottom.

The third group of critics, who came from the National Institute of Economic and Social Research (NIESR), argued that the needs of employers did not sufficiently dominate the teaching done under the TVEI.

Within this general thesis Bierhoff and Prais (1993, pp. 25, 26) were critical of the teaching of technology, which was a major element in the Craft, Design and Technology (CDT) syllabus. Specifically, they were critical of the lack of attention to the teaching of technical skills, and of the emphasis of courses upon so-called 'research, design and evaluation', which was the result of the 'intellectualisation' (or 'depracticalisation') of the subject. This, they argued, allowed insufficient opportunity for students to develop practical skills. In particular, disadvantaged pupils with practical aptitudes but below-average academic abilities were prevented from gaining the skills which would have helped to suit them for the world of work. Many of these problems arose from the *National Curriculum Statutory Order on Technology*, which greatly widened the subject and 'put an end to any remaining teachers' efforts to teach practical skills' (Bierhoff and Prais 1993, p. 27). In 1991, a report was published which was highly critical of the performance of British teaching of technology. It was based on comparisons with continental European schools (Prais and Beadle 1991). In 1992, the Engineering Council published a report which began: 'Technology in the National Curriculum is a mess' (Smithers and Robinson 1992 quoted in Bierhoff and Prais 1993, p. 2). In June 1992, HMI issued a critical report (HMI 1992a) which was accompanied by a paper from the National Curriculum Council entitled 'The case for revising the Order', ie, the National Curriculum Statutory Order (Bierhoff and Prais 1993, p. 2 footnote 4).

Under the weight of these criticisms the government called in July 1992 for a review of the teaching of technology as provided for under the National Curriculum. The HMI review was published in December 1992 (HMI 1992b), and the proposals for change which it contained were scheduled for implementation in 1994 and 1995. These changes included a greater emphasis upon 'making good quality products', but work on planning, organising, testing, modifying and evaluating – mainly paper-work 'of the intellectualised kind which has caused problems hitherto' (Bierhoff and Prais 1993, p. 33) – would still account for two-thirds of the marks allocated. Bierhoff and Prais argued that these proposed changes did not go far enough, and that what was needed was a review that questioned the conceptual approach taken to teaching technology in Britain.

There have been some achievements for the TVEI. The following have been assembled from several different sources:

1 There were positive effects on teaching styles and 'little doubt that TVEI has greatly increased the range of practical and applied activity in the classroom' (HMI 1991).

2 Of a cohort of post-16 year old TVEI students, nearly 10% took up

Certificates of Pre-Vocational Education (CPVEs), 25% BTEC National Diplomas in business, computing or engineering, and over 50% had taken GCE 'A' Level courses (HMI 1991, p. 10).
3 Eighty per cent of TVEI students received work experience, compared to 37% of those outside the scheme (*The TVEI Experience*, MSC, 1987; quoted in Luck 1991, p. 545).
4 Helsby (1989, pp. 78, 79) reviews the results of a study (by the Institute for Research and Development in Post-compulsory Education, University of Lancaster) to examine the effect of the TVEI on the attitudes of young people to the benefits which their schooling under that scheme conferred on their employment outcomes. Twelve LEAs were covered and 3000 young people, who were matched for ability, completed questionnaires. One thousand of these were ex-TVEI students. They were more likely than the others to agree that their work at school had prepared them with the skills they needed to find a job (41.8% against 31.7%), and to perform a job (33.7% against 17.3%).
5 There appears to be quite a strong connection between the TVEI and the YTS. Over a third of the 1000 ex-TVEI students in the sample (quoted in Helsby 1989, p.79), entered the YTS. They considered that the TVEI had helped them to decide what they did on work placement (52% against 43% non-TVEI), and that it had prepared them well for their off-the-job YTS training (21% against 14%).

The results of the survey referred to in points 4 and 5 show that the differences between TVEI students and non-TVEI students of equal ability were not great in respect of their attitudes to the TVEI as a preparation for their further training and employment, but they are consistent across both sets of results from this survey.

In parallel with the extension of the TVEI to all state secondary schools, links were set up, in more formal terms than previously, between school pupils and business. They are examined in the next section.

Compacts

Education–business partnerships called Compacts were initiated by the Department of Employment. The idea for this scheme came from the United States, where a form of schools-business partnership was set up in Boston in the early 1980s, with the aim of reducing the high (50%) drop out rate from schools in inner city areas.

The first Compacts were established in Britain in 1987 in six London Docklands schools by the Inner London Education Authority and the London Enterprise Agency (Opie 1991, p. 598). The movement was expanded in 1988 and in subsequent years. Compacts were at first confined to inner city areas, but later (in 1992) extended to other areas of the country.

Compacts are generally for 14–16 year old school children. In addition to normal class work, they sign up in the Fourth Form for a range of performance and attainment goals. From the age of 14 a typical Compact would include one or several experiences of the world of work, including:

1 Two weeks' work experience.
2 Class visits to local companies.
3 Special project work using materials and expertise provided by local firms.
4 Help from local employers in self-presentation.
5 Careers guidance linked to completion of an individual Record of Achievement.

The Department of Employment (DE) offered schools a grant (in 1991) of £50,000 to start up a Compact, and £100,000 covering the first four years. The total cost of running a Compact at that time was estimated at £180,000, the balance coming from participating employers and other sponsors. In return the DE required: (i) that upon pupil achievement of goals at the end of two years of study, a job or training position must be offered, and (ii) that the Compact must include all pupils in an age group irrespective of ability.

The results of the early Compacts in 1989 were encouraging. For the schools in the original Docklands project, 82% of students met the goals they had signed up for, and the proportion of students staying on at school after age 16 to pursue further vocational studies rose from 35% in 1988 to 56% in 1990. While there was evidence that the scheme was successful in improving motivation and outlook, it appeared to do little for the demotivated and less able. 'Compact plus', a programme aimed to help such pupils, was piloted in 1991 (Opie, p. 597).

A view from the side of the employers was given in a report by the Confederation of British Industries (CBI 1992). It was noted that by 1990–91 about 78% of Local Education Authorities (LEAs) had set up formal partnerships with businesses, and that was largely due to the success of Compacts, but the report was critical of the fact that most LEAs had not integrated work experience into GCSE courses. More than a third of participating LEAs used no more than a form of debriefing or informal essay to exploit the experience, demonstrating 'a large untapped potential for business links'. However, the report expresses the view that the extension of Compacts was providing 'a major opportunity for businesses to develop a more sustained involvement [with school education] throughout the country'.

Another evaluation of Compacts in England and Wales was conducted in 1991 by the National Foundation for Educational Research (NFER) (1992) as part of a four-year study running from 1990 to 1994. The 1992 report of the NFER found that Compacts had improved pupil motivation and increased employer involvement in inner city schools. More than half the Compact schools surveyed had noted improvements in student motivation and behaviour which they attributed wholly or partly to Compacts. Of more than 400 employers surveyed, one quarter reported that involvement in Compacts had improved their links with schools – chiefly by arranging work experience. Where employers had, as required by Compacts, offered a job guarantee in 1991, 'there was often a marked drop between the number of jobs initially offered by employers and those definitely committed in the event' (*Employment Gazette*, August 1992, p. 375).

While Compacts and the TVEI are guided by similar philosophies and goals they are distinct programmes and are separately funded.

In April 1992 the Training and Enterprise Councils (TECs) in England and Wales, and the Local Enterprise Companies (LECs) in Scotland, took over the management of Compacts, which by then had become available nationwide.

This completes the review of the first stage in the sequence of government intervention to promote increased investment in vocational education and training. This stage is the preparatory one and is for school-aged pupils, chiefly those in the age range 14–16. The next stage in the sequence is the major intervention in the form of the YTS (later YT). That scheme is assessed in Chapter 9, and the methods of assessment are explained in Chapter 8. Before doing that it seems useful to consider the framework of vocational qualifications which are relevant to YTS attainments, and which have been subject to considerable changes in recent years.

Three routes to post-school education and training

At age 16 there now exist three alternative routes available to young people who wish to achieve educational or vocational qualifications beyond those obtained at school: (i) the general academic route via 'A' Levels and on to full-time higher general or vocational education of several years' duration; (ii) the route to National Vocational Qualifications (NVQs), which are occupational qualifications designed for those in employment or in training positions (such as YTS) with an employer; (iii) the route to what have been named 'vocational 'A' Levels', which are obtained by staying on full time within the school and further education system and studying for vocational qualifications named General National Vocational Qualifications (GNVQs).

The first route, that leading to general academic and higher vocational qualifications, is not pursued here. The development of the other two routes is considered below.

National Vocational Qualifications

In parallel with the development of the TVEI, but before its extension to all state secondary schools in 1987, the government took a further initiative in 1985 by setting up a committee (Chairman Mr. H. G. de Ville) to review the whole system of vocational qualifications. The outcome was a White Paper: *Working Together – Education and Training* (1986) which recommended the setting up of a new National Council for Vocational Qualifications (NCVQ). That was done in the same year, and a framework of National Vocational Qualifications was established with four levels of practical competence and theoretical knowledge ranging from that needed for jobs entered by 16 and 17 year olds up to that required at higher technician level. In the specific terms which were formulated later these levels are as follows:

Level 1 is competence in the performance of a range of work activities, most of which may be routine and predictable.
Level 2 is competence in a significant range of work activities, some of which are complex or non-routine, and require some autonomy and responsibility.
Level 3 is competence in a broad range of work activities performed in a wide variety of contexts, most of which are complex and non-routine.
Level 4 is competence in a significant range of complex technical or professional work activities performed in a wide variety of contexts with a substantial degree of personal responsibility. (*Employment Gazette* 1991, July p. 398)

A fifth level concerned with professional and managerial competence was added later.

The aim was to bring needed cohesion, classification and order to the many and varied vocational qualifications awarded by about 300 bodies. However, it must be noted that these included the long-standing and highly regarded City and Guilds of London Institute (CGLI), the Royal Society of Arts (RSA), and the Business and Technician Education Council (BTEC). The NCVQ's policy is to change as well as to co-ordinate methods of vocational teaching for a wide range of occupational skills, and also to change the methods of assessment and validation and to require the three main traditional examining and awarding bodies to comply with them.

That process has been going on, with results which have met with wide-ranging criticism by academics, and by opposition from some employers and employers' organisations. The framework of the new NVQs encompasses the existing vocational qualifications in craft, office and other skills, but the new system is changing the teaching and assessment system in a radical way. A substantial amount of research has been carried out by the National Institute of Economic and Social Research and by others (see, notably, Mason, Prais and Van Ark 1992; Prais 1993; Smithers and Robinson 1993; and Smithers 1993). Many of their findings are based on studies which involve comparisons with the vocational teaching and training practices of continental European countries, and with their methods of assessment for the award of qualifications.

The basic problems which appear to be arising from the new NVQ system are that the craft skills are to be learnt almost wholly on the job. Much less teaching of theory and methods is involved than for the earlier qualifications. That is done because 'the theoretical knowledge required to carry out the tasks is said to be "embedded" in them' (Smithers 1993, p. 20). So all that is seen to be needed is competence in a range of tasks, and qualifications are awarded after assessments of such competencies by internal and external 'verifiers'. Because the background knowledge of mathematics and of theory is seen as being insufficiently taught, doubts arise about competence after training over a wide range of skilled tasks, some of which will be new and will not have been covered by on-the-job training. A comparison with the highly regarded City and Guilds Craft Certificate is unfavourable to the NVQ. The City and Guilds award requires both the formal classroom teaching of theory as well as on-the-job supervised work; furthermore, it is examined by written and practical tests by external examiners who make graded awards of pass, credit and distinction, compared with pass/fail of the NVQ (Smithers 1993, pp. 22–3).

There was a need for rationalisation of the earlier very heterogeneous system of awarding bodies and awards, and there was and remains a need to increase greatly the number of those qualified at the intermediate levels, that is those below the level of degrees and diplomas. It has been estimated that in Britain only 27% of the workforce have such qualifications, while the proportion for Germany, France and the Netherlands ranges from 40 to 63% (Mason, Prais and Van Ark 1990, p. 57). However, it is abundantly clear that the changes being made to teaching, training and assessment methods for the first, second and third levels of NVQ need to be re-appraised by government.

The YTS system is linked into the NVQ format of qualifications, and YT entrants have to attend courses designed to reach NVQ Level 2 (see Chapter 12). The shortcomings of the NVQ are therefore relevant to the assessments made of the YTS and YT in later chapters.

General National Vocational Qualifications

A further step was taken by the government in May 1991, when a White

Paper was published (*Education and Training for the 21st Century* 1991). This paper proposed policies aimed at improving full-time education and training for 16–19 year olds. It included some proposals that would have implications for the TVEI:

1 A national framework of vocational qualifications would be established, and accreditation of all levels of learning would be promoted.
2 Equal status for both academic and vocational subjects would be promoted through the development of new diplomas, and the action of moving between academic and vocational subjects would be made easier.
3 The range of qualifications offered in the Sixth Form would be widened. In particular, schools would be allowed to offer BTEC from September 1991 in addition to the CPVE, which was already available via the City and Guilds.
4 Employer–school links would be promoted and the acquisition of 'an understanding of the world of work' before leaving school would be promoted. In particular the 'Compact' model of industry–school co-operation (explained above) would be supported.

These proposals were linked with the TVEI for those school pupils who wish to stay on at school and to continue their vocational studies on a full-time basis.

In November 1991, the government instituted a new set of NVQs in accordance with the White Paper. These were named General NVQs. They are designed to be 'A' Level equivalents, and accordingly require a much broader and deeper understanding of general principles than the occupationally-specific NVQs, which are for those who have left school and are engaged in training. It was projected that by 1995 about 25% of all 16–19 year old students would be working towards GNVQs. Initially, the subjects offered qualifications in five areas: manufacturing, business administration, leisure and tourism, health care, and art and design. Later, it was envisaged, 12–15 subjects would be offered. It was recognised that much staff training would be required and that the quality of the courses, and the rigour of assessment, would determine the credibility of the qualifications as 'A' Level equivalents (*Employment Gazette*, November 1991, p. 568).

There have been severe criticisms of the teaching for these new vocational courses, and of the methods of testing and assessment for the GNVQ, thus questioning the validity of the new qualifications. The grounds for criticism are that the courses are too shallow and that the teaching of the principles, particularly mathematics and knowledge of theory, which are the foundation for the technologies, is seriously deficient (Smithers 1993, p. 32). The latter has made some comparisons between the new British GNVQ syllabus and teaching methods on the one hand, and the vocational teaching arrangements in main continental European countries on the other. The conclusion he has reached is as follows:

Compared with the comparable qualifications of our continental neighbours, GNVQs appear lightweight, ideology ridden and weak on general education. European experience is that theoretical and academic learning is a vital complement – not a distraction – to vocational studies. While Britain moves away from formal academic and theoretical studies in vocational education, elsewhere they are placing even greater emphasis on them. (Smithers 1993, p. 39)

It seems clear that much yet needs to be done to establish in an effective way 'equal status for both academic and vocational subjects', which was among the aims set out in the White Paper on *Education and Training in the 21st Century* (1991).

The establishment of three clearly signposted routes to general and vocational qualifications at post-school leaving age may be seen as progress in the organisational sense, and the addition of teaching in technology and other applied, career-based subjects in schools as early preparation for later studies and training after age 16 may be welcomed in principle. However, it is abundantly clear that the quality of school teaching under the TVEI and for the new GNVQs is seriously deficient in terms of both syllabus and method, and particularly in respect of the teaching of mathematics and the knowledge of theory which is needed for a complete understanding of the applied, vocational subjects which are contained in the GNVQ courses. It is also clear that changes in the distribution of time between the teaching of theory and practical work on-the-job have been to the disadvantage of quality in the occupationally-based NVQ system.

8　Methodology of assessment

The analytical methods used in the present study to assess the economic effects of YTS draw to some extent upon a study of the economic effects of the Temporary Employment Subsidy (TES), an adult employment subsidy (Deakin and Pratten 1982). The methods used in that study, in turn, drew upon earlier work which was in terms of 'general economic considerations' for evaluating subsidies to industry (Prest 1976).

Subsidies to industry or to individuals may be classified as either general or selective. Both the TES and the YTS were selective to the benefit of individuals falling within defined categories. Hence the relevance to the present study of the earlier work.

The YTS was paid both to individuals, and also to firms which thereby gained financial and other benefits. The general economic considerations which are relevant to a study of the economic effects of such a subsidy may be summarised as follows:

1 Effects upon employment, output and productivity.
2 Induced changes in resource usage within an industry and between industries.
3 Effects upon relative prices, which are likely to be affected by the degree of competition in product markets.
4 The 'balanced-budget effect', which brings into consideration the effect of additional taxation to meet the *net* spending on the subsidy.

The methods of assessment, which are described below, are applied (in Chapters 9 and 10) to the British experience of the YTS, but they are of general applicability to subsidies in support of youth training.

The economic effects of a government-financed intervention in the youth labour market (or other area of economic activity) can be assessed only if the alternative, no-policy position can be compared with the actual outcome of the policy which is adopted and put into operation. This is clearly not an easy task. It involves seeking answers to hypothetical questions, among other problems, but it has to be attempted.

It is necessary to know first the aims of the policy, and next to consider how far those aims would have been met without the policy, and finally how far the policy has accomplished what it aimed to do.

The aims of the YTS may be summarised as follows:

1 To provide school leavers with at least one year (later two years) of high quality training and work experience as a bridge between school and work.
2 To provide employers with a better-trained young workforce with competence and practical experience in a range of related jobs or skills.
3 To provide experience and skills which are transferable between employments.

Microeconomic effects upon employment and employers

Distribution

The YTS was designed to be selective in its support for young people of a specified age range, but it was open ended in the sense of the skills it aimed to encourage and train. The second aim of YTS (given above) would not be achieved if the trainees supported by the scheme entered only a few industries in the country. So an assessment of the accomplishment of the aims of YTS should include an analysis of the distribution of YTS trainees across all goods and service industries and a comparison made with the distribution of all employees.

That comparative analysis is not intended to beg the question of the effectiveness of YTS as a mode of training (which is considered separately, in Chapter 11). It is, however, a necessary but not a sufficient condition for the attainment of the second aim that the distribution of YTS should be similar to the distribution of all employees, and that the two distributions should change approximately in step as the pattern of demand for the products of labour changes over time. In so far as they match closely, it is reasonable to conclude that employers in general are being provided with one opportunity at least for acquiring 'a better-trained young workforce with competence and practical experience in a range of related jobs or skills'.

The induced training effect

In order to assess the direct effects of YTS upon employment and employers, and the attainment of stated aims in the sense of enabling more training and employment of young people to take place than would have occurred in the absence of YTS, it is necessary first to estimate how many of the YTS places filled represent additional new training places, and not ones which would have been filled by school leavers in the absence of YTS. This is named the *induced training* effect.

To make estimates of this effect it is necessary to estimate both the *deadweight* and *substitution* effects. Those training places which would have been filled in a no-policy situation represent the *deadweight* effect. Also, employers might in some cases take in YTS trainees who are capable of some output while receiving training, in the place of older workers who would have been recruited in the absence of YTS. This is named the *substitution* effect.

In further detail, the survey method for obtaining estimates of the *deadweight* and *substitution* effects of YTS requires field research with a representative sample of firms participating in the scheme. Managers of these firms need to be asked the hypothetical question as to whether they would have engaged fewer trainees if YTS had not existed. If they reply yes, they are asked how many fewer. From the answers to these questions it is possible to make quantitative estimates of the *deadweight* effect – the number of vacancies which would have been filled by young people had there been no YTS. It is necessary also to ask managers if they would have engaged more employees in other age groups in the absence of YTS. From answers to this question it is possible to estimate the *substitution effect* – the jobs for older workers which have been replaced by YTS trainees (Deakin and Pratten 1987b, p.13).

The number of YTS trainees taken in by each sample firm is known, and therefore the subtraction of the *deadweight* and *substitution* effects in quantitative terms will allow the number of training places induced by the YTS, named the *induced training* effect, to be reached, and so one aspect of the economic effects of the scheme can be estimated.

The employment effect

The employment effect of YTS is the outcome for trainees at the end of their YTS courses. This effect is measured first in actual terms by finding the proportion of the total number of trainees who have obtained jobs, either with the employer who arranged their training or with another employer. A further proportion continue training, and others go into unemployment. These results are then modified to take into account the *deadweight* and *substitution* effects in order to reach the *net* employment effect, which measures the employment outcome of YTS *net* of what would have been expected to occur in the absence of the scheme. Changes over time in the employment effect would be expected to occur as youth labour market conditions change, and the employment effect of the scheme should not be judged from a measurement at one point in time. Information on the economic activity of ex-YTS trainees can be obtained from employers participating in YTS, or from the trainees themselves by 'follow up' surveys. Results from these assessments are relevant to the third aim of YTS (set out above). Post-YTS experiences are examined in Chapter 11.

The effects of YTS on employers

These need to be estimated in terms of the *net* cost or benefit to employers over the period of the subsidy, and that should be done separately for the first and second year of YTS. The benefit in terms of average output produced by trainees (*net* of offsets due to 'makework' and loss of output by employees due to YTS), and the costs are those associated with on-the-job training and any 'top-up' paid to the trainees. Information on these benefits and costs are assembled from participating employers and the actual *net* cost or benefit estimated. Following the methodology previously described, the realistic effects of YTS in this respect can only be reached by estimating the actual and the no-policy positions. That is done by using estimates of the *deadweight* and *substitution* effects to find the *net* cost or benefit per trainee without subsidy. That shows the *net* benefit to employers of YTS on the assumption that in the no-policy situation without YTS they would have recruited the trainees they said they would have recruited and paid them the going rate. Both costs and benefits need to be adjusted to take account of trainee pay and changes in costs due to relief of managing agent's fees and other items. Further detail is given in Chapter 9.

The price effect

The price effect of YTS, which is allied to the effect on output, may distort product market competition, which would be an unintended and unwanted side-effect of the scheme. Estimates of this effect were made by interviewing a matched sample of non-participating firms of similar size in the same industry and region as YTS participants. The non-participants were asked to consider how far, if at all, their competitive product market position had been influenced by the receipt of the YTS subsidy by competing firms who may have used it, in part, to subsidise the price of the output produced by their trainees during their training period.

Strengths and weaknesses of these methods

Earlier methods, in particular those used by the Department of Employment and others, to evaluate the effects of the WEP, the YOP, and the RSSL and the YES (reviewed in Chapter 5), did not estimate fully the alternative, no-policy position and compare it with the actual effects of the subsidy. Estimates of the effects of the WEP and the YOP were *ad hoc*, and were of the actual effects. For the RSSL and the YES, estimates of the effects did include estimates of the *deadweight* and *substitution* effect, but went no further.

The shortcomings of the methods described in this chapter lie in the use made of answers to hypothetical questions asked of participating employers. This is also known as the 'counterfactual' nature of the assessment problem. There is also perhaps an element of self-presentation bias which may influence the answers to questions put to managers of participating firms in a direction which is favourable to the subsidy scheme.

As regards the hypothetical estimates of what would have occurred in the recruitment of trainees in the absence of YTS, many managers were found in the course of survey work to be reasonably sure of what they would have done in quantitative terms as regards the recruitment of trainees without subsidy – the *deadweight* effect. The same was true concerning estimates of the recruitment of other employees in the no-policy situation – the *substitution* effect. However, bias favourable to YTS may come in here, particularly with regard to the *substitution* effect which managers may have under-estimated, knowing perhaps that official policy was aimed at avoiding substitution.

Self-presentation bias as regards training programmes, and the value of output of YTS trainees, was no doubt also present. Attempts were made to limit and check this by cross-questioning and by asking basic questions of the YTS trainees themselves. There can be little doubt that the evidence on these and other aspects of YTS gathered from participating employers contained some self-presentation, pro-YTS bias, as well as a margin of error due to the need to estimate hypothetical figures, and that should be borne in mind when considering the estimates of the economic effects of YTS given in Chapter 9.

Self-presentation bias in the answers given by managers of non-participating firms may have influenced their opinions in an anti-YTS direction, although the survey results on the price effects of YTS contained very little evidence to support the existence of such an effect – an outcome which does not support an argument for this type of bias.

The method used here to establish the 'counterfactual' position and so, by comparison, the more realistic economic effects of the YTS, has the shortcomings which have been described. As a matter of reference, attention is drawn to others who have employed a different method, that of studying individual case histories coupled with the use of control groups.

An example is Main and Shelly (1990), where in a study of 'The effectiveness of YTS as a manpower policy' the experiences in the youth labour market of a group of ex-YTS trainees are compared with those of a control group of school leavers without YTS. There are shortcomings in this method too in terms of the difficulty of obtaining two groups accurately matched by ability, educational qualification and motivation. Lalonde (1986) also makes a claim for better results from experimental data using a method of random assignment to YTS in a 'genuinely experimental' setting. He claims that the method adopted by Main and Shelly is 'second best' to the one he proposes. Reference may also be made to Elias (1991) who has studied the 'methodological, statistical and practical issues arising from the collection and analysis of work history information by survey techniques'.

No judgement on the merits of various methods of trying to establish the counterfactual is attempted here, but the route has been opened for those who wish to pursue this matter.

Macroeconomic effects

A subsidy to support youth training will have macroeconomic effects upon the government, business, personal and overseas sectors of the economy, and they need to be traced and estimated to provide a complete assessment.

The methods used are described below. The details of the way each individual estimate is made is given in Chapter 10, where they are placed adjacent to the estimates given there of the macroeconomic effect of YTS.

First-round macroeconomic effects

These first-round effects can be estimated in detail on the basis that they occur during a period one year after the YTS has been in operation for several years. A notional £100 million of government subsidy to YTS is considered. The number of YTS trainees supported by this sum can then be calculated. Estimates are then made of the expenditure and income of, first, the *government* sector. On the expenditure side there are payments of the subsidy to firms, and social security benefits (*net*) not paid in respect of induced training positions created (that is, the benefits not paid to YTS trainees *less* the benefits paid to adult workers replaced by them). On the income side there are estimates of: (i) reduced tax and national insurance contributions by the young and adult workers who are replaced by YTS trainees (the *deadweight* and *substitution* effects); (ii) increased indirect taxes on supply-induced expenditure by the personal sector; (iii) increased tax revenue due on payments to training staff; and (iv) increased corporation tax.

In the *personal* sector on the expenditure side there are: (i) purchases of extra supply-induced output (output produced by YTS trainees); (ii) reduction in tax and national insurance contributions on behalf of replaced workers; (iii) increased indirect taxes on supply-induced output; and (iv) increased taxes on payments to training staff. On the income side there are: (i) payments to YTS trainees; (ii) wages not paid to replaced workers; (iii) payments to extra training staff and for training by firms; and (iv) social security not received in respect of induced training positions for YTS trainees.

In the *business* sector on the expenditure side there are: (i) payments to YTS trainees; (ii) wages not paid to replaced workers; (iii) national insurance contributions not paid for replaced workers; (iv) payments to extra training staff and for training; (v) increased taxes on payments to training staff; and (vi) increased corporation tax. On the income side there are (i) receipts of YTS subsidy from the government; (ii) receipts from the personal sector for increased supply-induced output; and (iii) receipts from the overseas sector for increased supply-induced output.

In the *overseas* sector the influence of the subsidy, which is not expected to be large in this sector, is represented by purchases of extra supply-induced output.

An application of these methods enables estimates to be reached of the shares in YTS training costs per trainee paid by the three parties involved: the government (acting on behalf of the taxpayer), the trainee and the participating employer.

Balanced budget approach

A more realistic assessment of the macroeconomic effects of a youth labour subsidy needs to include a balanced budget approach. That involves tracing the effect of an increase in taxes to meet the *net* increase in government expenditure on the subsidy. The balanced budget approach leads to modified sector balances, and from that to indications of the type and direction of the second-round macroeconomic effects upon each sector. That is done in Chapter 10.

Longer-term macroeconomic effects

It is also useful to estimate the longer-term macroeconomic effects of a youth labour subsidy upon the growth of GDP, changes in total employment and unemployment, and upon retail prices. This can be done by feeding the results from surveys of the outcome of the subsidy in terms of *net* jobs created and *net* government expenditure into a model of the British economy. Such an exercise has been done and the results of it are given in Chapter 10. The methodology involved is extensive and its description beyond the scope of the present work, but the relevant sources are given in Chapter 10.

9 An assessment of the economic effects of the Youth Training Scheme upon employment and employers

The inception of the Youth Training Scheme (YTS) was announced by the Manpower Services Commission in April 1982, and it came into operation in April 1983 in succession to the Youth Opportunities Programme (YOP).

The then Chairman of the MSC, Mr David Young (later Lord Young), speaking at a conference in Birmingham in June 1982, said: 'The YTS is not about unemployment: it is about bringing nearly half a million employed and unemployed young people into a single integrated programme giving high quality training for work' (*Employment Gazette* 1982, July, p. 275). This emphasises the policy change from the YOP, which aimed to reduce unemployment among young people by providing work experience, to a scheme where the aim was primarily one of training for skills.

The terms of the Youth Training Scheme (YTS)

The YTS has gone through several changes of form since it was started in 1983. The following was its initial form.[1]

1 It was for a period of 12 months and was open to 16 and 17 year old school leavers who remained unemployed, and to some employed 16 year olds.
2 There were two 'modes': Mode A places were sponsored by private sector employers and were centred on factories, offices and other places of work. These formed the large majority of all YTS places. Mode B places were in

[1] From the description of YTS given in *Training for Jobs* 1984.

107

community projects sponsored by local authorities and voluntary organisations, particularly those in inner-city areas where there was a shortage of employer-led schemes.
3 Some places under Mode B were provided at Information Technology Centres (ITECs) – a continuation of an existing programme, but with extra numbers under the YTS.
4 Each trainee was paid an allowance of £25 per week.
5 Some employers who participated in the Mode A scheme did so as Managing Agents for the YTS. They were paid initially £1950 per year for each trainee. This sum comprised a managing agent's fee of £100, £1300 for the trainee's allowance, and £550 towards training costs.
6 Under Mode A the training programme comprised on-the-job training at the employer's premises, integrated with 13 weeks off-the-job training at a technical college or training school, but the latter was not brought into effect at the beginning of the scheme.

The absolute and relative scales of the YTS

In quantitative terms the impact of the YTS may be compared first with the scale of the YOP which preceded it. This is shown in Table 9.1.

Because the duration per trainee of each scheme was different and the duration per trainee under the YTS changed over time (see note (d) to Table 9.1), large differences in scale arise from the use of figures for entrants to schemes when, as in the case of these comparisons, one scheme, the YOP, was normally for six months, and the other, the YTS, was for one year to begin with and then extended in 1986 to two years. This problem of estimating relative scale is reduced by the use of average annual figures for young people in training.

The YOP peaked in 1982/83 at 241,700 young people in the programme on average over the year to March 1983. The YTS started at the lower level of 161,500 in the year to March 1984, but then built up to a peak of 388,100 on average in the year to March 1989. This is a large number of young people, most of them entering direct from school, to be supported by a government labour market intervention. This support via YTS was 60% higher than the peak support by the YOP in 1982/83.

These absolute figures now need to be set in context with the whole youth cohort of 16–18 year olds who were engaged in various economic and non-economic activities over the same period. The relative scale of the government's intervention can then be seen (Table 9.2).

The figures given in col. 2 of Table 9.2 show that there has been a decline since 1983 in the total number of young people in the 16–18 years cohort. There has concurrently been an increase in the proportion of this cohort

Table 9.1 *Number of young people in training on YOP and YTS, 1978/ 79–1990/91, GB (annual averages)*[a]

	Years to March
Youth Opportunities Programme[b]	
1978/79	53,900
1979/80	77,900
1980/81	127,500
1981/82	188,400
1982/83	241,700
1983/84	4,100[c]
Youth Training Scheme[d]	
1983/84	161,500
1984/85	266,700
1985/86	263,800
1986/87	296,300
1987/88	375,500
1988/89	388,100
1989/90	368,900
1990/91	314,200[e]

Notes:
[a]Based on monthly averages. Figures to nearest 100.
[b]YOP started in February 1978.
[c]A residual figure. YOP closed for entrants in March 1983.
[d]YTS began in April 1983. Courses were initially for one year. Two-year YTS began on 1 April 1986. YT replaced YTS on 29 April 1990.
[e]Figure for March 1991.
Source: Employment Department 1992.

entering further full-time education after the school-leaving age of 16. So the number available to the labour market has declined. The relative scale of the employment and training schemes in this period, which is shown here, may be seen from the rising proportion of this cohort taking YOP or YTS places. However, the relative importance of these government interventions is greater than these figures show because the number of young people available in any year to enter the labour market has been falling for the reasons which have been given. In 1982 the number of young people available for the labour market was 1,897,000, and of these about 242,000, or 13.2%, went on to the YOP. In 1988 about 1,637,000 young people were available for the labour market, and of these 397,000, or 24.3%, went into the YTS. This percentage was 23.9% for 1987 and 23.4% for 1989. So nearly

Table 9.2 *Trends in the educational and labour market status of 16–18 year olds, 1976 and 1981–90, GB*

(1) At January each year	(2) Number of persons aged 16–18 years (000s)	(3) In full-time education (%)	(4) In employment and others[a] (%)	(5) On youth employment and training schemes (%)	(6) Unemployed (%)
1976	2409	27	64	1 (RSSL)[b]	8
1981	2748	28	53	5 (YOP)	13
1982	2757	31	46	7 (YOP)	16
1983	2789	32	42	9 (YOP)	17
1984	2753	30	42	10 (YTS)	17
1985	2679	31	42	10 (YTS)	16
1986	2633	31	43	10 (YTS)	15
1987	2577	32	43	12 (YTS)	14
1988	2547	33	42	16 (YTS)	10
1989	2480	34	40	16 (YTS)	10[c]
1990	2386	36	37	15 (YTS)	12[c]

Notes:
[a]This column is a residual obtained by subtraction after the proportions for the other columns have been estimated, thus reflecting any errors in other estimates. Also included are the unregistered unemployed and those economically inactive but not in full-time education.
[b]Recruitment subsidy for school leavers.
[c]In September 1988 16 and 17 year olds became ineligible for income support and are therefore excluded from col. 6 figures. The figures shown for 1989 and 1990 are the estimated unemployment rates for the cohort of 16–19 year olds.
Source: *Education Statistics for the United Kingdom* (1992 and earlier years), Tables 19 and 21.

a quarter of all 16-18 year olds who did not stay in full-time education were taken into the YTS in these years.

The proportion shown, in col. 4 of Table 9.2, as being 'in employment' should be treated with caution, as explained in Note (a) to the Table.

The YTS was clearly important in terms of size and comparative scale against the total number of 16–18 year olds seeking employment. It constituted a link of one year and, later on, two years between school and employment with the purpose of learning skills, acquiring work experience, gaining qualifications, and thence employment in a trade requiring the skills acquired, and also of gaining a measure of transferable skill which would enable the possessor to move into other, related work.

How successful has YTS been in providing this important link? An answer cannot be a short one, because the economic effects of government intervention in labour markets, as in other areas of the economy, are hard to assess. The ramifications of such actions are widespread and are difficult to disentangle from other, contemporaneous changes occurring for other reasons. The methodology of assessment which is applied in this chapter has been explained in Chapter 8.

The microeconomic effects of YTS upon employment and employers

The methods of assessment of the economic effects of YTS were applied to a study of the impact of the scheme at three points in time: the first in 1986 when the labour market, and particularly the youth labour market, was relatively slack and youth unemployment (among 16–18 year olds) was at about 15%; the second in 1987, when youth unemployment was beginning to decline; and the third in 1989 when the labour market and the whole economy were more buoyant, and youth unemployment was considerably lower at about 10%. These studies of the scheme under widely different labour and product market conditions enabled a balanced assessment of these effects of YTS on the youth labour market to be made.

The following microeconomic assessment of the YTS and of an associated intervention, the Young Workers Scheme (YWS), is divided into six stages which are set out below:

1 The industrial distribution of YTS compared with the distribution of all employees in employment, and changes in both distributions over time and their significance.
2 Estimates of the *induced training* effect of the scheme to show how far the YTS created *net* new training positions under different labour market conditions.
3 The associated role of the Young Workers Scheme (YWS).
4 The *employment effect* of the scheme, showing the destinations of ex-YTS trainees in terms of jobs, further training or unemployment.
5 The costs and benefits of YTS training to employers.
6 The product market influences of YTS.

The industrial distribution of YTS

This is shown by the industry divisions of the Standard Industry Classification 1980 in section A of Table 9.3, and is compared with the

Table 9.3 The industrial distribution of YTS trainees in training compared with that of all employees in employment, 1985–86 and 1988, GB

Industry Division (SIC 1980)	A. Distribution of all YTS trainees in training (%)		B. Distribution of all employees in employment (%)		C. Ratio of % distribution of YTS trainees to % distribution to all employees	
	1985/6 Average March 1985– April 1986	1988 December	1985/6 September 1985	1988 December	1985/86	1988
0 Agriculture, Forestry and Fishing	3.0	2.2	2.8	1.3	1.1	1.7
1 Energy and Water	1.8	1.6	2.8	2.0	0.6	0.8
2 Metal manufactures, Minerals (other than fuels) and Chemicals	2.0	1.6	3.7	3.6	0.5	0.4
3 Engineering and Vehicles	11.6	10.5	12.3	10.1	0.9	1.0
4 Other Manufacturing	4.3	3.3	9.9	9.5	0.4	0.3
5 Construction	11.2	16.9	4.5	4.6	2.5	3.7
6 Distribution, Hotels and Repairs	22.2	13.1	21.1	20.9	1.1	0.6
7 Transport and Communication	3.3	3.5	6.1	6.3	0.5	0.6
8 Banking, Insurance and Finance	11.1	6.7	9.4	11.6	1.2	0.6
9 Other Services	29.5	40.6	29.5	30.1	1.0	1.3
Total	100.0	100.0	100.0	100.0		
Total YTS trainees in training	264,000	392,000				
Total employees in employment (000s)			21,075	22,330		

Sources: YTS Leaver Survey (1985/86); figures provided by the Training Agency (1989).

distribution of all employees in employment, given in section B of the same table.

The distribution of all employees broadly reflects the pattern of demand from home and abroad for the goods and services produced by British industry. Since a main aim of the YTS is 'to provide employers with a better-trained young workforce with competence and practical experience in a range of related jobs or skills' (aims of YTS quoted in Chapter 8), it would be reasonable to expect the distribution of YTS to reflect the distribution of all employees at any point in time, and to change as the pattern of total employment changes in response to present and expected future changes in demand for goods and services. How far is that true?

In both 1985/86 and 1988 the distribution of YTS trainees and of all employees in employment matched reasonably well. But the construction industry stands out in 1985/86, and more so in 1988, as taking a disproportionately large share of YTS trainees. One reason for this is that the industry retained its Training Board (CITB), and YTS was used, with the strong backing of the trade union involved, the Union of Construction, Allied Trades and Technicians (UCATT), to support apprenticeships and other training positions in the several skilled trades in demand by the building industry in these years.

The service industries (Divisions 6, 7, 8 and 9) expanded their employment in relation to the goods industries in the 1980s. The share of service industry employees in total employment was 64.8% in 1984. It rose to 66.1% in 1985/86 and to 68.9% in 1988. The share of YTS trainees in the service industries as a percentage of all YTS trainees precisely matched that of all employees in employment at 66.1% in 1985/86, but declined to 63.9% in 1988. The large share of YTS trainees in Division 6 in 1985/86 (it was also very high in 1984 at 41% of all Mode A YTS, when about 75% of all YTS trainees were in Mode A) was reduced by the MSC by 1985/86 and further by 1988. Retail distribution accounted for a large proportion of Division 6, and most of the skills in retailing were lower level ones, such as shelf-filling and cash-till operation, which could be acquired in a few weeks. YTS support in retailing was reduced for that reason.

The manufacturing industries as a group (Divisions 2, 3 and 4) are often regarded as being in the forefront of growth of output of high technology goods for both the domestic and overseas markets. These industries require a high proportion of craft skills, and their share of trainees is accordingly a matter of interest for an analysis of the aims of YTS as a provider of a better-trained, skilled young workforce. In the two years shown in Table 9.3 the share of manufacturing industry of all YTS trainees was 17.9% in 1985/86 and 15.4% in 1988. That industry group was contracting in terms of its share of all employees in employment over the same years. Its share in that respect was 25.9% and 23.2% in each of these years. It should also be noted that in the mechanical and electrical engineering and vehicles industries (Division 3) the share of YTS trainees was very close to that of all employees in employment in 1985/86, and was in fact slightly greater in 1988. However, not all these YTS trainees were recruited for skilled trades; indeed, many entered semi-skilled occupations in these and in other industries.

The change in the pattern of concentration[2] of YTS trainees, and the reasons which have been given for the policy change involving retail distribution, suggest that under relatively slack labour market conditions with high youth unemployment, as was the case in 1985/86, the main motivation of government was to get young people into YTS and off the unemployment register. Later, in 1988, when labour market conditions were tighter, YTS was more focused upon training for the skills which were then more strongly in demand. More evidence on this is given in the next section.

The induced training effect of YTS

The creation of new training places which would not have been created without the scheme was the central objective of the YTS. That effect is estimated and shown in Table 9.4. The *deadweight* and *substitution* effects have been estimated (from field research with employers) in order to reach this *net* outcome in terms of new training places and jobs induced by the scheme, named the *induced training* effect of YTS.[3]

The percentages shown in Section C of Table 9.4 represent the proportion of total YTS trainees who would not in the absence of the scheme have gained training places (including those with employee status). Except for the smallest firms, there is a marked reduction in this *induced training* effect of YTS over the period 1986–89.

The general economic conditions, and particularly labour market conditions, changed greatly between 1986 and 1989, and the labour market impact of YTS also changed. This may be seen in Table 9.5 where the *induced training* effect of YTS is shown against some macroeconomic variables in this period. In 1986 total unemployment was high at 11.6%, and although output growth was rising strongly the demand for labour,

---

[2] Shown in Section C of Table 9.3, where a figure greater than 1 indicates a greater than average concentration of YTS trainees in relation to the distribution of all employees in employment.

[3] Some YTS trainees were given 'employee status' by their employers, so a YTS place will count as a job in that case. But in this analysis induced training places include YTS trainees with 'employee status'.

Table 9.4 *The* induced training *effect of YTS by size of firm, 1986, 1987 and 1989, GB (percentages of the total number of trainees in training in each size band)*

| | Size of establishment or firm by number of employees | | | |
	1–99	100–499	500 and over	Whole sample
A *Deadweight* effect				
1986	42	49	29	29
1987	53	57	50	52
1989	53	73	76	71
B *Substitution* effect				
1986	20	2	4	5
1987	9	4	1	3
1989	15	5	8	9
C *Induced training* effect [100 *minus* (row A + row B)]				
1986	38	49	67	66
1987	38	39	49	45
1989	32	23	16	20

Sources: These data are from sample surveys. The figures for 1986 are from Deakin and Pratten 1987b; for 1987 from Begg *et al.* 1988; and for 1989 from Begg *et al.* 1991, Table 1.

shown by the growth of total employment, was virtually stationary. So the usual lag between growth of output and growth of employment was in operation in this period. The labour market generally, and particularly the youth labour market, was slack. In these economic circumstances it might be expected that the *deadweight* and *substitution* effects of YTS would be found to be relatively small. That was the case, and the *induced training* effect was correspondingly high at that time at 66%. There is, however, another point to consider here. In the early years of YTS, particularly 1983–86, the MSC urged employers to take on YTS trainees in addition to their normal recruitment of school leavers and other young people (known as 'additionality'). That influence might still have been at work in 1986 and have been one cause of the relatively low *deadweight* effect of YTS found to exist at that time.

Table 9.5 *The* induced training *effect of YTS compared with concurrent changes in national employment, unemployment and output, 1986, 1987 and 1989*

	Induced training effect of YTS, GB (%)[a]	Change in total UK employment over previous mid-year (%)	Rate of total UK unemployment (mid-year) (%)	Rate of youth unemployment, 16–19 years, (Spring each year). GB (%)	Change in UK Gross Domestic Product at factor cost over previous year (%)
1986	66	+0.1	11.6	20.4	+3.8
1987	45	+2.1	10.4	17.9	+4.6
1989	20	+3.0	6.1	10.3	+2.0

Note: [a]*Net* new training places (including YTS trainees with employee status) induced by YTS as a percentage of the total number of YTS trainees in training.
Sources: (1) *Induced training* effect of YTS from Table 9.4. (2) Change in total UK employment, GDP and the rate of UK unemployment from *United Kingdom National Accounts* (1992). (3) Youth unemployment from *Labour Force Survey, Historical Supplement* (1993).

As the British economy improved in 1987, and further in 1988 and 1989, conditions in labour markets tightened. The *deadweight* effect increased greatly, particularly in large firms, as did the *substitution* effect in 1989. So the *induced training* effect correspondingly declined from 66% in 1986 to 20% in 1989. The YTS was no longer an important means of reducing youth unemployment: employers would have taken four-fifths of the total number of trainees into training and employment without the inducements provided by the subsidy. The accent and emphasis of the scheme moved to training. That had always been the purpose of YTS, but in 1989 the emphasis upon training much increased as skill shortages increased owing to the higher level of economic activity and of demand in the youth labour market.

It is clearly best for youth training and employment policies to march together; equally, it is wrong to reduce the emphasis upon training when the labour market is slack. Jobs will be relatively scarce at such times, but if training is continued the employment policy is much more likely to be effective later, if not in the immediate post-training period.

If past experience on wage subsidies is put together with the cyclical impact of YTS outlined here, it may be seen that advantages might be gained from a counter-cyclical wage subsidy to young workers immediately after training. The TES was such a subsidy (Chapter 5), and so to some extent was the Young Workers Scheme (YWS). The latter scheme supported the employment of ex-YTS trainees and others aged under 18, but it was not designed as a counter-cyclical measure, being focused on young people for a different reason, which is explained below.

The associated role of the Young Workers Scheme (YWS)

The YWS was introduced in January 1982 and discontinued in 1986. The scale of the scheme was moderately large – 110,000 applications were approved by end September 1982 (*Employment Gazette* 1982, November, p. 488).

The objective of the YWS was to encourage the recruitment and retention in jobs of young workers under 18 by a wage subsidy which widened the differential between wage rates paid to young workers under 18 and the rates paid to older workers.

The scheme provided employers with a subsidy of £15 per week per YWS worker, provided the employee's gross earnings were not more than £40 per week. The duration of the subsidy for each entrant was limited to a maximum of one year (*Employment Gazette* 1981, September, pp. 402, 403).

The scheme applied to recruits and to all young employees under 18 years of age who were in their first year of employment, subject to the earnings limits described above. Young people leaving the YTS were eligible for support under YWS under these conditions.

In 1986 YWS was found to have a high *deadweight* effect, 64%, and a *substitution* effect of 14% (Deakin and Pratten 1987b, p. 13), so the jobs induced by the scheme were only 22% of those supported by it. Although the scheme was founded on the belief that in the 1970s one of the main causes of the high rate of unemployment among young people was the closing of the wage rate difference between young workers and older workers (Wells 1983), that conclusion has been disputed and it is not supported by the finding of a large deadweight effect for YWS at a time when the youth labour market was relatively slack in 1985/86.

In 1986 the YTS was extended from one to two years' duration. YWS was abolished then, because it could no longer serve as a sequel to YTS. It was replaced by the New Workers Scheme (NWS) in March 1986. Under that scheme employers could claim a subsidy of £15 per week per young worker taken on in his or her first year of employment at a wage of £55 per week or less if aged under 20, or £65 per week or less at age 20. The NWS was tailored to fit in with the extended YTS, and to maintain the purpose of the

YWS to reduce the absolute and relative wage cost of a young worker (Smith 1986).

The YWS and the NWS were not designed as instruments of youth manpower policy to meet the counter-cyclical role which the above analysis of YTS suggests is needed. But the TES, and the YWS and NWS experiences, provide empirical evidence which could help the design and formulation of an employment subsidy sequel to YTS for use when labour market demand is particularly weak. Such a subsidy would enable the training programmes under YTS to proceed more confidently, and the trainees themselves would feel more settled if future jobs were more assured. When labour market conditions are tighter, then the employment subsidy sequel to YTS would be less needed, because jobs would be more readily available after training has been completed, and the value of the subsidy could be reduced progressively as youth labour market conditions tightened.

The employment effect of YTS

The training provided by YTS aimed to improve the skills and therefore the employability of young people. Indeed, without YTS many who entered the scheme would have entered unemployment direct from school. The proportion who would have done so has been estimated from surveys (see Table 9.4), as 66% of those taken into YTS in 1986, 45% in 1987, and 20% in 1989. These are the figures for the *induced training* effect for these years. The complements of these percentages are the proportions of all YTS trainees recruited who would have been engaged in the absence of YTS: they are 34% in 1986, 55% in 1987, and 80% in 1989. These percentages include what have been named the *deadweight* and *substitution* effects of YTS.

An attempt can now be made to answer the question: What was the outcome of YTS in terms of jobs obtained after the completion of YTS training? This is the *employment* effect. (It should be recalled that YTS started in April 1983 as a one-year course and was extended to two years in April 1986). What is now offered is a microeconomic analysis of YTS in terms of employment. A macroeconomic analysis of the effects of YTS upon employment and output is given in Chapter 10.

As the YTS progressed, a rising proportion of ex-YTS trainees obtained employment. No doubt this was due in part to the influence of the cycle of economic activity which swung upwards from 1987 and led to tighter labour markets and lower unemployment (Table 9.5) and, from 1986, in part to the fact that the two-year YTS provided for higher levels of training. The actual *employment* effect of YTS is shown in col. 1 of Table 9.6. In

Table 9.6 *The actual* employment *effect of YTS: the destinations of YTS leavers, 1985/86–1991/92, GB (%)*

	(1) Employed[a]	(2) Engaged in further training[b]	(3) Other destinations and not known	(4) Unemployed
1985/86 (YTS 1 only)	56.3	9.5	6.3	27.9
1986/87 (YTS 1 and YTS 2 merged)	59.9	13.9	3.6	22.7
1987/88 (YTS 2 only)	60.2	15.4	3.9	20.6
1988/89 (YTS 2 only)	66.8	15.4	3.8	14.0
1989/90 (YTS 2 only)	66.1	14.9	5.1	14.0
1990/91 (YT only)	57.0	15.8	7.0	20.2
1991/92 (YT and Youth Credits)	49.8	15.7	10.0	24.5

Notes:
[a]Includes small percentages of self-employed and part-time employees.
[b]Includes full-time courses and further YTS placements.
Source: *YTS Leaver Surveys* and *YT Follow-up Surveys*, various years.

addition, some leavers from YTS continued their training in various ways. Some of them were apprentices whose training period was four years, with support from YTS for the first two years. Other leavers changed their job aims and were allowed to enter a new training placement in a different trade. These continuations, which might be expected particularly in the case of apprentices to lead eventually to jobs, are shown in col. 2 of Table 9.6.

The main trends shown are the rising proportion entering jobs either with the employer with whom they trained or with another employer and, until 1990/91, when the economic cycle reversed, the falling proportion entering unemployment.

Had there been no YTS some of the young people who entered the scheme would in any case have been recruited into training positions by employers. If it is now assumed that in the absence of YTS those taken into training would have had similar labour market destinations to those who

Table 9.7 *The actual* employment *effect of YTS on those taken into training compared with the estimated no-policy alternative outcome, without YTS, 1986, 1987 and 1989, GB (%)*

	In employment or further training			Unemployed	
	actual ex-YTS	alternative without YTS	*net employment effect of* YTS	actual ex-YTS	alternative without YTS
1986	77	27	50	23	73
1987	79	44	35	21	56
1989	85	69	16	15	31

Note and sources: The actual ex-YTS figures are from Table 9.6, adjusted by the removal from the total of the percentages in col. 3 of that table (other destinations and not known). The alternative (without YTS) figures are from Table 9.4 sections A and B. The figures for the *deadweight* effect (for the whole sample) are reduced by the percentage given in Table 9.6 for actual ex-YTS trainees in employment or further training (excluding from the total 'other destinations and not known'). This assumes that, in the absence of YTS, employers would have given similar training to those they said they would have recruited without YTS as they did in fact give to their YTS trainees, and that their ex-training employment experience would have been similar. The figures for the *substitution* effect are taken without any adjustment because employers estimated that in the absence of YTS they would have recruited that proportion of older workers into jobs.

had been trained under YTS, then a comparison can be made between the actual *employment* effect of YTS, and the alternative employment outcome without YTS. That comparison is set out in Table 9.7.

The *employment* effect of YTS can be seen in a more realistic light when it is compared with estimates of the employment outcome without YTS. It can be seen that the influence of YTS upon the employment of young people has been considerable, particularly when demand in the youth labour market was slack, as it was in 1986. In that year the *net employment* effect of YTS was 50%, and the scheme provided nearly three times as many jobs for young people after training as would have been provided by a free market regime without YTS. As the economy improved, the *employment* effect of YTS increased in actual terms. But on a comparison with the alternative, no-policy hypothesis the *net* employment gain was much less, falling to 16% in 1989.

It may be concluded on the evidence presented here that YTS had an impressive positive effect upon the job prospects for trainees aged 16 or 17.

Unemployment post-YTS was still too high, but it was much lower than it would have been without YTS. However, the influence of YTS varied greatly with movements of the economic cycle, and the scheme did not adjust well to the cycle. At times of economic depression YTS promoted much training which would not otherwise have taken place, but unemployment post-YTS remained high. At times of high economic activity, much of the support for trainees which YTS provided replaced expenditure which employers would have undertaken in the absence of YTS. So it appears that manpower and training policies for the youth labour market need to move more closely in step with each other, and in this regard consideration needs to be given to counter-cyclical employment support for post-YTS trainees at times of economic recession.

The costs and benefits of YTS to employers

The impact of YTS has been examined so far in terms of the supply of school leavers, the enhancement of their training by government intervention, and the jobs obtained by former trainees of the scheme. The scheme also affects employers in various ways. For them, YTS entailed both costs and benefits. A survey was undertaken in 1987 to attempt to evaluate the costs and benefits to employers participating in YTS (Begg et al. 1988).[4]

Table 9.8 *Estimates of the actual benefit of YTS to participating employers, 1987, GB (£s per trainee per week)*

	First-year YTS	Second-year YTS
Benefit from the output of YTS trainees	21.9	48.5
Less		
Output of trainees which is offset by lower output by employees	(3.8)	(1.1)
Output of trainees which employers estimate is 'makework'	(1.6)	0
Total *net* benefit	16.5	47.4

Source: Begg et al. (1988).

---

[4] Fieldwork for this survey took place between September 1987 and January 1988. Interviews were undertaken with a stratified sample (by size and region) of 101 firms in eight industries: Chemicals; Mechanical Engineering; Motor Manufacturing; Construction; Retailing; Hotels and Catering; Repair of Consumer Goods and Vehicles; and Personal Services.

The actual *benefits* of YTS comprise the average *net* output per trainee in the scheme, after adjustments have been made to gross output for the following factors which are estimated: (i) the proportion of the output of YTS trainees which is offset by lower output by non-YTS employees; and (ii) the output of YTS trainees which is not productive, but is 'makework' which would not have been done in the absence of YTS. Estimates of the actual benefits from the output of first-year and second-year YTS trainees are given in Table 9.8.

Estimates of the actual costs of YTS to employers for first-year and second-year trainees are given in Table 9.9, where it is shown that the chief differences between the cost to employers of first and second year YTS trainees is the reduction in supervision costs and the increase in top-up pay. The impact of YTS upon employers in terms of financial costs and benefits is shown in Table 9.10.

As was seen in the case of the *induced training* effect and the *employment*

Table 9.9 *Estimated actual costs of YTS to participating employers, 1987, GB (£s per trainee per week)*

	First-year YTS		Second-year YTS	
Costs of supervision	4.3		1.7	
Payments to Managing Agents	3.0		3.1	
Top-up pay for YTS trainees	8.1		18.4	
Other costs				
wastage of material		1.2		0.7
clothing and footwear		0.6		0.6
tools		0.2		0.6
meals		1.4		1.1
holiday pay		0.3		0.6
travel expenses		0.5		0.6
other items of cost		0.5		0.4
	4.7		4.6	
Total cost per trainee per week	20.1		27.8	

Source: Begg *et al.* (1988).

effect of YTS, it is more realistic to consider the alternative, no-policy position with regard to the costs and benefits of YTS.

If there had been no YTS, employers would have recruited some trainees and a few older workers. In the survey described, employers gave estimates of the number they would have taken on in that circumstance. That number corresponds to the *deadweight* and *substitution* effects which add up to 55% of the total number of YTS trainees actually taken on in 1987. It was

Table 9.10 *Estimated actual* net *cost or benefit of YTS to participating employers, 1987, GB (£s per trainee per week)*

	First-year YTS	Second-year YTS
Total benefit (from Table 9.8)	16.5	47.4
Total cost (from Table 9.9)	(20.1)	(27.8)
Total *net* (cost) or benefit	(3.6)	19.6

Table 9.11 *Estimated net cost or benefit of YTS to participating employers after account has been taken of the costs and benefits which would have arisen under the no-policy alternative, without YTS, 1987, GB (£s per trainee per week)*

	First-year YTS	Second-year YTS
Net output[a]	7.4	21.3
Benefit from relief of pay[b]	21.4	32.2
Estimated total benefit	28.8	53.5
Cost[c]	(9.0)	(12.5)
Total *net* benefit	19.8	41.0

Notes and sources:
[a]Figures from Table 9.8, reduced by 55% to allow for output which would have been produced in the alternative, no-policy situation.
[b]In the alternative, no-policy situation, employers would have had to pay the recruits they said they would have engaged. The method of estimating these figures is explained in the text.
[c]Total cost, from Table 9.9 reduced by 55%, for the reasons given in the text.

estimated, at the time of the survey from which estimates of these effects were obtained, that on average a 16 year old taken on directly from school would be paid £50 per week, and a 17 year old £80 per week. So employers obtained, indirectly from YTS, benefits equal to 55% of these figures per YTS trainee per week (*less* 55% of the Managing Agents' fees and the top-up pay which would not have been incurred in the alternative, no-policy situation).

As regards the average output per trainee per week, the alternative no-policy position is that the gain to employers from the output of YTS trainees is reduced by 55% of their gross output, because the output of the trainees who would have been engaged in the absence of YTS would have been obtained in that case.

As regards the costs of trainees to employers, 55% of these costs would have been incurred in the alternative, no-policy situation without YTS, so

Table 9.12 *Estimated actual* net *cost or benefit of YTS to participating employers compared with estimates of the* net *cost or benefit which would have arisen under the no-policy alternative, without YTS, 1987, GB (£s per trainee per week)*

	Actual *net* (cost) or benefit	*Net* benefits which arise when account is taken of the no-policy alternative, without YTS
First-year YTS	(3.6)	19.8
Second-year YTS	19.6	41.0

the costs to employers due to YTS are 45% of the gross costs per trainee per week given in Table 9.9. So it is possible to estimate the alternative, no-policy position as regards the costs and benefits of YTS to employers, and that is shown in Table 9.11.

Some reservations about the estimates given in Table 9.11 need to be made:

1 The part played by Managing Agents in placing YTS trainees much reduced the recruitment costs of employers, so without YTS greater recruitment costs would have been incurred by employers. These have not been estimated.
2 In the alternative, no-policy situation it might have been the case that employers would have gained more output from their trainees owing to less off-the-job training. But there would have been an offset by the probably lower rate of output of trainees who did not benefit from such training.
3 Recruits taken on in the absence of the *substitution* effect of YTS would have been older workers whose pay and output would have been greater than that of young people aged 16 or 17. But it is likely that the *net* benefit would not have been greatly changed.

Bearing in mind these reservations, the calculations of actual cost or benefit of YTS to participating employers can be compared with estimates of cost and benefit adjusted to take account of the alternative, no-policy situation without YTS. That is shown in Table 9.12.

On both these estimations of cost and benefit, the *net* benefits rise in the second year as trainees produce more, and costs rise only moderately (Table 9.11) for the reasons which have been given.

Employers incur a small actual *net* cost on each first-year YTS trainee, but nearly £20 of *net* benefit per week per second-year trainee. However, when the benefits to employers from not having to pay the trainees whom they would have engaged in the absence of YTS are brought into account, then the total *net* benefits to them of YTS rise substantially for both the first and second year of the scheme.

In the second year, training becomes more specific to the employer's business, and trainees may be rather less mobile in the youth labour market than they are towards the end of their first year during which they acquired some general, basic training. It may be thought that employers should therefore be less subsidised for the second year of training. However, in 1986, when the scheme was extended to two years, a greater emphasis was placed by policy makers upon YTS to train for higher skills, and correspondingly for higher levels of qualification. What is reflected here in these cost/benefit estimates is the financial boost and increased incentive to employers which that extension of the government's policy delivered. Whether or not the skills and the qualifications were delivered in the quantities demanded by the economy is examined in Chapter 11.

Product market influences of YTS

It might be expected that a subsidy to training young people on the scale shown earlier in this chapter (Table 9.1), which yielded financial benefits by way of subsidy of the proportion shown in Table 9.12, would cause some unplanned (by the MSC) and undesirable price effects in the markets for the products of firms which participated in YTS.

A survey was made in 1986/87 of the 'wider economic effects of YTS' (Deakin and Pratten 1987b);[5] interviews were undertaken with firms participating in YTS and also with firms in the same industries as participants which did not take part in the scheme. The response for the whole sample of 230 firms was that only three firms claimed that their relative competitiveness had worsened through their competitors receiving YTS. More important, none of the 90 respondent firms which did not receive YTS considered their relative competitiveness had declined because of the subsidy paid to others.

Answers to other questions in this survey support the conclusion that the effects of YTS upon competition were minimal. Managers of participating firms were asked if YTS 'enabled [them] to accept lower prices for some sales than [they] would otherwise have been able to do'. One hundred and nine participants answered that it did not and six that it did. Four of these six were hairdressers, where the 'density' of YTS was relatively high at the

---

[5] At the time of the survey the second-year YTS had been operating for only about nine months. There would have been some output effects of that change at the time of the survey, but not the full effects.

time of the survey, and the other two also had a relatively high proportion of subsidised trainees. (In the survey there were 23 firms in which more than 10% of total employees and trainees were subsidised by YTS. Seven of these were hairdressers.)

Thus, with the possible exception of one personal service industry (hairdressing), it can be concluded that the one-year YTS did not significantly influence the relative price competitiveness of firms which participated in it.

The macroeconomic effects of YTS are considered next, in Chapter 10, and the qualitative impact of the subsidy on training and on qualifications gained by trainees is examined in Chapter 11.

10 Some macroeconomic effects of YTS

The analysis of the economic effects of YTS which was made in Chapter 9 was in microeconomic terms. A macroeconomic analysis of YTS is made in this chapter. The effects of YTS upon sector income and expenditure are estimated first. The sectors of the economy which are considered are the government, personal, business and overseas sectors.

Estimates are made first for £100m of government funds spent at 1986/87 prices on Mode 'A' YTS.[1] The following points should be noted:

1 The effects of YTS are estimated on the basis of the first round occurring during a year after the scheme has been in operation for several years.
2 The estimates given in Table 10.1 do not include any longer-term effects of YTS, such as the output and employment effects attributable to YTS on the completion of training. That is done later in the chapter.

This simulation of the macroeconomic effects of YTS is intended to indicate orders of magnitude only. It provides guidance on the main macroeconomic effects of the subsidy, but can do so only in an approximate way.

Methodology

The first-round macroeconomic effects of YTS are shown in Table 10.1. A description of the methods used is given first.

1 Government expenditure of £100m on YTS would have supported 50,000 trainees. See Chapter 9, where total expenditure is shown to be £1950 per trainee. There would, in addition, have been some administrative costs. These have not been estimated.
2 Payments by the employer to YTS trainees (the training allowance) was

[1] Mode 'A' YTS was for private sector employers only. In 1985/86 Mode 'A' YTS accounted for 76% of all YTS entrants, and 78% of all YTS in training (Gray and King 1986). It should be noted that all references to YTS in this chapter are to Mode 'A' YTS.

Table 10.1 *First-round macroeconomic effects of YTS by sector, 1986/87*

INCOME	£m	EXPENDITURE	£m
GOVERNMENT SECTOR			
Reduced tax and national insurance contributions by replaced workers[5]	− 3	Payment to firms[1]	+ 100
Increased indirect taxes on supply-induced expenditure by personal sector[7]	+ 4	Social security (net) not paid in respect of induced positions for trainees[4]	− 22
Increased taxes on payments to training staff[9]	+ 5		
Increased corporation tax[10]	+ 23		
	+ 29		
Extra expenditure (net)	+ 49		
	+ 78		+ 78
PERSONAL SECTOR			
Payments to YTS trainees by firms[2]	+ 70	Purchases of extra supply-induced output[6]	+ 25
Wages not paid to replaced workers[3]	− 41	Reduced tax and national insurance contributions by replaced workers[5]	− 2
Payments to extra training staff and for training by firms[8]	+ 25	Increased indirect taxes on supply-induced expenditure[7]	+ 4
Social security (net) not received in respect of induced positions for trainees[4]	− 22	Increased taxes on payments to training staff[9]	+ 3
			+ 30
		Extra receipts (net)	+ 2
	+ 32		+ 32
BUSINESS SECTOR		Payments to YTS trainees[2]	+ 70
Receipts from government[1]	+ 100	Wages not paid to replaced workers[3]	− 41
Receipts from personal sector for increased supply-induced output[6]	+ 25	Contributions not paid for replaced workers[5]	− 1

Table 10.1 *(cont.)*

INCOME	£m	EXPENDITURE	£m
Receipts from the overseas sector for increased supply-induced output[6]	+3	Payments to extra training staff and for training[8]	+25
		Increased taxes on payments to training staff[9]	+2
		Increased corporation taxes[10]	+23
			+78
		Extra receipts (net)	+50
	+128		+128
OVERSEAS SECTOR			
Extra expenditure	+3	Purchases of extra supply-induced output[6]	+3

Note: Superscript numbers refer to the numbered points in the methodology section which precedes this table.
Source: This tabulated analysis and the associated methodology are based upon material from Deakin and Pratten 1987b.

£1400 per trainee per year at this period, for the first year of YTS training. This amounts to £70m for 50,000 trainees. Second-year YTS did not start until April 1986 and is not included here.

3 Where YTS trainees replaced other workers (the *deadweight* and *substitution* effects), firms saved the wages they would have paid to these 'replaced' workers. 50,000 YTS trainees would have replaced 17,000 workers (see Table 9.4, where it is shown that the *deadweight* and *substitution* effects added up to 34% in 1986). Wages (in 1987) per job saved were an average of £54 per week (a weighted average of £50 for 16 year olds 'replaced', and £80 for older workers 'substituted'). However, in 1987 most firms paid a 'top-up' allowance to their YTS trainees at an average weekly rate of £8. Making allowance for this top-up pay, the total saving to employers is £46 per YTS trainee per week, a total of £41m for 17,000 trainees 'replaced'.

4 The 33,000 *induced* training places resulted in less unemployment pay and in less social security benefits. Assuming 75% of the trainees would have claimed benefits averaging £20 per week if they had not gained YTS positions, the reduction in benefits is £26m. Social security benefits

would have been paid to the adult workers replaced (the *substitution* effect) by YTS trainees. These are estimated to be 5% of all YTS trainees supported. So 2500 adult workers would have been paid an estimated £35 per week in benefits, a total of £4m. So the *net* reduction on benefits paid by the government is £22m.

5 Where YTS trainees replaced other workers there was a loss of tax revenue to the government. Much of the replacement was *deadweight* involving 16 year olds, so YTS replaced youths whose tax and national insurance contributions were low. The loss of such revenue is estimated at 8% of £41m, which is £3m, and that is split 60:40 between the personal and business sectors (the business sector pays the employers' national insurance contribution).

6 YTS led to an increase in output by firms. The average *induced* output[2] is estimated to be £11 per trainee per week. This figure is reached after allowing for 'makework', and for lower output by employees (including supervisors) owing to YTS, and for a 'mark-up' by firms of 50% on YTS net output.[3] So output of £11 per week amounts to £28m a year for 50,000 trainees working 50 weeks. These extra, supply-induced sales are divided £25m to the personal sector and £3m to the overseas sector. The survey results indicated that the effect of YTS on exports was very limited.

7 The extra supply-induced output sold to the personal sector resulted in extra indirect taxes of £4m.

8 Most of the difference between Managing Agents' receipts from YTS (£100m) and the payments to YTS trainees was expended on training. Total training costs for 50,000 trainees are estimated at £25m.

9 The payments to extra training staff due to YTS resulted in extra tax and national insurance contributions of £5m, split £3m to the personal sector and £2m to the business sector.

10 Corporation tax is taken at 30% of the extra receipts by the business sector.

Short-term macroeconomic effects of YTS

The principal short-term macroeconomic effects of YTS are shown to be that *net* government expenditure increased and *net* expenditure by the business sector declined.

It is important to note that the *net* cost to the government of £100m of gross expenditure on the scheme was only £49m, and that the profits, *net* of

---

[2] *Induced* by YTS after allowance for output which would have been produced in the no-policy, alternative situation.   [3] From Chapter 9, Table 9.11 grossed up by 50%.

Table 10.2 Net *effects on sector balances of £100m of government expenditure on YTS, 1986/87 (£s million)*

Government sector	+49
Personal sector	−2
Business sector	−50
Overseas sector	+3
	0

Note: Plus signs indicate extra expenditure by the sector, a *minus* sign extra receipts.
Source: Derived from Table 10.1.

corporation tax, of the business sector increased by £50m. The main offsets to the gross YTS payments by government are shown to be a reduction in social security benefit payments (£22m), which occurred mainly because of the training places *induced* by the scheme, and the increased yield of corporation tax (£23m) due to higher business profits. The induced economic effects of the scheme reduced the cost of government investment in training via the YTS and at the same time increased the profits of the business sector. The *net* effects on sector balances are shown in Table 10.2.

The shares of total investment via YTS in the training of each trainee may be calculated for 1986 from the foregoing analyses. The *net* government share per trainee is £18.85 per trainee per week.[4] YTS trainees received pay of £27.30[5] and top-up pay of £8 per week (Chapter 9). Those trainees who would have been recruited in a no-policy situation directly from school at age 16 would have received £50 per week (point 3 in section on Methodology). So their investment in their YTS training was £14.70 per week. The employer, however, received a *net* gain of £19.20 per trainee per week.

The apparent imbalance in the shares of the three parties concerned in investment in YTS training should be viewed in the light of the investment made by employers in the trainees they recruit and train without subsidy. Nevertheless, theoreticians may wish to note the imbalance in the shares of investment in YTS. There is as yet no prescription from the economic theory of training as to how the costs and benefits of that investment should be divided among the participating investors (Chapter 1). However, the *net* gain by employers suggests that the YTS is considerably distorted in respect of the costs and benefits involved in the training processes supported by that scheme.

[4] By dividing the *net* cost of YTS to the government sector (£49m) by 50,000 (the number of YTS places supported) and converting to an average weekly cost, and similarly for the *net* gain by the business sector (Table 10.1).

[5] Effective from 1 April 1986 (*Employment Gazette* 1987, October, p. 493).

A balanced budget approach

Some of the positive effects of the scheme, which are shown in Table 10.1, are attributed to the *net* increase in government expenditure via the YTS, but the estimates made there ignore any changes in taxes attributable to YTS. In order to bring these tax changes into account, and therefore to present a more realistic assessment of the macroeconomic effects of YTS, a balanced budget approach is now considered, and a broad indication of the second round of £100m of gross government expenditure on YTS is given.

To maintain a balanced budget it is assumed that the government raised by income tax £49m for every £100m it spent on YTS. The sector balances would then have moved as shown in Table 10.3. The government might have raised the revenue needed by another tax or a combination of taxes, but those further hypotheses are not pursued. These balances show the transfer of the *net* cost of YTS to the personal sector, that is, to the taxpayer. A transfer of an extra £49m in income tax from the personal sector would have increased its *net* expenditure from −£2m to +£47m, and the government sector would have moved to a balanced position.

Table 10.3 *Sector balances with a balanced budget, 1986/87 (£s million)*

	Net effect of YTS on sector balances in terms of net expenditure	Effect of increased income tax on sector balances	Sector balances with a balanced budget
Government sector	+49	−49	0
Personal sector	−2	+49	+47
Business sector	−50		−50
Overseas sector	+3		+3
	0	0	0

Source: Derived from Table 10.1.

The sector balances with a balanced budget can now be used to indicate the main directions of the second-round effects of government expenditure on YTS.

The principal second-round effects would have been as follows:

1 The personal sector would have reduced consumption expenditure because of the increase in income tax.
2 The business sector would have increased dividend payments and investment expenditure in response to higher *net* profits. Firms do not allocate to investment profits arising from particular sources, but the

level of *net* profits as a whole is a factor influencing investment. However, there would in the longer term have been some offset to business profits in the form of reduced expenditure by consumers.

3 If YTS had been paid for out of increased income tax (or if income tax had not been reduced as fast as it would have been in the absence of YTS), imports as well as consumption would have been reduced. Working in the opposite direction, increased dividends and investment would have increased both consumption and imports. The propensity to save is relatively high for dividend receivers and for companies, and it is likely that in the second round the financing of YTS out of extra income tax would have had some *net* effect towards improving the balance of trade.

Longer-term macroeconomic effects of YTS

The longer-term macroeconomic effects of YTS, in particular the effects upon the whole economy in terms of growth of GDP and employment (via

Table 10.4 *Macroeconomic effects of YTS upon output, employment, unemployment, and retail prices. Annual averages for the years 1984, 1985 and 1986, UK*

	(1) Change due to the *net* employment effects of YTS[a]	(2) Change due to the direct government expenditure on YTS	(3) Total change due to YTS (col.1 + col.2)
GDP at factor cost and constant prices (% change p.a.)	+0.5	+0.2	+0.7
Total employment (% change p.a.)	+0.7	+0.2	+0.9
Unemployment (000s)	−118	−37	−155
Retail prices (% changes p.a.)	+0.2	negligible	+0.2

Note: [a]Col. 1 shows the macroeconomic effects of the cumulative change in employment due to YTS. That employment change is equal to the cumulative *net register* effect of YTS, which is estimated after taking into account both the *deadweight* and *substitution* effects of YTS, and also the *secondary substitution* effect, which is an estimate of jobs taken by ex-YTS trainees which in their absence would have been filled by others.
Source: Deakin and Pratten 1987b, ch. 11.

the multiplier) of extra government expenditure on the training scheme, the macroeconomic effects of former YTS trainees entering employment, and the effect on retail prices, were estimated by feeding data on total YTS expenditure and the estimated cumulative employment effects of the subsidy over three years into the Cambridge Economic Growth Model.[6] These effects of YTS are analysed in two parts. The first is the *net* employment effect of YTS, and the second the effect on the economy of the *direct* expenditure by government on YTS. The total longer-term macro-economic effects are the sum of these two elements, as shown in Table 10.4.

The results of this exercise are given in Table 10.4 and show the *net* changes due to YTS after taking account of the alternative, no-policy situation. From this further macroeconomic analysis, the effects of YTS are shown to be positive on both output and employment, the latter effect being greater since the major proportion of the increase in employment is due to the jobs gained by young people post-YTS whose output and pay is below the national average rates. The effect upon the rate of retail price inflation is to increase it slightly.

[6] This model's full title is the Multisectoral Dynamic Economic Model of the British Economy (MDM). It was developed by the Department of Applied Economics, University of Cambridge. Its properties and capabilities at the time it was used for this analysis are described in Barker *et al.*, 1980. The model has also been used to estimate the effects of a hypothetical marginal labour subsidy in comparison with those of other economic policies to increase employment. See Whitley and Wilson 1983.

11 The skill attainments of YTS trainees in relation to the demand for skilled labour

Educational background

To make a fair assessment of the skill attainments of YTS it is necessary first to understand the quality of the scheme's entrants. In the analysis shown in Table 11.1 they are the third group (out of four) of 16 year olds by subsequent educational or labour market status. The first group are those who stay on at school or go on directly to further full-time education, and the second those who are able to obtain jobs directly from school without the aid provided by YTS, although some would doubtless have gained from the training provided by YTS.

The educational qualifications of these three groups of 16 year old school-leavers, and of a residuary fourth group, who went directly into unemployment or 'something else', are given for October 1986 in Table 11.1.[1] Very few school leavers with Level 1 qualifications entered YTS, but of those with Level 2 qualifications a greater proportion entered YTS than went directly into jobs. About 40% of the young people in each of the lower levels of qualification, i.e. Levels 3, 4 and 5 (no grades), went into YTS.

In 1985/86 about 12% of all school leavers in Britain, approximately 96,000 young people, failed to obtain any grades at school,[2] and 38% of these (about 36,000) entered YTS. Total entrants to YTS numbered 406,300 in 1985/86,[3] so about 9% of them were without any grades at school. That statistic gives an indication of the magnitude of the challenge facing the trainers and vocational teachers working on and off the job within the YTS.

Some later evidence on the lower end of the range of ability of school

---

[1] This date is chosen in order to match the extension of YTS to two years. The 1986 date marks the beginning of the period when training under the scheme both on and off the job took place on a larger and more organised scale. The analyses of YTS skill attainment which follow may then be seen against the background of the general educational attainments of the trainees involved.   [2] *Education Statistics for the United Kingdom* 1992, Table 29.
[3] Statistical Services Division of the Employment Department 1992.

Table 11.1 *Educational qualifications of 16 year olds by subsequent educational or labour market status, October 1986, England and Wales*[a] (%)

Level of Fifth Form educational qualifications[b]	Full-time education	Full-time job	YTS	'Something else'	Unemployed
1 4+ ABC1 passes	83	9	7	1	1
2 1–3 ABC1 passes	45	19	30	2	4
3 No ABC1 passes, 5+ others	29	21	41	3	6
4 No ABC1 passes, 1–4 others	12	27	43	6	12
5 No graded passes	5	27	38	10	20

Notes:

[a]The schools examination system is different in Scotland.

[b]A,B,C refer to 'O' Level passes, and 1 to CSE grade 1 which is equivalent to 'O' Level grade C. So, for example, Level 1 comprises those with 4 or more 'O' Level passes at grades A to C, or at CSE grade 1.

[c]Rows do not in all cases add to 100 owing to rounding.

Source: Sime 1991.

Table 11.2 *Employers' reasons for not participating in YTS. Sample survey results,* 1989, *GB (number of answers)*

Poor quality of YTS candidates	23
Against company policy	16
Poor image of YTS	13
Too much administration	13
Conditions in our jobs unsuitable for YTS trainees	11
Able to recruit without YTS	8
YTS trainees not available	2
Other reasons	7

Source: Begg *et al.* 1990.

leavers is obtained from a comparative survey (Begg *et al.*, 1990) of employers who participated in YTS and of a matched sample who did not. At interviews with firms which did not participate, the views of managers were sought as to why they did not recruit young people via the YTS. Of the 124 firms in this sub-sample, 63 had previously participated in YTS and 61 had never done so. Managers of the 61 sample firms which had never participated in YTS were asked to give their reasons for not doing so. Some managers gave more than one reason. Their answers are given in Table 11.2. It may be noted that the most cited reason given for not recruiting via YTS is 'the poor quality of YTS candidates'. It is not known how many of those who left school with no grades applied for but failed to obtain YTS places. Lack of basic educational achievement in terms of literacy and numeracy was no doubt one reason for such failures, and there is some evidence, which is given below, on the lack of such achievement.

A survey of literacy and numeracy students aged over 16 was undertaken by ALBSU in 1992.[4] It found that 29% of the sample group of 10,000 were young people within the age range 16–20. Of this group of 2,900, 1,700 were young men and 1,200 were young women. They were receiving tuition in both literacy and numeracy. As regards teaching in numeracy, 23% of the sample were young men and 11% were young women.

Some teaching in literacy and numeracy had to be carried out by employers. In a local labour market survey, a sample of employers were asked what basic educational teaching they had to provide for their YTS and other trainees taken on direct from school, before training and vocational education could be started. Of all participating sample firms, 20% (36 firms) gave some basic educational teaching in literacy or

[4] Survey by the Adult Literacy and Basic Skills Unit (ALBSU)(1992). The survey covered 10,000 adult literacy and numeracy students in 22 LEA areas of England and Wales. The survey did not include English for speakers of other languages.

numeracy or both (see Deakin 1990).So on this evidence the educational system in 1990 and 1992 was producing a significant number of young people who did not have the basic educational qualifications on which to base the training provided by employers and the vocational education off the job provided by Colleges of Further Education. However, this evidence relates only to those who sought remedial teaching, or agreed to it when it was offered by training employers. There are likely to be many young people who have neither sought it nor been offered it as a part of a training programme.

Against this background of educational achievement, or lack of it, and of efforts by LEAs and employers to remedy illiteracy and innumeracy, the performance of the YTS is examined first in terms of the proportion of all trainees gaining qualifications, and that is compared with the general demand from participating employers for skilled workers from YTS. That is followed by an analysis of YTS supply of skills by type in relation to the more specific labour demands from employers.

Attainment of qualifications by YTS trainees and the general demand for skills from employers

In the early years of YTS when youth unemployment was very high (see Table 6.1 in Chapter 6), the chief effect although not the overt purpose of the scheme, which until 1986 was for one year only, was to relieve unemployment among school leavers, which had risen greatly in the 1979–82 recession. The vocational element in the YTS was slow to get under way, and in these early years there was no obligation upon Managing Agents to ensure that trainees attended off-the-job training and external courses, although some trainees did so.

The proportion of one-year YTS trainees who obtained a full qualification while in training was very low during the period 1983 to 1987. It is shown (Table 11.3) that 73% of all YTS leavers (including non-completers) failed to gain a full qualification in 1984/85, and 79% in 1985/86 and 1986/87. Even as late as 1987/88 the improvement in that regard was slight, but it should be noted that only the one-year YTS course was operating in these years. It is emphasised at this point that about 36,000 YTS entrants in 1985/86, or 9% of the total in 1985/86, had no grades when they left school, and were therefore much less likely than those with some school-leaving grades to obtain a qualification under YTS.

A considerably higher proportion of those who completed YTS training (Table 11.3 col. 2) gained full qualifications. From 1987/88 there was an overall improvement by all ex-YTS trainees as the two-year YTS introduced in 1986 became more widespread, but there was a considerable

Table 11.3 *The proportion of YTS/YT trainees who gained a full qualification: all leavers, and completers only, 1984/85–1992/93, GB (%)*

	(1) All leavers	(2) Completers only[a]
1984/85	27	n.a.
1985/86	21	n.a.
1986/87	21	n.a.
1987/88	29	56
1988/89	41	67
1989/90	43	68
1990/91	38	61
1991/92	33	53
1992/93	32	54

Note: [a]Those who left YTS no more than four weeks before the expected completion date.

Sources: Gray and King 1986; *Training Statistics 1994*, Table E6, and earlier years; *YTS Management Information System* and *YT Follow-up Survey*, Department of Employment.

reduction in the proportion gaining full qualifications after 1989/90. Over the latest three years for which data are available, 1990/91 to 1992/93, an average of 56% of those who completed YTS gained a full qualification, but only 34% of all leavers. It should be noted, however, that although there were 'drop outs' from YTS, many early leavers in fact transferred to another YTS placement, while some went into jobs and continued their training and gained qualifications later.

When trying to assess the impact of YTS in terms of qualifications gained during the training period, it is essential to note that for the higher skills, particularly those involving apprenticeships, the period of training is up to four years. YTS gives support to such training for the first two years, and the fact that the qualification is gained later does not detract from the value of the initial support to training which is due to YTS, and which may be crucial in individual cases to the initial decision to train via apprenticeships.

Employers did use YTS to help them meet their demand for skilled workers. In the survey by Begg *et al.* (1990), which was conducted in 1989 when labour market conditions were tight and skill shortages were acute in many trades, managers of 126 sample firms who were then participating in YTS were asked to assess the extent to which YTS helped them to meet their skill shortages. Fifty-two per cent of managers said that YTS was 'important' or 'useful' in this respect. Managers of firms were also asked for their most important reason for recruiting young people via YTS.

Fifty-four per cent said that they 'recruited for skilled jobs', 22% to 'provide opportunities for young people', and 15% 'to obtain financial benefits'. Nine per cent gave other reasons. About 30% of *all* workers recruited by sample firms were taken on via YTS.

The character of demand from participating employers should also be judged under slack labour market conditions. Such conditions existed in 1985 when a survey of employers' attitudes to YTS was undertaken by Sako and Dore (1986, pp. 195–204). It was found from that survey that, as regards the advantages to the firm, the chief reason managers gave for taking part in the one-year YTS, as it was then, was 'screening for good employees' (42%), and the second most important reason was 'saving on labour costs' (32%). The contrast with the 1989 survey results was chiefly in the 'screening' or 'sifting' approach, which is more likely to occur when labour and product market conditions are slack. No doubt managers in 1985 were chiefly *seeking* to recruit in order to train for skilled jobs but were taking special care to screen and choose carefully under those market conditions.

They were probably also taking extra care in selection because the proportion of YTS leavers gaining qualifications in 1984/85 and 1985/86 was particularly low (Table 11.3). A further point, which has been made by Sako and Dore (p. 197), is that the scheme was fairly new then and some employers may have been 'tasting' it to discover whether it suited their needs for skilled workers.

It should also be noted, from both these surveys, that firms indicated that they gained financially from YTS, a finding which is confirmatory of those set out in Chapters 9 and 10.

It may be concluded from these sample survey results, and from the broad picture of attainment of qualifications by YTS trainees, that the scheme was an important channel for the recruitment and training of skilled young workers, and that held true under both slack and tight labour market conditions, with a number of reservations which have been noted. The proportion of YTS trainees obtaining *full* qualifications started in 1984/85 at a very low level. After the two-year YTS was introduced in 1986 there was a marked improvement, but since 1989/90 there has been a setback.

Qualifications aimed at by YTS trainees

These are shown separately for trainees in their first and second years of the scheme (Table 11.4). It may be seen from these sample survey results that in 1989 just over half the first- year trainees were aiming for nationally recognised qualifications, and the proportion doing so in their second year of training was 77%. In some cases, as has been noted above, training was set to continue beyond two years before the qualification sought could be

Table 11.4 *Qualifications aimed at by YTS trainees, sample survey results, 1989, GB*

	Number of YTS trainees	Percentage shares
A First-year YTS trainees		
Total number	163	100
of which those aiming for:		
nationally recognised qualifications[a]	85	53
company qualifications awarded after examination	22	13
qualifications not known to company manager	18	11
no qualification aimed at	38	23
B Second-year YTS trainees		
Total number	144	100
of which those aiming for:		
nationally recognised qualifications[a]	109	77
company qualifications awarded after examination	18	12
qualification not known to company manager	8	5
no qualifications aimed at	9	6

Note: [a]Specifically City and Guilds (various trades), BTEC, RSA, ONC and the YTS Certificate (but only three trainees in the first year and four in the second year were aiming solely for this low-level qualification).
Source: Begg *et al.* 1990, Part I, pp. 65, 66.

obtained. Trainees not aiming for any qualification at all declined from 23% of the total in the first year to 6% in the second year of YTS. It is notable that this latter proportion was only two-thirds the proportion of trainees who entered YTS with no grades from their school education.

However, these results indicate that much more needed to be done to raise the level of qualifications aimed at, and to ensure that all YTS trainees did engage upon a training and vocational education programme leading to a nationally recognised qualification. Progress in that direction was made later, in 1990, when the YTS was converted into the YT. It was then arranged that all YT entrants should attend courses at a standard of at least Level 2 of the National Vocational Qualifications (NVQs). Later, when Youth Credits were introduced in 1991, it was made a condition of the new scheme that trainees reach qualifications at NVQ Level 2 or above before full payment is made to the training provider. These developments are considered further in Chapter 12. However, it should be noted here that the decline in full qualifications obtained by YTS leavers (Table 11.3) may be due to some extent to this process of raising the qualification standards for the trainees which took place in 1990 and 1991. Previously, many YTS trainees qualified at the lower level of NVQ1 or the simple YTS Certificate.

The supply of skills from the YTS in relation to the specific needs of employers

This section is concerned with the impact on the labour market of YTS trainees when the period of training had been completed. An answer is attempted to the question as to whether the skills they were being trained for matched the demand for skills in that market.

The sample survey (Begg *et al.* 1990) conducted in 1989 involved interviews with 126 firms participating in YTS. Information was obtained from these firms on the number and occupational type of vacancies they currently had for skilled (and semi-skilled) workers. This constituted their demand for skilled labour. At the same time they provided information on the number of YTS trainees currently in training with them, and the occupational skills which these young people were aiming to acquire.

An analysis of these data is given in Table 11.5, where about 800 vacancies, broken down by occupation, are matched with the supply of some 900 trainees in the same occupations who might be expected to enter the job market when their YTS training had been completed. An allowance, based on past experience, of 10% should be made for YTS 'drop outs', and from the evidence presented in Table 11.3 for the fact that about 35% of 'completers' would not gain full qualifications.

The general labour market background to the situation shown in Table 11.5 is of relatively tight conditions due to a high level of demand for skilled workers. In 1989, the CBI's *Quarterly Industrial Trends Survey* showed that about 25% of *manufacturing* firms 'expected a lack of skilled labour to limit their output over the following four months', and there had been a peak of 28% in October 1988. By contrast, the corresponding percentage in 1992 was 5.

The unevenness of the match seen in Table 11.5 is partly due to the different lengths of the training process. In the engineering trades the apparent excess of supply reflects the long training period, usually four years, for engineering apprentices, who are supported by YTS for the first two years only of their apprenticeships. The same factor – length of training which has to continue beyond the end of YTS – applies to the higher skills in the electrical and electronic trades, and the skilled building trades.

Table 11.5 *The demand for skilled workers and the supply from YTS training, sample survey results, 1989, GB*

Skills in demand	Demand: number of vacancies for these skills	Supply via YTS: number of YTS trainees in training for these skills
Clerical and other office skills	117	249
Computing skills	53	2
Engineering fitters and other engineering skills	198	363
Tool setters and operatives	108	55
Metal moulders and forgers	19	3
Assemblers	96	60
Electrical/electronic fitters and allied trades	35	35
Instrument workers and repairers	32	5
Retailing/selling skills	31	34
Skilled building trades	44	35
Cooks and chefs	12	34
Restaurant and other catering and hotel trades	42	38
Horticultural and agricultural skills	1	3
Total	788	916

Source: Data from Begg *et al*. 1990, Part I.

Therefore, in these two latter cases there is a greater shortfall in supply than is apparent from the figures.

The broad distribution of YTS trainees by occupation matches the demand for skilled labour reasonably well. However, it is clear that in some of the trades which require relatively high levels of skills the YTS did not at this time come very near to satisfying the demand. Perhaps the most obvious case of this is computer skills, but supply is also short of demand in tool setting, metal moulding, assembling, electrical/electronic engineering, instrument making and repairing, and in the skilled building trades.

On the other hand, there may have been an excess at this time in the YTS-sponsored supply of workers with clerical and other office skills, and of cooks and chefs, although it is probable that staff turnover is relatively high in this group of occupations, a situation which would lead to employers engaging more trainees than they would for an occupation with a lower rate of labour turnover.

It may be concluded from this evidence that the supply of YTS trainees in 1989 broadly matched the pattern of demand for skilled workers as expressed by current job vacancies, but that for some of the higher skills then in demand the YTS supply was insufficient to meet the demand. So, as in the previous section on the progress made by YTS trainees in gaining qualifications, it is concluded that further progress towards a greater supply of certain higher grade qualifications and skills is needed. The method of providing these higher skills in order to match demand more closely is likely to depend on progress in the wider field of general and vocational education. In addition, some gain to the process of matching the supply of young persons trained via YTS to the demand for skilled workers could be obtained by offering longer period training subsidies for those trainees who were aiming for higher qualifications. That was done under the YT system introduced in 1990, and there is some evidence from the results of the analysis given here (Table 11.5) that the 'same subsidy per place' format of the YTS in 1989 was not producing the best match between supply and demand for skills.

Changes in the demand for labour: an occupational analysis

In the broader terms of the national labour market, changes in the structure of demand arise from changes in the pattern of consumer demand for goods and services, and also from the technological progress which influences the demand for particular skills. In recent years the application of computer technology and the skills associated with it have much changed the pattern of the demand for labour in many occupations, in both quantitative and qualitative terms.

Work by the Institute of Employment Research at the University of Warwick has been concerned with these changes in the occupational structure of the British labour market. The past and likely future changes in that structure are shown in Table 11.6.

The demand for many of the skills and semi-skills which YTS and YT have been providing was in decline in the 1980s. That has been particularly true for the semi-skills of plant and machine operatives, and the forecasts to 2000 are for a more rapid decline in this type of demand. Similar broad trends can be seen for the craft group of skills in engineering and other trades, except construction, where only a very small decline in demand is expected. In the clerical and secretarial occupations, where advances in information technology are continuing to influence employment, the growth seen in the 1980s is expected to be followed by reductions.

Growth has occurred in the past and is expected to continue in future in the managerial and professional occupations, including science and

Table 11.6 *The demand for labour: past and expected future changes in the occupational structure, 1981–91 and 1991–2000, all persons, GB*

| Occupation | Average change p.a. | | Number engaged in each occupation, 1991 (millions) |
	Actual 1981–91 (000s)	Forecast 1991–2000 (000s)	
Corporate managers and administrators	+52	+66	2.2
Managers/proprietors in agriculture and services	+24	+21	1.6
Science and engineering professionals	+17	+17	0.6
Health professionals	+4	+3	0.2
Teaching professionals	+19	+2	1.2
Other professional occupations	+23	+32	0.6
Science and engineering associate professionals	+10	+12	0.6
Health associate professionals	+9	+6	0.7
Other associate professionals	+35	+29	1.1
Clerical occupations	+9	−8	3.0
Secretarial occupations	+3	−10	1.1
Skilled construction trades	+6	−1	0.6
Skilled engineering trades	−20	−14	1.1
Other skilled trades	−32	−42	1.9
Protective service occupations	+3	+3	0.3
Personal service occupations	+26	+20	1.6
Buyers, brokers and sales representatives	+4	+1	0.5
Other sales occupations	+20	+14	1.4
Industrial plant and machine operatives	−32	−42	1.6
Drivers and mobile machine operatives	−13	−7	0.8
Other occupations in agriculture, etc.	−4	−4	0.2
Other elementary occupations	−25	−35	2.4
All occupations	+137	+62	25.3

Source: Wilson 1993, Table 3.3.

Table 11.7 *Annual number of higher education qualifications obtained in the UK, 1980/81, 1983/84, 1986/87 and 1990/91, all persons (000s)*

	Below degree level[a]	First degrees[b]	Post-graduate degrees[c]
1980/81	62	124	37
1983/84	72	133	37
1986/87	85	143	46
1990/91	111	162	65

Notes:
[a]Includes higher TEC/SCOTEC, BEC/SCOTBEC, BTEC/SCOTVEC, HND/HNC, (These acronyms refer to the higher awards made by the following bodies in England and Wales (and by their equivalents in Scotland): Technician Education Council; Business Education Council; Business and Technician Education Council; Higher National Diploma and Higher National Certificate awarding body), first university diplomas and certificates, CNAA diplomas and certificates below degree level and estimates of successful completions of public sector professional courses. Lower level qualifications within the NVQ framework are excluded, together with certificates of training attainment.
[b]Includes university degrees and estimates of: validated degrees (GB), CNAA degrees (and equivalent), and successful completions of public sector professional courses. Also includes certain CNAA Diplomas in Management Studies.
[c]Includes universities, CNAA and estimates of successful completions of public sector progressional courses. Postgraduate Certificates in Education are included.
Source: *Education Statistics for the UK* 1993, Table G. The Department for Education enters the qualification, as regards these statistics, that the trends in qualification number may not be directly comparable because, *inter alia*, qualifications may not be assigned to the year in which they are achieved.

engineering. Similar trends are expected for the associate professional occupations. The trend towards a higher proportion of young people continuing beyond the age of 16 in further full-time or part-time education, particularly the former (shown in Chapter 3), will tend in general terms towards an improved match of supply to the shift in the structure of demand for skills which is shown in Table 11.6. The movements towards an increasing supply of young people with higher qualifications are shown in Table 11.7. These increases in numbers have occurred in spite of a decline in size of the age groups concerned (see Chapter 3, Table 3.3).

There remain major problems with regard to the majority of school leavers, namely those who do not continue into full-time further general or vocational education and who are available for direct entry to the labour market. The qualification achievement rate for YTS/YT trainees has been declining in recent years (Table 11.3). There is, moreover, the major handicap to trainers and vocational educators of the low standards of school leavers, involving illiteracy and innumeracy among the lower ranges of ability, a high proportion of whom enter YTS/YT.

So the task for government policy makers dealing with youth training programmes grows harder. There are factors which are exerting an adverse influence upon both the supply and demand sides of the youth labour market. On the supply side there are the shortcomings of the general education system and, on the demand side, a shift in demand towards jobs which require much higher qualifications than those needed in the 1980s, and a decline in demand for recruits for semi-skilled and manual jobs.

12 The devolution of intervention and the movement towards *quasi*-markets

Devolution

When it was set up in 1983 the YTS was organised by the MSC on a national basis and was directed centrally. Previous government interventions in the labour market had also been centralised, except for the Industrial Training Boards (ITBs), which had been set up in 1964 on an industry basis.

The concept of a national labour market has never carried a precise meaning. The divisions of the market by occupation, and increasingly by specialisms within occupations, as well as by its regional dimensions, led to official thinking that a more devolved, free-market approach to the administration of youth training and employment measures and to other government interventions in the labour market, would be more appropriate and likely to lead to a more effective implementation of official policies. To some extent this policy shift was due to an increase in the application of free-market economics, which gained in strength as the Conservative Governments of the 1980s and early 1990s were kept in power. There was also some evidence that the control of training under the YTS, which was exercised by Managing Agents in their role as Approved Training Organisations (ATOs), was of uneven efficiency (Lee *et al.* 1990, pp. 172, 173).

The first step in the devolution process was made when the MSC was disbanded and the Training Commission, later the Training Agency (TA), was set up in 1988. The administration of the YTS was thereafter organised through local, regional offices. Later, in 1989 and 1990, this process of devolution was taken an important step further by the establishment of 82 Training and Enterprise Councils (TECs) in England and Wales, and 22 Local Enterprise Companies (LECs) in Scotland; the TA was succeeded by the Training, Education and Enterprise Directive (TEED), which together with another newly established body, the National Training Task Force (NTTF), directed the setting up of the TEC and LEC system. The function of the NTTF was to vet the quality of the bids to set up the TECs and LECs (it was abolished in October 1992, when that job had been completed).

The TECs were organised on a local basis: local employers, local providers of vocational education and trade union representatives were invited to play an active role by becoming directors of the TECs and running the government's intervention in the fields of the YTS, Employment Training (ET) for adults out of work for more than six months, the Business Growth Training Scheme (BGT), and various types of information technology training. So six years after the establishment of YTS in 1983, devolution and integration with local private and public sector employers, and with local providers of vocational education, became the pattern of organisation for the government's major intervention in the youth labour market.

It is notable that the devolution movement did not take the form of national occupational groupings, as had occurred in the 1960s with the Industrial Training Boards (ITBs). That experience and its shortcomings have been examined in Chapter 4. The ITBs were nearly all disbanded in the early 1970s, although a few survived longer. The Construction Industry Board (a Managing Agent for YTS), re-formed as the Engineering Construction Industry Training Board (ECITB) in 1991, was one which remained in operation.

A further change was made at the time the TECs were set up, and was in fact linked to them. This was to change the YTS to Youth Training (YT), which was done in May 1990. The rationale for this change was to provide the new TECs with a youth training scheme which was basically the YTS with added flexibility to enable the TECs to match supply more closely with demand in the local youth labour markets, and also to raise attainment of vocational qualifications in terms of both level and number.

The main changes to convert YTS to YT were officially stated as follows:

i an emphasis upon outputs [of qualified young people] rather than training processes;
ii flexible design of individual schemes to achieve outputs instead of a fixed national design structure;
iii the two- and one-year YTS entitlements to give way to training programmes of varying duration suitable for particular types of courses and the types of trainee need involved;
iv the promise of courses at a standard of at least level 2 as laid down by the National Council for Vocational Qualifications (NVQ), or at equivalent occupational training or education standards. In addition, more purchase of training at NVQ levels 3 and 4;[1]

---

[1] Specification of the standards of achievement required at each level of the NVQ system is given in Chapter 7.

v allowances to unemployed trainees based upon age rather than cumulative time in training;[2]
vi improved assessment and endorsement procedures for special training needs; enhanced training opportunities to help unemployed trainees nearing the end of training to secure jobs;
vii extension of the guarantee [of a YT place] to include certain groups whose entry into training had been unavoidably delayed;
viii more scope for discretionary entry for people not covered by the guarantee; greater financial discretion to use YT funds to build up local training arrangements, improve local marketing and to give specific support for individual young people on assessment, action plans and similar matters. (Secretary of State for Employment in answer to a Parliamentary Question, 20 February 1990, *Employment Gazette* 1990, p. 227)

The new YT scheme was drawn in broad, flexible terms with a wide range of discretion allowed to the local TECs to administer it in accordance with their judgement of local demand for youth labour, local training arrangements, and the particular aptitudes and needs of individual local school leavers. In particular, the differential funding arrangements whereby longer subsidies are offered to trainees aiming for higher qualifications may be seen as an improvement over the 'same subsidy per place' structure of the YTS in terms both of meeting the needs of trainees and of the greater demand for various higher skills.

The outcome and relative success of YT in achieving its aims largely remain to be seen. The number of young people training within the YT scheme was 350,000 in July 1991. At that time, just over a year after its inception, 89% of those who had completed their training under YT had gained jobs, and 67% had obtained some vocational qualification (Bridges 1991). Later figures on full qualifications gained, which are for all leavers, are less encouraging, and particularly so when compared with results achieved in earlier years by YTS trainees. It has been shown (Chapter 11, Table 11.3) that 43% of all YTS leavers gained a full qualification in 1989/90. YT was introduced in April 1990 and the rate of attainment of full qualifications for all YT leavers fell each year to reach 32% in 1992/93, but, as explained in Chapter 11, the pre-1990 qualifications under YTS were generally at a lower level.

The devolution process for the supply of government-sponsored youth training had run a full course by 1991, and a revised view has therefore to be

---

[2] The minimum values of the lower and higher levels of the YT allowance remained as for YTS immediately before the change to YT at £29.50 and £35 per week respectively. However, YT included the change that the higher rate of allowance became payable to YT trainees when they reached their 17th birthday, instead of after completing a fixed period of training. In consequence, most trainees were expected to qualify for the higher level of allowance earlier than under the YTS.

taken of the role of government intervention in the youth labour market. Central direction had been reduced to what appeared to be a minimum level. One central body, the National Training Task Force (NTTF), existed until 1992 to oversee and guide the TECs and to advise government, and the Department of Employment continued to administer the total budget for youth training, but it was intended that administrative control should be effectively in the hands of the TECs.

More decision-making power was also devolved to the trainees. This was done by a system of Youth Credits (originally called Training Credits or Vouchers). A pilot scheme[3] to test these was announced in the House of Commons on 27 March 1990.

The Youth Credit scheme was designed in the following terms:

1 Young people aged 16 or 17 who plan to leave school discuss their job prospects with their school careers adviser.
2 If they decide to take a Youth Credit it is supplied by their local TEC. It is available to them to use until their nineteenth birthday.
3 School leavers may obtain a job straight away. In that case they discuss with their employer how to use their Credit. They may use it for day release classes, evening classes or distance learning. Those unable to find a job are found a guaranteed YT place approved by the TEC.
4 During training employers pay the trainees the standard YT allowance, where that applies, and record their progress.
5 On completion of training, trainees receive their qualifications at NVQ Level 2 or above as required by the conditions of the Youth Credit scheme.[4]

The value of the Youth Credits at the time of their introduction was within the range £500–5000 according to type of occupation. The trainees are in greater control, under this scheme, of the process of investment in their own skills. There are, however, some constraints upon choice of occupation in that the TECs channel the 'spending' of Credits, which have 'real cash value', towards training places which are relevant to the current demands of local employers, and trainees have to gain training places through the usual recruitment process, which entails the exercise of choice by the employer. The TECs provide an information and advisory service on vacancy availability.

The Youth Credit system extended the range of choice of career open to new trainees, and it conferred upon them a significant degree of decision

---

[3] Ten TECs in England and Wales and one LEC in Scotland were chosen to run the pilot scheme.
[4] The final tranche of the Credit is not paid to the employer or training provider if a qualification at NVQ Level 2, or higher, is not obtained by the trainee.

making at the earliest and perhaps most crucial stage in their working lives.

The new Modern Apprenticeship system was announced in 1994. It is expected to be in operation by September 1995, and will be supported financially by the government through the medium of the Youth Credit scheme. The Modern Apprenticeships will be administered by the TECs and will be for two or three years. They will aim to 'equip young people with technician, craft and supervisory skills at NVQ Level 3 and above'. The target size of the new scheme is 150,000 young people at any one time (*Employment Gazette* 1994, April, p. 99). The government claims that it is a move to close the skills gap between Britain and its international competitors. It will undoubtedly prolong intervention in support of the higher level skills which were shown (in Chapter 11) to be needed in the 1990s and beyond.

The YTS system, the Youth Credits and Modern Apprenticeships are funded on an output-related basis, under which the government finances training provided by others: employers, colleges of further education and private providers of training services. Output is measured largely by the NVQ system, and the new output-related basis for funding is likely to put pressure upon the integrity of assessment for the NVQs which are already the subject of much criticism in terms of their structure and content (see Chapter 7).

In sum, the process of devolution from centralised to local control of government-sponsored youth training proceeded rapidly from 1989. It started with the establishment of the TECs, went on to the conversion of the YTS to YT, then to the introduction of Youth Credits which could be used either within YT or outside it, and in 1995 to the Modern Apprenticeship system. The devolution process was accompanied by a liberalisation of labour market processes by conferring greater market freedom upon new trainees and by the introduction of output-related funding. The government remained the *financer* of youth training services but it was effectively no longer the *provider* of those services. In 1990 there was a decisive policy shift towards the establishment of a *quasi*-market for youth training services. That development is examined later in this chapter. First, the nature of *quasi*-markets is examined.

Quasi-markets

In the late 1980s there were some important changes in the way the British welfare state was organised. Before 1988 centralised control by very large bureaucratic mechanisms was exercised over the vast non-market sector of the economy, which in 1979 consumed almost a quarter of the gross domestic product. Little change took place before 1988; such change as did occur was in permitting the sale of council houses to their tenants (Le Grand 1991).

The main changes in the welfare state apparatus have occurred since 1988. The first were in the National Health Service and in education.

The early changes in the National Health Service, before 1988, were in the privatisation of ancillary services, such as cleaning. A major change, initiated in April 1991, was the choice for hospitals and some other service units to opt out from health authority control to form hospital trusts. They were then free to compete by tender for contracts from health authorities and from General Practitioners (GPs) who, if their practices were of a certain minimum size, were allowed budgets for each of their patients. These budgets can be 'spent' by GPs on behalf of their patients, to purchase the services of competing providers of medical services, chiefly the independent hospital trusts. A *quasi*-market was thereby established. It is one in which the government remains the financer, but not the provider of services. The providers are independent units in competition with each other, in this case trust hospitals. The consumers have greater choice, which is exercised on their behalf, because of the technical nature of the service required, by their GPs. This, in effect, is a voucher or credit system and may be seen as similar to the Youth Credit system which has been described in the previous section of this chapter and which is examined further in the next section.

The educational system, which is necessarily linked to the vocational training system, has also been changed by a process of decentralisation of control, and of widening consumer choice leading to *quasi*-market status. The *Education Act 1988* dismantled the system of control and organisation of education, which had for long been in the hands of central and local government in respect of both finance and provision of education services. The new system, which devolves control locally to schools, is named the Local Management of Schools (LMS) system. The arrangement for funding is that the number of pupils entered into a particular school will attract proportionate funding. The Local Education Authority (LEA) retains a proportion (15%) of total funding to provide certain centralised services, such as inspection services and special units for disruptive pupils. Schools are also permitted to opt out of LEA control completely. In such cases funding is as for non-opted out schools, together with extra funding as compensation for not receiving the LEA's central services.

The degree of competition introduced by these means will, in theory, increase efficiency in ways which are explained below. Decision making at school rather than at LEA level is expected to improve resource allocation in terms of staff and of books and equipment. The pressures of competition for pupils, and thence income, is also expected to work strongly towards the same end. However, other considerations may lead to less favourable outcomes in terms of equity, as selection bias acts against less able pupils (Glennerster 1991).

Quasi-markets introduce market signals into a number of public services, with the general aim of improving the efficiency of the service and of its delivery. Consumer choice is broadened by a *quasi*-market structure and the probability of greater consumer satisfaction thereby increased. In so far as *quasi*-market conditions approach freely competitive market conditions, they tend to increase both *allocative efficiency* and *X-efficiency*.

It may be useful to explain briefly that *allocative efficiency* is attained when the economy is Pareto-efficient. That means that no reallocation of resources can be made that will make someone better off without making at least one other person worse off. The conditions for allocative efficiency are exceptionally stringent. For satisfaction they require that marginal cost must equal price in all markets, and that the sum of producers' and consumers' surplus is maximised. These conditions are fulfilled only under universal perfect competition.

X-efficiency requires the condition that all firms produce on, rather than above, their long-run marginal cost curve. For full productive efficiency it is a necessary further condition that all enterprises producing the same product must have the same marginal costs. Profit maximisation is sufficient to produce X-efficiency, but perfect competition is necessary to ensure equal marginal costs for all producers.

Providers of hospital and other medical services in the reformed National Health Service, and schools operating under the Local Management of Schools system, will come under some of the pressures which arise from competitive market conditions. Where their services are priced above cost, or where their costs, although equal to their prices, are higher than their competitors' costs, they will suffer some loss of revenue. They may then endeavour to move nearer to their X-efficiency, by reducing their costs and prices.

Allocative efficiency is even harder to achieve, but the introduction of competition into the markets for provider services will tend to move prices for the same services towards equality with long-run marginal costs, and so enlarge consumer surplus by that means and also by extending consumer choice, notwithstanding that such choice is made by a proxy, such as a GP making a purchase of hospital services on behalf of a patient.

In education, increased competitive pressures will oblige managers (headmasters and governors) of schools to use the powers devolved upon them to reduce costs by improving the match between staff, books and equipment on the one hand and the needs of pupils on the other. That would also be expected to increase pupil numbers, and revenue, and so tend towards maximisation of profit and improved X-efficiency, as well as producing greater allocative efficiency.

The extent to which the more competitively oriented *quasi*-market can deliver welfare services more efficiently than the previous, long-standing centralised system requires further study and testing, but a start on that process has been made.

How the application of a *quasi*-market structure is changing the market for vocational education and training services, and thereby influencing the youth labour market, is examined next.

The *quasi*-market for youth training services

On the supply side in this market are the providers of training services. These are public institutions (particularly Colleges of Further Education) and private firms which provide off-the-job training, and also public and private sector employers who provide on-the-job training and work experience. Not all of these are yet subject to full-scale competitive market conditions, but competition is increasing and the trend towards an improvement in X-efficiency should continue.

The demand side of this *quasi*-market comprises trainees. Some are in employment, having obtained jobs directly after leaving school, and others are YT trainees as yet without jobs. Both groups have access to Youth Credits, which have cash value and can be 'spent' at the providers who supply training services on and off the job. To some, rather limited extent the customers, i.e. the trainees, do decide how and where to spend their Credits, but they are advised and strongly guided by the TECs, who stand in relation to trainees in somewhat the same position, but less completely, as GPs stand in relation to their patients. The trainees are also limited in their choice by employers who have to act in accordance with their need for skilled workers of specified types.

The greater consumer choice, such as it is, which is entailed by the system of Youth Credits does in principle tend to promote greater allocative and productive efficiency (including X-efficiency) by releasing the consumers of training services from a single source of supply and providing wider choice. There is, however, a barrier on the supply side. This is the relatively monopolistic situation of most Colleges of Further Education. Although these are being disconnected from LEA control, they remain very large suppliers to a market which is local. So they will remain the dominant and therefore monopolistic suppliers of training services. Private suppliers of some training, many in the field of clerical training, do exist, but competition in the areas of training for the more technical trades of the goods and service industries and construction will remain weak. That will tend to slow the progress towards lower and more equal marginal costs, and thence towards increased allocative and X-efficiency in this *quasi*-market.

In the outline given earlier of the *quasi*-market in educational services, it was noted that less able pupils could be at a disadvantage because of the extra teaching cost which would be borne by the opted out, independent school whose revenue is based upon pupil numbers without differentiation. Some degree of selectivity by schools is also likely to occur as the pressures of competition lead to the need to achieve high standards of educational service. That involves selectivity at entrance and acts to the disadvantage of the less able who would have to be educated in schools where general standards of achievement may be lower.

In the *quasi*-market for training services the Youth Credits are variable in value according to the training costs involved in different occupations. There remain the hard-to-train youngsters who may be of less ability or have special needs, and whose training costs may be high for reasons unconnected with choice of occupation. A problem of selectivity may therefore arise in this *quasi*-market too. Indeed, the introduction of competition into previously bureaucratic structures is likely to lead to the problems which arise from selectivity. This involves the general problem of equity which needs to be addressed with regard to all the new *quasi*-markets.

One solution, which has been proposed by Le Grand (1989), is the Positively Discriminatory Voucher (PDV) for education services. Individuals with markedly less natural endowment and/or with greater needs for other reasons are given higher value vouchers or budget allocations. This would provide an incentive for the providers of services to take on such individuals, who would thereby have gained the necessary market power to buy the best services available. In the market for training services the differential value of the Youth Credits already allows for cost differences due to occupational choice, and further consideration needs to be given to the differential value of Credits for specially hard-to-train individuals. For the less able, including those who leave school with no grades in educational examinations, there is a clear need to provide a Positively Discriminatory Credit to increase their market power, and to enable them, under guidance from the TECs, to 'spend' a part of the Credit first on remedial classes in literacy and numeracy, which have been shown (Chapter 11) to be necessary in some cases before or during the early stages of training with employers. Corrective action can thereby be taken to improve the equity aspects of the *quasi*-market for youth training services. By these means the best abilities of the less able and of those disadvantaged in other ways are more likely to be realised in later training processes and employment.

13 Some critics of the government's youth training intervention

There have been many critics of the YTS/YT over the first ten years of its operation, 1983–93. The more prominent of them fall largely into four groups.

The *first*, a relatively large group, concentrate upon the poor general and vocational education and training system in Britain compared with that in main competitor countries, and more specifically with the lack of attainment of qualifications by trainees in the YTS and YT, and also with the related matter of the predominance of the internal labour market (ILM) for ex-YTS trainees, that is the job market within the firms which provide the training, and the corresponding lack of supply to the external labour market, also named the occupational labour market (OLM), which is the wider market involving demand from many employers.

The *second* group criticise the YTS for the emphasis which, it is held, is placed upon free market forces, which do not provide the type of training needed for young people who leave school without securing jobs.

The *third* group are concerned with the priority of policies: the priority given to the government's training policy over its manpower policy is seen as damaging to the central aim of manpower policy, which is to provide the desired equilibrium in the youth labour market, and as damaging also to training policy which, without a successful manpower policy, may lead to young people completing their training but then having no jobs to go to.

The *fourth* group, comprised of the three authors of one book (Bennett *et al.* 1994), are concerned with the structural and management problems, as they see them, of the Training and Enterprise Councils (TECs) in England and Wales and the Local Enterprise Companies (LECs) in Scotland, and with the policies of the government departments and their central agencies which control them.

The criticisms are appraised first and then set in context with contemporary and later developments in order to show those changes in the YTS/YT system, or in the general conditions of the youth labour market, which have

157

met some criticisms and have lent force to others. It is not intended to suggest that the critics lacked foresight, but to illustrate the evolution of policy, or the lack of it, in relation to the criticisms made.

Lack of attainment of qualifications by YTS trainees

In the *first* group, one of the more constructive critics of the quality of YTS training (Jones 1988) points first to the very poor levels of qualifications gained by those on the original one-year YTS: less than a quarter gained any qualifications at all. Most of those who did qualify gained no more than Level 1 of the NVQ system or its equivalent. However, in the comparison which he makes with what went on before YTS was introduced in 1983, the new scheme is seen to have led to an increase of about 50% in the total number gaining qualifications approximately equivalent to Level 1 of the NVQ (Jones 1988, p. 60). The extension of YTS to a second year was made in April 1986. By 1986–87 (the latest year available to Jones) there was little evidence from his analysis of an increase in qualifications above NVQ Level 1. More evidence was available later (see above, Chapter 11, Table 11.3), and that did indicate a rise in full qualifications until 1989/90. To improve the number and level of qualifications obtained, Jones proposed, bearing in mind the low educational standard of YTS entrants from schools, that entry requirements be introduced. These would be at minimum levels in the basic subjects – English and Mathematics. This proposal matches the point, made earlier in the present study (Chapter 11), that the poor educational attainments of YTS entrants were and continue to be a serious handicap to the attainment of vocational qualifications. The main drawback to a policy of minimum entrance requirements must be the problem of dealing fairly and effectively with those who then fail to gain YTS entry. The argument for equity (see Chapter 12) would apply. Further constructive proposals by Jones included incentive payments to trainees to gain qualifications, and improvements in arrangements to train the trainers. A final and important proposal, since implemented, was to extend the two-year term of YTS when the (then contemplated) full NVQ framework was in place. That has been achieved and the terms of the later YT provide the flexibility of longer-period support for training (Chapter 12), coupled with the requirement for the attainment of a specified level of qualification.

Another critic of the quality of training standards and attainment of qualifications (Raffe 1987, 1988 and 1989) maintains that, in the one-year YTS, little weight was given in the vocational education element to the broad-based curriculum, and that the scheme was 'employer-led', serving employers' short-term needs by providing low-level skills of narrow scope. A serious further disadvantage of YTS is seen by Raffe in the attraction it may have had for school-leavers who joined the scheme when they might have gained broader vocational education by continuing in TVEI, or on other full-time vocational courses. Some of Raffe's criticisms of the vocational education standards obtained were met in later developments: since 1989, the proportion of 16 year olds staying in full-time education has increased steadily (Chapter 3, Table 3.4), and since 1986 YTS has provided two years of training. Raffe also criticises the lack of supply to the external labour market of trained workers ex-YTS. The internal labour market is seen as being supplied with 'narrow skills' but the wider, external market which, it is suggested, requires the higher and more transferable skills (to produce which it was and remains the aim of YTS/YT) was poorly served. In fact, the evidence is that both markets were served about equally by ex-YTS trainees (Table 13.1).

Table 13.1 *Internal and external labour market destinations of YTS and YT leavers who obtained full-time jobs, 1985/86–1990/91, GB (percentage market shares)*

Years to 31 March	Internal labour market	External labour market[a]
1985/86		
YTS1 only	52.2	47.8
1986/87		
YTS1 and YTS2 merged	48.9	51.1
1987/88		
YTS2 only	39.9	60.1
1988/89		
YTS2 only	51.3	48.7
1989/90		
YTS2 only	53.4	46.6
1990/91		
YT only	54.5	45.5

Note: [a]Includes those who went into self-employment.
Source: Based on data from the *YTS Leaver Survey* and *Follow-up Survey*, various years.

The economic theory of training, based in this respect on Becker (1975), would suggest that as soon as the longer, two-year YTS courses had become firmly established, the internal market would retain a high proportion of the total number of ex-YTS trainees who gained jobs (Chapter 1). That would be so, according to that theory, because the training in the second year would be more specific to the business of the employer undertaking the training, thereby reducing the ex-trainees' labour market mobility. That thesis is not very strongly supported by the evidence given in Table 13.1. The share of the internal labour market did expand steadily, but modestly, after the two-year YTS (which was introduced in 1986) began to produce more fully trained young people from 1988/89 onwards, but the external market largely retained its share in comparison with what occurred under the one-year YTS which was in operation in 1985/86.

So ex-YTS trainees, and particularly those with two years' training, clearly have labour market mobility. Whether more or less mobility than in fact existed in this period (as shown by these data) is desirable, is an open question. It may be that Becker's theory is valid, but the evidence in Table 13.1 does not unequivocally support his thesis.

Further analysis and assessment of the youth labour market in its internal and occupational (external) aspects is given by Marsden and Ryan (1988, 1989) and by Marsden (1990). They maintain that the access of young people to the more secure and better paid skilled jobs ('primary employment') is via apprenticeships, or equivalent longer-term training, and then into the external, occupational market. In their view, internal markets provide, through on-the-job training, jobs which are likely to be relatively low skilled and are 'secondary employment', and which are less secure and have poorer prospects for advancement. Ex-trainees entering secondary employment may be paid more highly at age 18, when their training for lower skilled jobs will have been completed and adult wages become payable, than an apprentice who has to train for four years from age 16 before receiving adult wages for a job in primary employment. However, the remuneration of a newly-qualified apprentice is then likely to be higher than that for secondary employment, and more job security and satisfaction are likely to be obtained. These critics maintain that the decline in apprenticeship in Britain, particularly in manufacturing industry (shown in Chapter 6, Table 6.2), has decreased youth labour mobility and the supply to the occupational market. The training system of the YTS has not, it is claimed, produced a fully satisfactory substitute so far. In its two-year form YTS is much shorter than the normal four year apprenticeship, although it is used to support the first two years of apprenticeships, notably in the construction industry, and does therefore provide some support for the older system.

Improvements on these shortcomings are not yet fully in place, but the longer training available under the Youth Credits goes some way to extending training beyond two years with financial support from government, and the new intervention to support Modern Apprenticeships via Youth Credits (see Chapter 12) will go further to meet these criticisms. The extra labour mobility and associated access to primary employment for the young trainee is likely therefore to be much improved in future. The longer-term support for youth training should also bring some improvement in access to more highly skilled and better paid jobs in the internal market.

Finegold and Soskice (1988) make severe criticisms of the whole of the UK educational and training (ET) system. The economy is seen as getting low skills for mass-produced modes of production which are no longer economically viable. Emphasis is laid by these authors upon the low level of training produced by YTS, and the lack of measures to undertake the depth of ET which is needed in a rapidly restructuring world and national economy. The countries with successful ET systems devote substantial resources to research in that field while the UK policy, which has become highly centralised, is seen to be based upon limited information and research.

Further examination of some trends and consideration of later developments may be seen to answer some of these general criticisms, but clearly not all; and there have been some later developments which strengthen the points made by these critics.

The establishment of the TECs, and the accompanying devolution process in both education and training, has much reduced centralised control in Britain. Other countries which have 'successful ET systems' may not be so remarkably advanced in this respect as these authors believe. International comparisons of ET are particularly hard to make in precise and fully comparable terms. However, data on the rates of participation in ET can be given for the Group of Seven countries. These provide a broad view of *engagement* in ET, which is shown in Table 13.2.

These comparative data, which are quantitative only, give no grounds for complacency, particularly in respect of the 16–18 age group. But neither do they suggest that the UK is playing in an altogether different league, where neglect of vocational education and training is endemic.

Although qualitative measures of general and vocational education qualifications across countries run up against many problems of comparability, trends within a country can be measured more satisfactorily. In the UK there has been a large and sustained improvement in the number of qualifications obtained at degree level and in those below degree level. Between the academical years 1980/81 and 1990/91, the number of first degrees awarded increased by 31% and the number of higher vocational

Table 13.2 *Participation rates in education and training, 16 year olds, and the 16–18 age group, 1990, Group of Seven countries (%)*

Rank order of Group of Seven countries for participation by 16 year olds	16 year olds	16–18 age group
Canada	100	78
Germany	99	89
USA	96	82
Japan	94	79
UK	94	71
France	90	82
Italy (1983)	69	65

Source: Education Statistics for the United Kingdom 1993, Table BB.

qualifications by 79% (see Chapter 11, Table 11.7 where these vocational qualifications are specified). Further data on trends in the acquisition of vocational qualifications are available for the United Kingdom. These are for National Vocational Qualifications (NVQs) at Levels 2 and 3. These are given in Table 13.3.

Evidence on the comparative national participation rates in vocational education (Table 13.2), together with the upward trends of the five levels of qualifications shown in Tables 11.7 and 13.3 should be set alongside the more pessimistic assessments of the British education and training system and its performance which have been outlined.

However, these data on the NVQs conceal major problems concerning their quality and the control of their quality. Academic research conducted by the NIESR and by others (see Chapter 7) has produced results which are severely critical of the methods of academic and vocational teaching at schools under the TVEI, which is designed to be preparatory for the NVQs, and of that for the NVQs themselves. Furthermore, changes made from 1986 onwards in the methods of examining for the award of vocational qualifications within the NVQ system are also open to the doubts about their validity which were outlined in Chapter 7. Much criticism on these lines has been sustained, and corresponding reforms are clearly needed.

These problems of the poor quality of vocational teaching, together with the shortcomings of basic educational teaching in terms of literacy and numeracy (Chapter 11), are bound to be very influential upon the

Table 13.3 *Annual percentage of certain age groups qualified to Levels 2 and 3 of the National Vocational Qualification or equivalent, 1985, 1987, 1989, 1991 and 1992, UK*

	Level 2[a] or equivalent. Age 16–24	Level 3 or equivalent. Age 20–24
1985	42.5	25.9
1987	45.5	26.9
1989	48.1	28.2
1991	51.4	30.0
1992	55.1	33.5

Note: [a]NVQ at Level 2 is the required qualification for YT trainees (see Chapter 11, where a description is also given of the qualifications required at each NVQ level).
Source: Bilsborough and Ross 1993, p. 359.

subsequent training system under the YTS and its successor schemes, and upon the quality of the results from them.

Reliance of YTS on free-market forces

The *second* group of critics may be represented by Lee *et al.* (1990). They have produced an assessment of YTS based upon a survey of an urban area in South-East England. They state (Lee *et al.* 1990, p. 186) that the area surveyed contained chiefly service industries: those they specify include retail outlets, warehouses, building societies, hotels, and finance offices. There was little manufacturing in the area surveyed. The main conclusion reached is that the training offered by YTS was low level due to a *laissez-faire* policy, which entailed poor standards of training and poor supervision of the scheme generally. This seems to be a valid criticism of the one-year YTS, for which control of training standards was originally vested in the MSC. In 1986, when the two-year YTS was introduced, responsibility for the institution and maintenance of training standards was passed to approved Managing Agents, who became Approved Training Organisa- tions (ATOs) after MSC inspection and staff training at an Accredited Training Centre (ATC). In the country as a whole the service industries, particularly the distribution industry, took a large proportion of the total of those entering YTS in the period up to 1986 (see Chapter 9). The skill level required was low as was the training offered, and, as concluded by Lee *et al.*, a surfeit of these semi-skills was created. That was partly corrected by 1985/86, when a smaller proportion of YTS places was approved for Division 6 industries (Distribution, Hotels and Repairs, but chiefly Distribution), and that policy continued thereafter.

The criticism that a *laissez-faire* policy is to be blamed for the perceived failure to train under YTS seems to need further consideration. The YTS was, and as YT continues to be, a major government intervention in the youth labour market - that action is not voluntarism. However, the chief criticism by these authors is that employers should not be free to specify their demands for youth labour because their views are short term, and because training is too important to be left to them. It is true that the *quasi*-market in youth training services started on the supply side, which favoured the employer, but it has now moved to include the demand side by the introduction of Youth Credits. Therefore, such benefits of *laissez-faire* as appear in *quasi*-markets, which at first favoured employers, now favour the young people, who are equipped with the financial resources to 'purchase' training for high level skills. Thus there is a more even balance of labour market advantage. The very important need to maintain and improve training standards to match the national demand for youth labour remains a government responsibility. That is now carried out within a *quasi*-market structure.

The priority of policies

The *third* group of critics are concerned with apparent and real disparities between national manpower and training policies.

In general terms, it is the role of a manpower policy to ensure full use of a nation's labour resources by economic management methods. Training policy has as its aim the supply of vocational education and on-the-job training to enable best use to be made of the talents of young people, particularly school leavers, but also those of other employed and unemployed members of the labour force, so that they may be engaged in employment of a type which suits both their talents and the demands of the economy for the production of goods and services which meet the demands of consumers at home and abroad. These two policies should complement each other to attain the aims of both, and training policy should reinforce manpower policy. In practice that has not always happened. Exogenous economic shocks, such as the oil crisis of 1973, and endogenous malfunctioning of the economic system as well as errors of policy have led to the training policy operating under conditions of failure of manpower policy. The early years of the YTS, 1983–86, are an example of this. In 1984 the weak demand for youth labour led to some waste of the investment in training via YTS and other schemes.

Although later increases in demand relieved that situation, a reversal of priorities is seen by one of these critics to be needed (Ryan 1984). In his view training policy is secondary to manpower policy: 'in the longer term training policy would gain from being relieved of having to deal simultaneously with youth unemployment' (Ryan 1984, p. 44). However, in the absence of a successful manpower policy – and so far no country has been able consistently to find and apply such a policy – training should not be subject to a 'stop-go' policy which follows the business cycle. Training policy needs both short-term and long-term dimensions. In particular, consideration needs to be given to counter-cyclical bridging mechanisms for youth training schemes to provide support for youth employment in economic recessions and thereby support the long-term dimension of training policy.

Critics of the Manpower Services Commission (Ainley and Corney 1990) point to its failure to establish and apply a national manpower policy. It has been shown earlier (Chapter 5) that unemployment, and particularly youth unemployment in the 1970s, led the MSC into short-term crisis reactions, exemplified by the YOP. The switch in the early 1980s to a training policy for youth labour, and to a much more limited extent for adult labour, may be regarded as a reinforcement of manpower policy, because it aimed to enhance the employability of youth labour. But according to Ainley and Corney the MSC was a failure: it failed both on manpower policy and on training policy, which was over-concentrated on youth labour. It failed also to convert employers to the need to train and to finance training. Furthermore, it adopted an enterprise philosophy and what these authors call a 'work relevant practicalism' which is seen as inappropriate for Britain's needs. The MSC was abolished in 1988 and replaced by the Department of Employment's Training Agency (TA) and later by the Training, Education and Enterprise Directive (TEED). As explained in Chapter 12, the management of YT was largely decentralised in 1990 when control was vested in the TECs. Policy has shifted towards devolution with the accent upon local labour markets. At the same time, the management of training for youths and adults has been brought together at the local level, and more influence and control have been given both to trainees under YT and Youth Credits, and to local employers.

The direction and control of policy on training, particularly training for the higher skills to supply the occupational labour markets, was still centralised in 1988, and Marsden and Ryan (1988) took the view that the training for these skills was better organised by the Industrial Training

Boards in the late 1960s and early 1970s, since they were in a position more fully to appraise the occupational labour market. This is a valid point in principle, but the ITB framework was misconceived and failed in operation (Chapter 4). The Youth Credit system operated by the TECs may partly meet the need for training for the higher skills and the later Modern Apprenticeships (to be operating from September 1995 and financially supported by government through the medium of Youth Credits) will go further (Chapter 12), but basically the need for training for higher skills remains and the intervention policy does not yet fully meet it.

Structural and management problems of YT

The *fourth* group of critics (Bennett *et al.* 1994) have made a detailed study of the organisation of TECs and LECs, and of their central and local managements. They find that 'there are fundamental deficiencies in the structure of TECs, and to a lesser extent of the LECs, as a result of unclear mission, inadequate empowerment, conflicts in local leadership, gaps in personnel skill to deliver and ability of the Boards [of the TECs] to manage, cost inefficiency and budget uncertainties' (Bennett *et al.* 1994, pp. 8 and 9). The 'inadequate empowerment' criticism relates to the retention of central control by the Employment Department and its central agencies. It follows that, in the view of these critics, the intended devolution of power to the providers of training services, the TECs, remains incomplete. These criticisms and those which follow apply to the LECs as well as the TECs. There are further criticisms which relate to the size and geographical coverage of the TEC areas, and some which are concerned with 'significant gaps' in all the main fields of local TEC activity.

These criticisms are well supported by evidence and, rarely for critics of this area of government activity, the criticisms are constructive and advice on how the system should be developed in future is given. Basically, the failures are seen as organisational, and therefore open to amendment and reform. The devolution process should be advanced further to give more power to the TECs, and particularly to local employers. That advice is coupled to one which would effect a merger of the TECs with local Chambers of Commerce, with a view to making the TECs better able to act as providers of training services. It was originally intended that the TECs should do that, but these critics claim that the TECs have been acting as no more than purchasers and facilitators of such services, and that is seen as inadequate as a method of advancing the processes of youth training to the higher standards which are now, and will in future be even more urgently required by the British economy.

Summary

Qualitative improvements in training are in progress but it is clear that much more needs to be done, particularly with regard to raising the quality of the associated vocational education. Only one of the critics whose views have been considered (Jones 1988) attached any importance to the poor educational standards of YTS entrants. The scale of that problem, indicated in Chapter 11, needs to be borne in mind in the making of youth training policy and in assessing the value of the criticisms made of it.

14 Collaboration and opposition from trade unions

The recruitment of school leavers and other young people into training positions and jobs has for a long time been regarded by trade unions as a threat to the job security of adult workers. The young people produce output, but their remuneration is relatively low and the jobs of adult workers are therefore seen as being in danger. When governments intervene by subsidising the pay of the young workers, even when the conditions of the subsidy include off-the-job vocational studies as well as work experience and training on the job, the concern of the trade unions representing the adult workers is likely to be that much greater, and some of them may encourage active opposition to such interventions. It is therefore only prudent for government to seek the collaboration of the trade unions in their efforts to promote the training and employment of young people by special measures involving subsidies.

In this chapter the policies of government and the views and actions of trade unions are examined for the influence they have had upon the implementation of youth training schemes.

The means by which governments have sought the collaboration of the trade union movement, and of employers, in their interventionist youth labour market policies are outlined first. That is followed by treatments of (i) TUC policy towards government interventions in the youth labour market, 1977 to 1988; (ii) the reasons for the subsequent breakdown of the collaboration which the TUC and MSC had built up over this period; (iii) the reasons for the division between unions, in their views and actions towards YOP and YTS, into two groups, one of which collaborated, via the TUC, with the MSC and the government's policy, though seeking to change it, and the other which opposed that policy; and (iv) the extent of the opposition, in terms of individual unions voting for boycotts and strikes against YTS and acting on those decisions.

The evidence given here is from debates at the annual Trades Union Congresses (TUC), and from the annual conferences of individual unions which took a particularly strong stance for or against the government's policy. Some evidence is that of the views of union representatives at the TUC, and some the views of ordinary union members when the affairs of individual unions were considered at their annual conferences, or as set out in their journals. (The acronyms and abbreviations for the trade unions referred to in this chapter are given in the chapter appendix.)

Collaboration

Government policy on the establishment of relations between its own officials, employers, trade unionists and educationalists was to ensure that all three external interests were represented on the MSC and its associated bodies, and particularly on the Youth Training Board. By that action it aimed to ensure that a policy-debating and liaison forum was established, and that its interventions in the youth labour market were supported by educationalists and by both sides of industry.

Government intervention in the youth labour market started on a very small scale with the Recruitment Subsidy for School Leavers (RSSL) in 1975/76, the Youth Employment Subsidy (YES) in 1976/78, and continued on a larger scale with the Work Experience Programme (WEP) in 1976/78 (see Chapter 5). A much larger-scale intervention took place when the Youth Opportunities Programme (YOP) was introduced in 1978, and from that year the debates at the annual Trades Union Congress became increasingly concerned with the government's programme to support youth employment and training.

TUC policy

At the 1977 TUC, the MSC's proposals for YOP were endorsed (TUC 1977, p. 453). The TUC strategy adopted at that time was one of co-operation combined with pressure for various changes, but the shape of the strategy evolved over time: there was never a fixed set of objectives.

At first there were broadly two groups of unions with different reactions to the government's intervention. In the first group were the teaching unions, particularly the National Union of Teachers (NUT), who were positive in pressing for wider, educational reforms, and in particular for (i) mandatory educational allowances for young people continuing in full time schooling after age 16, (ii) improved education and further education opportunities, and (iii) mandatory day release for training both on and off the job for those already in full-time employment. The thinking behind these proposals was that YOP would draw young people away from school earlier than they would otherwise leave (TUC 1977, p. 453). A broad policy objective was then formed and a statement was submitted by the TUC to government in 1978 to the effect that all young people should either be in employment, training or education (TUC 1978, p.177). The craft unions in the private sector were also generally positive in their approach, as will be shown from their attitudes which are identified later in this chapter.

The second group of unions adopted a negative stance to government-sponsored schemes to provide youth employment and training. The first line of opposition was on the *substitution* of YOP trainees for union members in jobs – also named (in TUC debates) the *displacement* of existing adult employees by YOP trainees. The representative of the Civil and Public Services Association (CPSA) produced the following statement at the 1978 TUC:

> The ingredient that is worrying us is work experience. We feel that there is something of a conflict between work experience and, on the other hand, the staffing ceilings and public expenditure cuts that we have experienced in our sections of the civil service. In the areas covered by the CPSA the use of young people would mean – and this is quite blunt – that they would be doing work mainly associated with the clerical area covered by CPSA. (T. G. Ainsworth (CPSA), TUC 1978, p. 621)

The General Council strove to maintain a united union front by a change of strategy. That is, it acted not so much to secure detailed improvements, as it saw them, to YOP, but to move into a position based on collaboration with the MSC over YOP, without which the programme could not be implemented, in order to influence in wider terms the direction of the government's policy on education and training as a whole (TUC 1978, pp. 621–2).

In 1979, the General Council's policy changed back to its original form and it tried instead to work for improvements in the YOP through the active involvement of union members in the work place, by influencing the MSC through the TUC's three commissioners on that body, and by direct representations to government ministers.

The election of a Conservative Government in 1979, and the cutback of MSC funding which followed, led to heightened tension between the TUC and the government; the collaborative policy of the TUC was strained but unbroken. However, throughout the early 1980s there was increased tension at annual TUC meetings between representatives of those unions who would and those who would not collaborate in a positive way on the issue of youth training.

Some stronger dissenters from TUC policy appeared in several affiliated unions in 1981. The main reasons for their dissatisfaction with the YOP were variously stated to be as follows:

1 Job *substitution*, estimated (it was said by employers) to be as high as 30%.

2 Exploitation of trainees as 'a source of cheap labour'.
3 Inadequate, or complete lack of training.
4 Threat to union integrity in co-operating with a scheme with which the young people were dissatisfied.
5 Collusion with a scheme which allegedly did no more than disguise unemployment, and which had in the first place been created by the government: the YOP was no more than a palliative. (TUC 1981, pp. 440–2).

A public sector union, the Society of Civil and Public Servants (SCPS), proposed a motion, which was carried, calling for radical improvements in the YOP, and recommending the withdrawal of TUC co-operation if no acceptable improvements were forthcoming. Various other improvements were sought by other unions.

Another objector, the Transport and General Workers Union (TGWU), proposed that the TUC should seek (i) to secure the right of union veto on all applications to set up a YOP, (ii) to organise trainees into unions, (iii) to prevent YOPs in non-union work places (A. Kitson (TGWU), TUC 1981, p. 441).

Where it occurred, the shape of trade union opposition to government policy on youth labour market intervention was becoming clearer, and it was to some extent a successful opposition because the government was at that time anxious to retain the co-operation of the TUC. At the 1982 TUC, the General Council was able to report that the MSC had been persuaded to introduce (i) tighter controls on YOP in non-union work places, (ii) a procedure for investigating complaints, and (iii) a requirement for employers to secure approval from appropriate unions for applications in unionised work places.

The government incorporated these and other changes to YOP in 1982: the rate of allowance to young people was raised, the programme was extended to a full year (previously six months), and both work experience and off-the-job training were included. But this was no more than a prelude to the introduction of a completely re-designed scheme which placed much more emphasis upon training. The YTS was introduced in April 1983, and it replaced YOP in September 1983.

The General Council had endorsed the MSC's paper 'A New Training Initiative' (MSC 1981), which foreshadowed the YTS, but the government's White Paper 'A New Training Initiative: A Programme for Action, 1981', which set out the first draft terms of the YTS, was 'totally unacceptable' to the General Council (TUC 1982, p. 43). The main objections were twofold: (i) the new scheme would be for all unemployed school leavers, but as the right to Supplementary Benefit would be withdrawn the YTS would in effect be compulsory, and (ii) the allowance would be reduced from the YOP level of £25 to £15 per week.

The General Council worked, through its membership of the Youth Task Group (YTG) of the MSC, to improve the terms of the YTS. The YTG was charged with the task of producing guidelines for the MSC. As a result of these processes the MSC advised the government that the new YTS should include the following terms (TUC 1982, p. 43):

1 A guarantee of a place for every school leaver for one year.
2 A minimum of 13 weeks' vocational education off the job.
3 An allowance equal to the real value of the then current YOP allowance, or at a rate negotiated with employers to top up the allowance.
4 Tougher approval procedures for places, with a clearer role for trade unions.
5 The scheme should be voluntary, with young people retaining the right to Supplementary Benefit.

The government accepted these proposals from the MSC, but made it clear that it would not guarantee that entitlement to Supplementary Benefit would continue, or that the real value of the allowances would be maintained.

At the 1982 TUC the introduction of YTS was welcomed, as was the General Council's role in shaping the terms of the scheme.

It was thought by the General Council that YTS would support the first year of apprenticeships, and so help to reverse the decline in the number of apprentices. The view of the Amalgamated Union of Engineering Workers: Engineering Section (AUEW:ES) at this time was positive and supportive of TUC policy.

The TUC was playing a constructive role in trying to ensure that the very insidious attacks by employers cutting back on training are put to an end . . . we are saying to employers that now is the time, recession or no recession, to invest in training, to invest in young people. (G. H. Laird (AUEW:ES), TUC 1982, p. 486)

Not all affiliated unions welcomed the YTS. Some of them applied and maintained pressure for a substantial increase in the allowances to trainees, for union participation to negotiate on behalf of trainees, for holiday rights, for sick pay, and for the coverage of trainees by the statutory health and safety regulations.

Meanwhile the General Council worked to change YTS, as it had done in the case of YOP. YTS was built into the TUC's organisational structure, and the General Council asked affiliated unions to appoint a liaison person in their organisations who would be responsible for YTS matters. It also published a handbook on the YTS to guide trade unionists and to help them to ensure that YTS schemes were only accepted if the recommended standards and safeguards were in place (TUC 1983). This advice and the power of approval of YTS in any unionised work place, which was written into the scheme, provided the opposers of YTS with both an opportunity and the means to block schemes at the place of work.

The opposers continued to argue at the 1983 TUC for a break in the collaboration between the TUC and the MSC, which was seen as an agent of government policy. However, the General Council was able to continue its strategy of collaboration as an instrument for seeking change in the YTS. At the 1984 TUC it was able to report some progress: YTS trainees had gained the same grievance procedure rights and the same health and safety protection as employees, and MSC agreements with sponsors (employers) had been amended to include equal opportunity and anti-discrimination instructions (TUC 1984, p.148). Other changes the TUC had aimed for, notably an increase in the allowance to trainees from £25 to £34 per week, were not achieved.

The opposers now moved more forcefully against the General Council's policy of collaboration. The National Association of Teachers in Further and Higher Education (NATFHE) proposed:

Congress notes that the TUC has been unsuccessful in obtaining most of the improvements in YTS called for at the 1983 Congress, and that there have in fact been further developments of a retrograde nature . . . Congress resolves that unless immediate evidence of a willingness on the part of Government to meet these criticisms is forthcoming the General Council are instructed to consult all affiliated unions. (Seconded by the Amalgamated Union of Engineering Workers:Technical Administrative and Supervisory Section (AUEW:TASS)

This motion had an Amendment proposed by the National and Local Government Officers Association (NALGO) and seconded by the CPSA, which read: 'with a view to withdrawing support for the YTS by March 1985' (TUC 1984, p. 476).

The debate on this motion divided the 1984 Congress into those who tried to press the General Council to a stay-or-go decision on collaboration, and those who, while dissatisfied with YTS, took the view that the General Council should be reasonably free to continue to work for changes in the scheme which matched the views of Congress. The motion was carried but the amendment was lost.

The General Council then moved to try to influence the two-year YTS. It made it a condition of future TUC support for the scheme that the government accept an allowance to trainees of £35 per week in the second year of training. The government agreed. Some of the other Congress demands from the 1983 and 1984 meetings were met by the new form of YTS as it was when introduced in 1986 (TUC 1985, p. 68).

At the 1985 Congress NATFHE put forward a motion on education and training which condemned the two-year YTS (YTS2) as 'an underfunded extension of an already flawed programme'. In moving it, the NATFHE delegate, P. Dawson, said:

My union has been amongst those who have been critical of the scheme, but we have argued at the same time that the answer has been an improvement through the trade union movement . . . but it has got to be said that the experience of the last year has radically increased the criticism of the scheme, and the call from teachers and other trade unionists . . . for outright opposition are stronger and stronger. (TUC 1985, p. 508)

The NATFHE gave no detailed reasons for this motion. Clearly it was not a fear of *substitution*, which could not have applied in further and higher education. The motion on this occasion was carried, but an amendment to instruct the General Council to withdraw TUC endorsement for YTS was defeated, and no instruction was attached to the motion.

At the 1986 Congress NATFHE again proposed a motion, which was seconded by the TGWU, which condemned YTS and, while it supported the General Council's attempts to press for improvements, it (inconsistent-ly) required a campaign for the scheme's replacement and also for a change in the 'political and economic context' (that is, a change to a Labour government) (TUC 1986, p. 537). In the event, Congress did not withdraw support for the strategy of the General Council.

The breakdown of collaboration

In 1987 the government, acting through the MSC, used intervention to try to relieve adult unemployment by the introduction of the Job Training Scheme (JTS). It refused on this occasion to agree to TUC conditions for co-operation, and at the 1987 TUC a motion calling for active opposition to the JTS was carried (TUC 1987, p. 488). This was a significant break, and the General Council's positive policy of co-operation with the MSC and the government in order to try to improve the terms of the YTS and other government interventions in the labour market finally ended in 1988. The actions and reasons involved in this major change were as follows:

1 The government changed the benefit rules in the *Social Security Act 1988* to remove entitlement to Supplementary Benefit from 16–17 year olds. It was replaced with a 'bridging' allowance of £15 per week for up to eight weeks for those awaiting YTS places. The General Council unsuccess-fully opposed this change.

2 JTS was unsuccessful and was replaced by Employment Training (ET). The General Council tried to give ET conditional support but, under pressure from affiliated unions, withdrew support and took up a stance of non-co-operation.

3 The *Employment Act 1988* changed the name of the MSC to the Training Commission. In response to the TUC's decision to withdraw support from ET the Training Commission was abolished and its functions, including the management of ET, YTS and TVEI, were placed with the Training Agency (TA) which was within the Employment Department Group and therefore an organ of government. The TA included representatives of employers, and provision was made for trade union representation, but no invitation was issued to the TUC.

So the TUC's positive policy failed when the government refused to make the changes to the ET which the TUC wanted. The General Council and the government had kept this form of collaboration going for more than ten years. It was a workable compromise which yielded some changes in the government's intervention policy in the youth labour market, which may be judged to have been improvements.

Up until 1988 the General Council of the TUC had largely 'kept the lid on' the affiliated unions who really opposed both the YOP and the YTS, and who were uninterested in trying to reform the schemes by negotiation with the MSC. After 1988 the opposers were freer to pursue their policies.

Divisions between the unions

The views and policies of individual unions affiliated to the TUC are considered next. In broad terms, the unions in the private sector were constructive critics who supported the General Council's policy of trying to modify the government's interventions in support of youth training. However, some private sector unions consistently opposed YTS, although they were not prepared to withdraw their support of the TUC's position. They criticised various aspects of YTS and urged reasoned changes upon the General Council, who largely took up their points of criticism and proposals for change at meetings of the MSC and its associated groups. Some private sector unions also obtained, through negotiation with employers, the grant of 'employee status' to YTS trainees. That enabled them to recruit trainees to union membership and then to undertake negotiations on their behalf for various benefits, including 'top-up' pay. On the other hand, the affiliated unions in the public sector adopted a much more negative approach to the government's measures of support for youth training.

There were general reasons for the differences between the policies of the private and public sector unions. In the private sector, the higher grade technical skills needed in many industries, coupled with a greater degree of competitive pressure in their product markets, appear to have influenced most private sector unions to adopt a more positive attitude towards YTS in particular. They desired and worked for changes and improvements as they saw them, but generally YTS was accepted and integrated into their training and more general policies. In the public sector, on the other hand, the competitive pressures were largely absent. Jobs were not under threat for that reason, but there were actual job losses and fears of future ones due to concurrent government policy to reduce employment in the public sector. Labour market intervention in the form of YOP and, particularly, YTS was seen by many unions in this sector as a threat to their members' jobs owing to the *substitution* effect. However, these unions also represented some workers with high grade skills who were less threatened by YTS substitution.

In the private sector, the leading craft union by size of membership, the engineers in the AUEW:ES (Engineering Section), which had about one million members in 1985 (TUC 1986), viewed training for engineering skills as best accomplished by the four-year apprenticeship. Early in the government's intervention process they criticised YOP and YTS for inadequacy in the duration and quality of training, although G. H. Laird (TUC 1982, p. 486) did approve of YTS in principle as a way of getting employers to 'invest in training'. The Engineering Industry Training Board (EITB) was one the few ITBs to survive the 1981 cutback. It administered a module-based system of off-the-job engineering craft training. The MSC and EITB promoted the use of YTS to support apprenticeships, or as a substitute for them. For the AUEW the introduction of YTS was accompanied by pressure from its parent body, the Confederation of Shipbuilding and Engineering Unions (CSEU), to move to apprenticeships based on training to standards rather than the older system of training for a set period of time, usually four years. YTS and training to standards was seen by the AUEW as a threat to the existing apprenticeship system, leading to a dilution of craft skills and to alterations in the existing skill/wage relativities (Rainbird 1990, p. 29). From 1983 to 1986 the AUEW opposed training to standards, but thereafter it accepted that system. At factory level YTS2 was used to fund the first two years of engineering craft apprenticeships, but the traditional apprenticeships remained in operation alongside YTS and also continued on after the first two years of training supported by YTS. There was pressure by the AUEW membership, contrary to the views of the union's leadership, to oblige employers of ex-YTS trainees who moved to apprenticeships after one year on YTS to pay the trainees (at the start of their year of training) the extra wages they would have received had they been apprentices from the start (Rainbird 1990, p. 31). That pressure was kept up until 1988, when it was dropped without having much influenced the situation at factory level.

Another smaller, craft union, the Electrical, Electronic, Telecommunication and Plumbing Union (EETPU) recognised the importance of training, and in particular of apprenticeship training. The union was fully aware that the speed of technological change in its field was such that training and re-training were essential if the jobs of its members were to be retained and if employment and its membership were to be expanded. The union welcomed YTS, and it continued to collaborate with the Employment Training (ET) system even after the TUC had withdrawn its support in 1988. In earlier years it had been a militant union. In the 1980s its political ideology changed towards 'new realism' in industrial relations. The Training Committee, which the union established, negotiated with the Joint Industry Board the incorporation of YTS into apprenticeship training, so as to avoid any possibility that employers would try to use YTS as a substitute for apprenticeship training. The agreement involved the maintenance of apprenticeships in exchange for lower rates of youth pay. In the late 1980s it was the only union to make training central to its organisational structure (Rainbird 1990, p. 137). It did not become dissatisfied with government youth training policy until 1992, when the devolved TEC structure made it impossible to negotiate funding for the union's *national* agreement with the electrical contracting industry.

Another craft union, the Union of Construction and Allied Trades and Technicians (UCATT) had a representative on the Youth Training Board (YTB) of the MSC. This representative, speaking against a proposed amendment at the TUC 1984 which aimed to oblige the General Council to withdraw the support of the TUC for YTS, said:

If we pull out of the YTS, where there is a line up of TUC and other youth organisations on the one side and the CBI on the other, who will then represent the real interests of the young people? We are the anchor line. The youth organisations and the local authority representatives on the YTB look to the TUC to show the way to create better training arrangements for young people.

He went on later to argue that the view that YTS had been all bad was quite wrong:

In the construction industry, unions have welded the YTS on to our scheme of training through the Construction Industry Training Board and of the 20,000 places which are assessed each year, we have a 97% take-up . . . (L. Wood (UCATT), TUC 1984, pp. 480, 481).

These three craft unions in the private sector of the economy were the most supportive of the positive policy of the TUC.

The focus of the study now turns to those unions which were the chief opposers of the government's policy at the period of greatest opposition. The main opposition came from four unions in the public sector of the economy; one of these was the NATFHE, whose members were teachers in Colleges of Further and Higher Education.

The FE colleges had an essential dual teaching role to play in the YTS: remedial education in English and Mathematics, and off-the-job vocational education in technical subjects. In effect, the union recognised the national problem of large numbers of unemployed and untrained school leavers, but they opposed the government's policies to deal with them.

Some members of NATFHE held strong views on 'remedial' teaching of young people. It was felt that members' control of the curriculum was under threat, and that remedial teaching would bring ' a disruptive element' into FE colleges which would demotivate other students and divert staff from teaching to controlling students (NATFHE Journal October 1979, p. 16).

A motion highly critical of YTS was narrowly defeated at the NATFHE conference in 1983. The General Secretary reprimanded delegates for their outspoken opposition, asking them

to consider the implications of opposing TUC policy, of campaigning against the apprenticeships which some unions had negotiated through YTS, and of the reactions of the MSC and others who have accused teachers [at FE colleges] of inflexibility and remoteness from industry. The result would be more privatisation [of FE teaching] and loss of more members' jobs. (NATFHE Journal, June/July 1983, p. 20)

A policy of opposition without withdrawal of participation was the generally preferred option in view of members' fear of the possible privatisation of FE teaching, loss of jobs for that reason and also because demographic changes were beginning to reduce the intake of all young students to FE colleges. At the same time, the union called for more funding for the YTS training scheme and more off-the-job training. This seems to indicate that the union wanted the teaching jobs supported by government funds, but did not want the problems associated with teaching young people who were seen as 'difficult' in one sense or another, but who were essentially in need of remedial teaching if they were to gain from the vocational courses which were also provided by the FE colleges, and from the training provided by employers.

Official NATFHE policy at the Trades Union Congresses was one of opposition without withdrawal, but there is evidence of boycotts by some members, the Workers Education Association (WEA) in particular, who were affiliated to NATFHE.

I am surprised at the lack of support or comment in your pages on a long overdue rebellion of the concerned educators in the WEA against the educational Victorianism of the YTS . . . The WEA tutors are perfectly correct in refusing to co-operate in this immoral deception of our young people. (Letter to the Editor, Desmond Mason, *NATFHE Journal*, June/July 1983, p. 42)

Thus some NATFHE members, as distinct from the leadership, strongly opposed YTS. Other unions opposed YTS and in some instances prevented the entry of YTS trainees into training places at the place of work. The National Union of Public Employees (NUPE), whose membership in 1991 was 551,000, down from 664,000 in 1985 (TUC 1986 and 1992), represented a large number of workers in low skill occupations, and the threat of YTS substitution for these workers and of erosion of wage rates and conditions was seen to be particularly great. Up to 1988, the NUPE position was one of opposition in principle but co-operation in practice with schemes which met criteria agreed at the union's annual conference, and opposition in practice to schemes that did not. In practice this must have involved a large measure of opposition to YTS because these criteria were generally far beyond the terms of YTS. They required (NUPE 1981, p. 325; NUPE 1983, p. 212) that:

1 Work experience places should not be at the expense of permanent jobs.
2 Where there were cuts in permanent jobs there should also be cuts in work experience places.
3 Trainees must be guaranteed a job at the end of their training.
4 Trainees must have union rights and negotiated wages and conditions.

It would have been hard to alter either the YOP or the YTS at any work place to conform to all these conditions, although pressure from NUPE and also from some unions in the private sector did lead to the granting of 'employee status' to YTS trainees, which met the requirement under item 4 above.

The 1983 NUPE conference opposed both the New Training Initiative and the YTS, and condemned the TUC Handbook on YTS for praising the scheme and for encouraging members to promote YTS at their work places.

At the NUPE Conferences in 1983, 1984 and 1986, motions proposing outright opposition to YTS were put but rejected. In 1987 there was strong resistance by NUPE to a proposal for YTS to be incorporated into training programmes for NUPE members working in the National Health Service, and for new 'helper' grades of YTS trainees who would perform some tasks previously carried out by NUPE members. At the 1988 NUPE Conference consideration was given to a proposal to instal a 7000-YTS-places programme in the NHS. A resolution opposing that programme was carried and some very stringent conditions for participation in it were agreed, but effectively YTS was boycotted by NUPE at this time (*NUPE Journal* 1988, No. 6, p. 8).

The views of the Confederation of Health Service Employees (COHSE) were similar to those of NUPE in respect of the threat of substitution due to YOP and YTS. At the union's conference in 1981, delegates carried, without debate, a resolution that COHSE should call on the TUC to look closely at reports of the government's YOP being abused by employers who were using unemployed young people to fill jobs in place of other workers (*Health Services* 1981, July/August, p. 7).

An unsuccessful attempt was made at the 1984 COHSE Conference to call for TUC withdrawal from collaboration with the MSC over YTS, but a year later those making a similar proposal were successful and a motion rejecting YTS was carried. 'COHSE's total opposition to Youth Training Schemes was sealed' (*Health Services* 1985, July/August, p. 13). The National Executive Committee tried to get the motion remitted, but without success. At the 1986 Conference, a motion calling for a reversal of the 1985 decision was lost (*Health Services* 1986, p. 12). Another attempt at reversal was made at the 1987 Conference, but again was lost, and a motion reaffirming the union's boycott of YTS was carried, despite a plea for co-operation from the General Secretary:

If our present policy was successful, YTS would not be in hospitals to-day but they are there . . . We must not abdicate our responsibility to these youngsters. This is not a vote for every duff scheme but a vote for your right to negotiate locally about whether it is a good scheme. (The General Secretary of COHSE, quoted in *Health Services*, 1987, August, p. 8)

This is another example of the membership of public service unions being more oppositional to YTS than the union leadership.

Perhaps the most adversarial of the unions to YTS and the policy of cooperation pursued by the TUC was the CPSA. For the CPSA, the government's youth training intervention had been the object of long-standing opposition, beginning in 1977 when the early work experience programme WEP was in operation. Opposition was confirmed by CPSA Conferences in 1979, 1982, 1983, 1984, 1988 and 1989. The chief ground for the opposition was the fear of substitution. The civil service was a major employer of school leavers, and it was expected that youth work experience and training schemes on subsidised terms would have adverse effects upon the volume, terms and conditions of employment of union members (*Red Tape* 1979, July/August, p. 310). The divisions within the union wrought by the series of debates on YTS, and the not always corresponding actions by the union's National Executive Committee (NEC), were great. After the 1984 Conference, the General Secretary, Alistair Graham, wrote in a letter to members: 'we must ensure that this issue does not surface again. The argument is now well and truly over' (*Red Tape* 1984, July, pp. 2 and 9). Thereafter, YTS did not feature in conference debates for two years.

In 1987 the Department of Employment moved to place 120 YTS trainees in its own regional MSC offices without the prior agreement of the CPSA. In May the CPSA members went on strike at the Bolton Vocational and Educational Training Group of the MSC. This strike initiated a prolonged period of YTS-related strike action by the CPSA (*Red Tape* 1987, June (2), p. 3; August (1), p. 1). In October 1987, the union's NEC drew up plans for nationwide strike action against the Department of Employment's premises, and put them to a ballot of members. Support for them was gained and a one-day strike took place on 27 November. Strikes continued into 1988 up to July: one by members working at the MSC headquarters in Sheffield lasted from January to March 1988 (*Red Tape* 1988, March, p. 12). In July 1988, the national executive of the CPSA, which then included some new, less radical members, suspended all YTS-related action and tried to secure a negotiated settlement. It did reach 'a framework agreement on YTS in the Civil Service', and in 1989 this was put to a ballot of members. It was rejected, and at the 1989 Conference opposition to YTS was restated, but the impetus for strike action had been lost. In 1990, attention was turned to Employment Training (ET), which was also rejected and the national executive of the union was instructed to support any member who wished to oppose the introduction of ET (*Red Tape* 1990, July/August, p. 13).

The extent of union opposition

The main opposers of government intervention in terms of size were the three public sector unions whose attitudes and actions have been traced: NUPE, COHSE and CPSA, together with opposition of a different type from NATFHE, a considerably smaller union, although one with a key dual-role in the remedial and vocational education which was closely associated with the government's intervention to improve youth training and employment. Opposition from these unions occurred at various times over the period from 1978, when YOP was introduced, to 1993 when some opposition continued, but the peak was in 1987 and 1988. At that time the average total membership (at 31 December 1987 and 31 December 1988) of the three largest opposers was 1,002,000, and they represented 11.4% of the average membership of all unions affiliated to the TUC over the same period. The addition of NATFHE would raise this percentage only moderately, to 11.9%.

On a longer time perspective, 1983–88, Ryan (1991, p. 235) finds that 'those [TUC affiliated unions] espousing total boycott of YTS [at some time in the period 1983–88] accounted on their own for more than one fifth of the [TUC] membership'. Ryan (1993 p.13), working with a sample comprising the 42 largest unions, finds that over the period 1983–88 'the conferences . . . of 20% of unions with 18% of members [voted] at least once to endorse action against it [YTS], normally a boycott . . . and that one union in one year – CPSA in 1987/88 – decided to endorse strikes against it'. However, Ryan casts a wider net in terms of the number of unions, and deals with a longer time period than is done here, where the focus is upon the major opposers at the period of greatest opposition.

After 1988, the General Council of the TUC lost the use of the MSC as a vehicle of influence over the government's youth training arrangements, but it instituted new policies. It urged trade unionists to accept invitations to serve on the new National Training Task Force (NTTF) and on the Training and Enterprise Councils (TECs) (Chapter 12), but only on the basis that 'they [trade union representatives] would follow TUC guidelines on the performance of their duties and report back to the TUC on their actions and decisions made' (TUC 1989, p. 120).

The TUC also established new Regional Training Committees to match the government's new regional structure of the TECs. Members of the new committees were the trade union members of the TECs, and other union representatives concerned with training. By 1991, the elements of the new policies were in operation and the Education and Training Committee of the TUC was exercising an overview of the YT; it addressed concerns about gender imbalance in the take-up of YT places, and about the relatively low proportion of YT trainees gaining formal qualifications at the end of training (TUC 1991, p. 86). In 1992, the General Council reported that the TUC was represented by a trade union officer on 62 out of 82 TECs (TUC 1992, p. 57).

The government invited the collaboration of the trade unions in the new devolved mechanisms for implementing its youth training policies, and the General Council of the TUC adopted policies which ensured a measure of collaboration with the TECs while maintaining its influence over the form of the YT and Youth Credit interventions.

Appendix: List of acronyms used to refer to trade unions in this chapter

AUEW:ES   Amalgamated Union of Engineering Workers: Engineer-
              ing Section

AUEW:TASS   Amalgamated Union of Engineering Workers: Technical,
              Administrative and Supervisory Section

COHSE   Confederation of Health Service Employees

CPSA   Civil and Public Services Association

EETPU   Electrical, Electronic, Telecommunications and Plumbing
                Union

NALGO   National and Local Government Officers' Association

NATFHE   National Association of Teachers in Further and Higher
                Education

NUPE   National Union of Public Employees

NUT   National Union of Teachers

SCPS   Society of Civil and Public Servants

TGWU   Transport and General Workers' Union

UCATT   Union of Construction, Allied Trades and Technicians

Since the events which are the subject of this chapter took place, there have
been some amalgamations of trade unions. The chief of these are as follows:

COHSE, NALGO and NUPE have merged to form UNISON, AUEW:ES
and EETPU have become AEEU, and AUEW:TASS have joined with
ASTMS to form MSF.

15 Results and conclusions

In this final chapter, the main results of the historical studies and economic assessments of government intervention in the youth labour market which have been made in the book are summarised and drawn together. Conclusions are reached and key points of evidence supporting them are given, with reference made to other relevant material in earlier chapters.

The empirical assessments which have been made here of the role of government intervention have included reviews of policies and analyses of the impact of particular interventions aimed at promoting the vocational education and training of young people. The theoretical basis for such intervention, which is contained in human capital theory and in a branch of that theory – the economics of training – has also been examined. Conclusions from theory are given first.

Human capital theory and the economics of training

Human capital theory, and some empirical evidence relating to it, was examined (Chapter 1) and found to support the conclusion that economic growth and prosperity depend essentially upon investment to enhance the quality of the labour factor of production. The qualitative component of labour input, which arises from general education, vocational education and training, as well as from technical change and improved organisation which in turn are due to labour quality, has accounted for approximately 70% of the rate of growth of national output per unit of total factor input, on evidence from British and United States data.

Most investment in labour quality takes place early in the span of human life. Hence the importance of general and vocational education and of youth training, which have long-term consequences and which also in the shorter term greatly influence the operation of the youth labour market, which is responsive to both *qualitative* and *quantitative* factors. It is at this stage that major interventions by government occur and affect the youth labour market.

The economics of training deals also with vocational education, which includes the acquisition of the higher craft skills by off-the-job vocational studies as well as by on-the-job training. The economic theory of training is relatively new, and although not fully developed it makes a contribution to understanding the basic reasons for these processes. The chief theorist is G. S. Becker (1962, 1964, 1975). He regards the training process as investment and applies general investment theory, with modifications to allow for a tripartite role, the investors being the young people themselves, the employer, and the government. Special risks are involved. For the trainee it is the risk of loss of investment through subsequent unemployment, and/or possible erroneous choice of occupation. For the employer there is the two-stage training process: the basic training and the training for specialised skills. The risk of loss of the employer's investment in the first stage through youth labour being 'poached' by other firms is thought to be great, greater than in the second stage when the skills acquired are expected to be much more specific to the employer's business, although the problem of 'poaching' of recently trained young skilled workers occurs here too, and further increases the risk to the employer's investment.

The thesis of the economic theory of training is that when 'poaching' is prevalent after the first, basic stage of training has been completed, as it is when there is competition in that section of the youth labour market, the training employer tends, because of the large degree of risk involved, to transfer the costs of training to the trainee. Two market externalities are involved here: the first is that between training firms and non-training firms, which generates uncertainty on both sides about actions on training and on 'poaching'. The second externality concerns the trainee's access to financial credit in a free market situation, which is likely to be hard to obtain or unavailable. In both these cases the decision to train is likely to be affected in a negative direction. This situation tends to lead to a low volume of training, because of the deterrence engendered by the high risks to both the training employer and the trainee. The consequences are likely to be disequilibrium in the youth labour market, entailing a high rate of youth unemployment. That in turn entails private and social costs as well as losses of the short-term and longer-term private and social benefits from trained and employed young people. In the second stage of training, if and when it can be reached in these circumstances, the costs and benefits of training between employer and trainee are shared in proportions which are as yet undetermined by theory. A third market externality is involved here. It concerns the uncertainty regarding the future productivity of the second stage trainee in relation to expected wage rigidity. This uncertainty may lead to loss of mutually beneficial training contracts, and thereby a tendency towards disequilibrium in that segment of the youth labour market which is concerned with the higher levels of skill.

It may be concluded from these considerations of theory, summarised above, that intervention by government to invest in training by subsidising both the trainee and the training employer is necessary, under all but exceptional circumstances (such as the very high macroeconomic demand conditions in Britain in the post-war period up to the early 1970s), to get the training process started if all young people seeking work on leaving school are to have an opportunity to acquire training and employment. A no-policy alternative, involving a free market or 'voluntarist' regime, would entail youth unemployment and associated social costs which are too great to accept.

The results from the empirical studies which have been set out in earlier chapters divide into two broad categories: the *quantitative* and the *qualitative* aspects of the youth labour market in relation to the role of government intervention in it.

The quantity of youth labour supply, which is seen as a 'vehicle' for quality, moves erratically causing major problems for intervention policy. The findings on that aspect are given next.

Quantitative obstacles to equilibrium in the youth labour market

The goal of equilibrium in the youth labour market in Britain was particularly hard to obtain in the 1970s and early 1980s. Two of the main obstacles were demographic factors and economic activity rate changes.

The main demographic factor was the 'generational crowding' effect which arose, after a time lag of some 16 years, from a sharp increase in the number of births. In Britain the proportion of the youth cohort (aged 16–19) of the total labour force increased from 12.6% in 1971 to 14.8% in 1983. This was due to the 'boom' in births in the 1960s. The relative size of the cohort has since declined.

The economic activity rate factor is the 'age crowding' effect. That involved a large increase in the economic activity rate and employment of women (both full-time and part-time), which was partly in substitution for the employment of young people. In 1971 the proportion of women in the total civilian labour force was 35.3%, in 1983 it was 40.0% (Chapter 3).

It is concluded that these two effects contributed largely to the massive disequilibrium in the youth labour market which occurred in this period. There were 14,800 unemployed school leavers in 1971, 99,800 in 1977 and 120,100 in 1980. This disequilibrium challenged governments, and led to direct state intervention in the youth labour market.

Fluctuations in youth labour supply for demographic reasons are forecast to continue in the future to 2020, but after a decline from 1987 to the mid 1990s a recovery is forecast, and the 'late schooling and training cohort' (15–19 years) is expected to increase only moderately to the year 2020 in absolute number and in its share of the working population of Britain (Chapter 2).

That steady future trend may be contrasted with those for Britain's main European competitor countries where, particularly for Germany and Italy, but also for the EEC(12) as a whole, an absolute and relative decline in the size of this important youth cohort is expected over the same period.

These results from demographic studies are of particular relevance for the British economy because, unlike some main competitor countries, Britain is relatively more dependent upon labour resources, since national resource endowment is poor and the country trades internationally to a relatively large degree. The importance to future economic growth of a well-educated, highly trained and positively motivated supply of youth labour is emphasised by these findings (Chapter 2 and the Appendix on resource endowment).

Youth labour quality: historical perspectives

Investment by the private sector and by government to enhance the skills of young people by vocational education and training is not a recent development. It has been shown (Chapter 4) that the subject occupied governments, and many Royal Commissions in the nineteenth century. A free enterprise regime prevailed for most of the century, even in the field of general education. Vocational education and training were in the hands of employers for even longer, but the subject was regarded as increasingly important as the Industrial Revolution progressed.

In the second half of the century, competition in world markets was rising fast to challenge the first industrial nation. The work of the Royal Commission on Technical Instruction (the Samuelson Commission) was particularly extensive and thorough. The chief outcome was the *Technical Instruction Act 1889*, which empowered local authorities to levy rates to establish technical schools administered by school boards. Two of the Commission's recommendations are relevant to modern conditions: (i) to introduce some vocational subjects into schools, and (ii) to encourage the attachment of practical work done in the daytime to theoretical work done in evening classes. The first foreshadows the TVEI 1982, and the second the on- and off-the-job training arrangements of the YTS 1983.

Improvements to general and vocational education and training did not move forward together. In the 1890s and until the *Education Act 1902*, general education was insufficient to support the vocational education which was needed. The 1902 Act greatly advanced both secondary general education and vocational education. Trade Schools were established then and the two processes advanced more closely in step with each other. It may be doubted how far lessons can be learned from history, but the modern British system is out of step for the same general reason – that the school system is failing pupils, particularly those of below average ability, by not providing them with an adequate basis for vocational education and training (Chapters 4 and 11).

The two economic depressions of the inter-war period (1920–21 and 1930–32) were influential in maintaining and increasing government intervention in the youth labour market. The aims were those of manpower policy to promote the employment of young people who would otherwise have remained unemployed.

In the post-war period up to the early 1970s, macroeconomic demand was exceptionally buoyant and all labour resources were fully employed; some economists even maintained that there was over-full employment. Training was very largely performed by employers, and government intervention was limited to providing youth labour market information via a careers service.

The 'bulge' in births in the early post-war years led to a large increase in youth labour supply in the early 1960s. That was foreseen, and the Carr Committee reported in 1958 on training and other measures to deal with it, but no intervention to support youth employment was undertaken because demand for youth labour in the early 1960s rose to match the increased supply. However, skill shortages became acute at that time and with the aim of supplying the demand, the *Industrial Training Act 1964* established the Industrial Training Boards (ITBs). Employers were required by this Act to provide training for skills, which was financed by a levy/grant system. The employers paid the levy and received the grants; no significant public funds were involved in this system. It did not work well. Small firms had to pay the levy but were not able, chiefly for scale reasons, to make use of the grants. The larger firms did increase training, but the form of it often did not match the changing demands for skilled labour, and criticisms of 'short termism' were sustained. The ITBs in effect failed to provide the training which was needed, and policy was radically changed in the early 1970s when a new beginning in government intervention was made.

New policies of intervention

A new start was made with the *Employment Training Act 1973*, and the beginning of an interventionist policy-learning process can be detected at that point. The 1973 Act set up the Manpower Services Commission (MSC). The Commission had two executive arms: the Employment Service

Agency and the Training Service Agency, with a view to producing manpower and training policies respectively.

The long period of full employment in post-war Britain came to an end at this time. There was also a shift in the pattern of labour demand as technologies changed, but the main government interventions in the whole labour market in the 1970s were predominantly manpower policies. These were of three basic types:

1 *Job preservation* subsidy. This was the Temporary Employment Subsidy (TES) 1977–79. It was a counter-cyclical marginal wage subsidy for employees about to be made redundant. The aim was to preserve jobs in the longer term by keeping employees in employment over the period of depression in trade. It was on a large scale: a cumulative total of 500,000 workers were supported by it.
2 *Job sharing* subsidies. There were two, of which the chief one was the Temporary Short Time Working Compensation Scheme (TSTWCS) 1979. The aim was to reduce redundancies by offering subsidised short-time working as an alternative. Nearly a million workers shared jobs under this scheme.
3 *Job creation* subsidies. There were two: the Small Firms Employment Subsidy (SFES) 1977–80, and the Adult Employment Subsidy (AES) 1978–79. Both were on a much smaller scale than the job preservation and job sharing subsidies.

With the exception of the AES, which was halted promptly, there was a fair measure of success for these early schemes of intervention to support general employment during the economic recession of the mid to late 1970s. But the policies were piecemeal, and the policy- learning process appears to have been one of trial and error rather than of progressive modification and improvement in the light of experience, but it was 'learning by doing'.

Youth labour market policies

The same economic recession in the 1970s that had induced manpower policy interventions in the whole labour market also created the need for intervention in the youth labour market, but conditions in that market were made exceptionally unfavourable by the 'generation crowding' and the 'age crowding' effects which have been noted. The main increase in youth unemployment came quite suddenly – the total number of school leavers without jobs increased sixfold from 13,300 in 1974 to 81,600 in 1976 (Chapter 5).

The MSC acted, first in terms of manpower rather than training policy.

Two types of youth employment subsidy were introduced in the first phase. Results and conclusions from assessments of them are as follows:

1 *Recruitment subsidies.* There were two: (i) the Recruitment Subsidy for School Leavers (RSSL) 1975, which was of general non-marginal application to all school leavers; and (ii) the Youth Employment Subsidy (YES) 1976, which was more marginal in that it was available only to young people aged 16–20 who had been unemployed for six months or more. Both schemes were on a small scale: 29,000 for the RSSL by June 1976, and 38,497 for the YES during the period of the scheme. These subsidies were not successful. For the RSSL it was found that less than 20% of those supported would not have been recruited in the absence of the subsidy, and for the YES 75%, but additionally 12.5% were substituted for other workers.
2 *Work experience subsidies.* There were two: (i) the Work Experience Programme (WEP) 1976–78, which provided work experience for six months for unemployed school leavers. No training was involved. There were 47,500 participants in total; and (ii) the Youth Opportunities Programme (YOP), 1978–83. This was similar to the WEP, but on a much larger scale: a total of 1,834,700 participated in it . No training was involved in the scheme until near the end. In 1982 a training element was introduced but that accounted for only a small part of the total programme (15% of those on YOP in 1982/83). These two schemes achieved a partial success in that in both cases approximately 60% of those who participated throughout the period of support or for part of it obtained employment, or subsequently went on to courses which improved their employability, but because no training was involved the jobs obtained were at best semi-skilled ones, and so the talents and abilities of the young people were less than fully developed by these programmes.

It may be concluded that these early manpower policy interventions in the youth labour market achieved little success in terms of investment in youth labour quality.

The general economic situation deteriorated further from 1979 to 1984, when youth unemployment rose from 8.9% to 25.1%. The supply of school leavers was still rising at this time and demand in the youth labour market was falling. This escalation in adverse circumstances led to a re-assessment of government policy on intervention in the youth labour market.

A Conservative Government had been elected in 1979. It began to apply a *laissez-faire*, free market approach to much economic policy, but not in the youth labour market where it was thought right to continue the previous Labour Government's interventionist policies. However, there was soon a comprehensive re-appraisal. A White Paper entitled 'A New Training Initiative: A Programme for Action' (1981) provided the basis for the training and youth labour market policies for the 1980s, and they underlie much policy today. The new policies set in place a sequential linked programme for the vocational education and training of young people (Chapter 6). They entailed tripartite investment: by the trainees, the employers and the government, and they were a substantial advance upon the YOP, a work experience only scheme.

The new policies led to the Technical and Vocational Education Initiative (TVEI) in 1982. That was followed by the Young Workers Scheme (YWS) in the same year, and the Youth Training Scheme (YTS) in 1983. Under these three schemes the planned sequence began at school at age 14 with technical and vocational education for those whose abilities and talents lay in that field, rather than in the general academic stream of education, and continued with the YTS for those who could not obtain employment after leaving school at age 16. The YTS offered a year's (and later two years') training both on and off the job with continuing support from the YWS, and later the New Workers Scheme (NWS), for the employment of young people ex-YTS for one further year. The YWS and NWS also aimed to assist unemployed young people into jobs which were accompanied by some training, although that was not a condition of these two schemes.

Results and conclusions from reviews and appraisals of this sequence of interventions are given below.

Policy reviews and appraisals

The Technical and Vocational Education Initiative (TVEI) 1982

This vocational education scheme was organised within schools. It has been heavily criticised on both organisational and educational grounds (Chapter 7). Many organisational changes were involved in its implementation, the chief being the introduction of the National Curriculum in 1988, which disturbed the TVEI and reduced its effectiveness. The method of teaching technology in schools, one of the main elements in the TVEI, has been severely criticised as being unsuited to the needs of both employers and pupils. The methods and outcomes of TVEI have been compared very unfavourably with the teaching of technology to the same age-groups in some other European countries. The main criticism has been directed at the 'depracticalisation' of the subject, which has worked particularly to the disadvantage of pupils with practical aptitudes but of below average academic ability, but neither have the basic principles been taught effectively. Following from actions by HM Inspectorate of Schools and the

Department of Employment in 1992, some organisational improvements have been made in the TVEI. There have also been some achievements. Research by others has shown that, compared with non-TVEI students of equal ability, ex-TVEI pupils were better adapted to the world of work and were better prepared for their choice of occupation and for their training both on and off the job.

The occupational qualifications designed for those in employment or in YTS or other training positions with an employer were re-organised in 1986 into the NVQ system (explained in Chapter 7). The teaching for these qualifications, and the revised methods of examination for the awards, has been much criticised by academics and employers. It was generally agreed that organisational change was needed – previously there were some 300 awarding bodies – but changes to teaching methods which put the emphasis upon workplace practice and which are insufficiently supported by teaching in mathematics and knowledge of theory are judged from research carried out at the NIESR and elsewhere to produce results which are of poor quality, and well below the standards of qualifications awarded by continental European countries for comparable occupational skills.

In 1991 a new system of full-time vocational education for post-16 year olds was set up leading to General National Vocational Qualifications (GNVQs). It was designed as a follow on from TVEI, and more generally as a vocational education path with status comparable to 'A' Level courses. It has also met severe criticisms on the grounds of shallow content and lack of coherent teaching principles, and it has also been compared very unfavourably with some continental European systems designed to meet the same need.

It is concluded that comprehensive re-assessments and reforms are clearly needed in these two important areas of occupational qualification (NVQs), and of vocational qualifications taken after full-time courses (GNVQs).

Young Workers Scheme (YWS) 1982–86

This was a continuation of the earlier regime of manpower measures. It was based on the view, current at the time, that the wages of young workers had risen, under earlier full employment conditions, so high in relation to adult wages that increased youth unemployment resulted. The subsidy was paid to employers of previously unemployed young people aged 17, conditional upon the pay of the recruit being below a stipulated level. It was taken up by unemployed school leavers, and also by post-YTS trainees who had failed to find employment. An appraisal of the subsidy in 1986 found that 64% of participants would have been employed in the absence of support. The extent of this *deadweight* effect shows that the premises of the scheme were without a sound foundation. Nevertheless, when the YTS was extended to two years the YWS was succeeded by the *New Workers Scheme (NWS) 1986–88*, which aimed to serve a similar purpose.

Youth Training Scheme (YTS) 1983–90

This was the main and by far the largest government intervention in the youth labour market. It was in operation for seven years and was succeeded by Youth Training (YT), which is a modified version of the YTS, and that has continued in operation since then. YTS supported one year's training on and off the job 1983–86, and two years' training 1986–90. Nearly a quarter of all school leavers who did not continue in full-time further education were in training on YTS in each of the years 1988, 1989 and 1990 (YOP accounted for only about 13% of the comparable total in its peak year 1982). The methodology of assessment of the employment and other economic effects of a government subsidy to training and/or employment is given in Chapter 8. In brief, an assessment of a subsidy to training involves estimating both the actual effect of the subsidy and the no-policy, hypothetical alternative, and comparing the two sets of estimates to reach the *induced* training effect (the *net* new training places created by the subsidy), and the *employment* effect (the outcome of the scheme in terms of jobs obtained or of progression into further training). The no-policy alternative position is reached from estimates of the *deadweight* effect (the number of trainees who would have been recruited in the absence of the subsidy), and the *substitution* effect (the number of YTS trainees who have been substituted for adult employees). The conclusions reached in Chapter 9 from the application of these methods to the YTS, based on sample data for 1986, 1987 and 1989, may be summarised as follows:

1 The *induced training* effect of the subsidy fluctuated markedly with the economic cycle, being 66% in 1986, when the demand for labour was slack and youth unemployment high, to 20% in 1989 when labour demand was much stronger.
2 The actual *employment* effect of YTS (which includes progression to further training) was 77% of all ex-YTS trainees in 1986, and 85% in 1989. Under the no-policy alternative without YTS, the *employment* effect was that only 27% would have found employment in 1986, and 69% in 1989. Therefore the *net employment* effect due to YTS was 50% of all YTS trainees in 1986, but only 16% in 1989. So, although YTS was designed as a subsidy to training it acted more as a means of reducing youth unemployment in 1986, reverting in 1989 to a subsidy for youth training when labour demand was stronger.

3 The costs and benefits of YTS to employers have also been assessed, using the same methodology (namely comparing the actual costs and benefits with those under the hypothetical, no-policy alternative). The conclusions from that assessment are that the actual *net* cost in 1987 was £3.60 per trainee per week in the first year of YTS training and the *net* benefit £19.60 in the second year. In the no-policy situation employers would, by their own estimation, have recruited and trained a specified number of young people without subsidy (the *deadweight* estimate). On this more realistic basis the *net* benefit to employers is estimated to be £19.80 per trainee per week in the first year and £41.00 in the second year. The conclusion reached from this microeconomic analysis of costs and benefits is that employers gained a substantial *net* benefit from YTS, particularly in the second year of the subsidy.

4 A macroeconomic analysis of the implications of YTS (Chapter 10) confirms the finding from the microeconomic analysis, and shows that the business sector of the economy increased its *net* profits as a result of YTS by £50 million, and also that the *net* cost of YTS to the government sector was £49 million per £100 million of gross expenditure on the subsidy. This was basically due to the increased yield of some taxes and the reduction in certain state benefit payments. In terms of cost per trainee per week of training in the first year of YTS (when basic training was undertaken) the *net* cost to the government was £18.85, and to the trainees, who accepted a lower wage than they would have got had they been recruited in the absence of subsidy, it was £14.70. The *net* benefit to the employer was £19.20.

5 Further macroeconomic analyses reach the conclusion that YTS induced an increase in the growth of total output (GDP) of 0.7% per annum, due chiefly to the *employment* effect of the subsidy but due also in part to the gross government expenditure on it. Employment due to YTS increased by 0.9% per annum, and unemployment fell by 155,000.

In terms of its *net employment* effect it is concluded that YTS achieved a good measure of success, but it did not adjust at all well to the economic cycle. It has been shown that on a *net* basis the cost of investment in training in the first year, when basic training was given, fell on the government (taxpayer) and the trainee; the employer gained a *net* benefit. No prescription on the proper shares of these three parties in the investment in training process has been laid down by theoreticians, but a *gain* of this magnitude by employers would seem to be a design fault in the YTS. However, it should be noted that concurrently employers invested in the training of other young people (and adults) who were not supported by subsidy.

Skill attainments

It must be borne in mind when considering conclusions about the attainments of YTS in terms of skills and qualifications acquired that the educational qualifications of some YTS entrants were and continue to be very poor. In 1985/86 about 96,000 young people, 12% of all school leavers in Britain, failed to obtain any grades at school, and about 36,000 of these entered YTS (9% of total entrants at that time). The failures of school education in terms of basic literacy and numeracy greatly handicapped YTS trainers and vocational education teachers as well as the trainees themselves. Employers, local education authorities and colleges of further education had to organise classes in literacy and numeracy before training could be started. The vocational education of YTS trainees was also slow in getting started for administrative reasons, particularly between 1983 and 1985, when YTS was for one year only. The proportion of all YTS leavers (including those who left before completion) who gained a full qualification was only 21% in 1985/86. In 1989/90 this proportion rose to 43%. Since then there has been a disappointing decline, to 32% of all YT leavers in 1992/93, although it should be noted that the qualifications obtained before 1990 were of a lower quality than those obtained by YTS trainees since then.

Under both slack and tight youth labour market conditions surveys have shown that employers aimed to recruit via YTS to train for skilled jobs. Labour market analysis (Chapter 11) shows that at a time when market conditions were tight (1989), the supply of trained youth labour via YTS broadly matched demand for skilled labour in various trades (as shown by all vacancies), although that supply was deficient in some occupations which required a relatively high level of skill. The YTS had at that time been of two years' duration for about three years, but the training period was still too short to provide some of the higher skills which were then in demand.

An analysis of the likely future pattern of demand for skills to the year 2000 shows a shift towards managerial and technical skills of many types (Chapter 11). Demand for the lower skills in both factory and office environments is expected to decline. That outlook, coupled with the poor level of general educational attainment of many of those who enter government-supported training schemes, challenges the training system, which will also have to cope with an increase in numbers as demographic influences lead to a larger cohort of 16 year olds from the mid 1990s onwards.

According to the economic theory of training, youth labour is more mobile after basic training has been completed in the first year, and less mobile after a second year, say, in which skills more specific to the employer's business have been acquired. But for government-supported training of two or more years' duration the theory is less tenable, and the evidence from the employment outcomes of YTS does not support it (Chapter 13). The proportion of first-year YTS trainees gaining jobs in the external market did not differ greatly from the proportion remaining with the training employer and obtaining employment in the internal market (within the training employer's business). When the two-year YTS had been in operation for two years there occurred only a modest increase in the proportion who gained jobs in the internal market.

One of the aims of YTS/YT (given in Chapter 9) is to encourage more mobility and greater career opportunities for young workers who have been trained under schemes which have been sponsored and largely financed by government. Later developments, in the form of longer and improved training under the YT, Youth Credits and the Modern Apprenticeships (see below), aim to provide the higher skills which are clearly needed. Whether or not ex-YT trainees will then move in greater proportion into the external labour market remains an open question.

There have been criticisms of the quantity and quality of the educational and training (ET) qualifications of all young people in the UK compared with those in other countries. These are particularly hard to confirm or refute, owing to problems of comparability. In terms of rates of *participation* in post-school education (both academic and vocational) and training, the UK was ranked equal fourth with Japan in the Group of Seven countries in 1990, with a rate of 94% of all 16 year olds, behind Canada (100%), Germany (99%) and the USA (96%). That small differential does not, as some critics allege, put the UK in an altogether different league where neglect of post-school education and training is endemic.

In the more important qualitative terms, international comparisons are even more hazardous. Comparisons can more usefully be made over time within the UK. At the upper end of the scale of qualifications, the increase in the number achieving first or higher degrees in the UK rose by 41% between 1980/81 and 1990/91. For those gaining qualifications below degree level, but excluding those who obtained only the lower levels of National Vocational Qualifications (NVQs), the increase over the same period was 79% (Chapter 11). The lower two levels of NVQ qualifications are particularly associated with YTS trainees but are also obtained by ex-YTS trainees and others. Over the shorter period 1985–92, the proportion of all young persons in the age group 16–24 years who obtained NVQ Level 2 or equivalent increased from 42.5% in 1985 to 55.1% in 1992 (Chapter 13). But the views of the critics are supported by the poor standards which have more recently afflicted the NVQ system.

It may be concluded that the main youth training intervention, the YTS/YT system, has boosted the quantity of youth training, but has a poor recent record on qualifications, both in the proportion of all trainees gaining them and on the quality of those obtained, and the rate of youth unemployment post-YTS/YT has been and remains far too high. Measures have been taken to improve the quality of training output, but there are as yet few signs of improvement.

The devolution of government intervention

Central control over youth training intervention was devolved in 1990 from the government's Training Agency and Employment Department to 82 regional Training and Enterprise Councils (TECs), and to 22 Local Enterprise Companies (LECs) in Scotland. From a study of these changes (Chapter 12) it is concluded that a *quasi*-market structure has been established, with the government remaining the *financer* but ceasing to be the *provider* of youth training services.

At the same time (1990) the YTS was changed to Youth Training (YT) and Youth Credits were introduced, and from September 1995 a new intervention, Modern Apprenticeships, will extend government-sponsored training by two or three years beyond what was previously available. Youth Credits conferred greater freedom of choice upon the trainees, who were offered a Youth Credit (also available to non-YT trainees) to 'spend' upon the training they wished to undertake. The TECs provided new trainees with advice and guidance on choice of trade and training employer, and although that was an aid to choice, it also necessarily imposed some limitations which arose from the pattern and size of local employers' demand for yet-to-be trained youth labour.

The national movement towards the establishment of *quasi*-markets, which has been in process since 1988 in health services and in general education as well as in youth training services, is not yet complete. No definitive economic assessment of *quasi*-markets has yet been carried out, and their advantages and short-comings remain to be assessed. The essential change is from a centralised form of bureaucratic management, with the productive and allocative inefficiencies which are thereby entailed, to a devolved and localised market-oriented system. Gains in productive and allocative efficiency are expected, but have yet to be convincingly established. Furthermore, safeguards against the occurrence of the inequities which are bound to arise in a freer market system are not yet in place. A form of positively discriminatory voucher for training has been suggested for those who, owing to physical disabilities or educational disadvantage, are hard and relatively expensive to train, but that has not been implemented. Colleges of Further Education, which provide a large volume of vocational education services, are no longer controlled centrally, but their monopolistic powers remain, and that may limit the gains from increased efficiency which the *quasi*-market structure is expected to induce.

Opposition to government intervention

Some trade unions in the public sector actively opposed the YTS in the second half of the 1980s, and boycotts and even strikes were undertaken to oppose the implementation of the scheme (Chapter 14). That led to a diminution of the effectiveness of the subsidy, and to some skewing of the distribution of YTS trainees away from the public sector industries concerned. However, the policy of the General Council of the TUC until 1988 was to collaborate with government policy. TUC representatives sat on the MSC, and particularly on the Youth Task Group of the MSC, and they worked for improvements, as they saw them, to the YOP and YTS. There was a break in collaboration in 1988, when the TUC refused to collaborate over a new adult training scheme. The MSC was abolished then and the government proceeded to direct its interventions without participation from trade unions. With the arrival of devolution of control of the YT, and other interventions, the TUC was invited back, and it now has directors on most TECs. It has also formed regional training committees of union officials to match the government's devolved arrangements.

TUC/government collaboration has been resumed and it seems likely to continue to the benefit of youth training supported by government subsidy.

General conclusion on government intervention in the youth labour market

Until 1983 direct government intervention in the youth labour market had been mostly in reaction to various particular circumstances:

1 Major wars and the contingent, urgent demand for skilled and semi-skilled labour of various types.
2 Economic depressions, in the inter-war period, and later in the 1970s particularly, which induced interventions designed to relieve youth unemployment.
3 Demographic changes which massively increased the supply of youth labour in relation to the total work force, causing 'generational crowding'.
4 The consequences for youth employment of 'age crowding', which involved increased competition in most sections of the labour market due to the increased willingness of women to enter that market on a full-time or part-time basis.
5 An increase in youth wage rates relative to adult wage rates.

In the mid 1970s, the circumstances referred to at points 2, 3, 4 and perhaps also at 5 above combined to produce a marked failure of the youth labour market and very large scale youth unemployment. The reaction of government was first to intervene in terms of manpower policy. The first interventions were small scale, even experimental, *recruitment* subsidies. They were ineffective and were followed by much larger scale *work experience* interventions, which were short term both in duration of subsidy and in effect. These reduced youth unemployment, but they involved little or no training (until a later stage when it was added to work experience), so full-scale investment in human capital, and the longer-term employment which might have been achieved from it, was not secured by these measures. The policy-learning process as regards intervention in the youth labour market began here and it advanced by a large stride in 1983, when *training* rather than *manpower* policy was implemented with the YTS. That had been preceded by extended policy studies, and was more a government initiative than a reaction to circumstances.

One of the forms which the learning process in policy intervention has taken is a reduction in the ineffectiveness of subsidies, and the consequent loss of public money, which arose in part from paying employers to do what they would have done in the absence of subsidy (the *deadweight* effect). This improvement was to some extent achieved by switching from recruitment subsidies to work experience and then to training schemes, and by greater supervision of training both on and off the job. The policy-learning process also involved reducing the scale of *substitution* of subsidised young workers for existing adult workers. That was achieved by switching subsidies to support supervised training on the job and for specified periods off the job, thus reducing the work output of trainees, and thereby their usefulness as substitutes for adult workers. But there were and continue to be limitations in this remedy in cases where the training content is small because the employment aimed at involves little skill.

The switch to interventions to support training may be seen to be advantageous in these ways, and it also has important advantages as a longer-term policy which should aid the manpower policy aim of fuller youth employment in the future. However, a shorter-term manpower policy is seen to be needed to complement long-term training policy. This is so because the YTS and YT schemes have not adjusted at all well to the economic cycle. It has been shown that *deadweight* is relatively low in economic recessions and high at times of strong demand and fuller employment. That implies that in recessions employers are responding to the inducement to train which is offered by YTS, although there are fewer jobs available at the end of the training process. This suggests that a short-term manpower policy to complement the long-term training policy is needed to avoid the economic losses and frustrations which follow when trained young people enter unemployment as soon as their training has been completed (Chapters 9 and 13).

The policy-learning process has also advanced with the greater flexibility which was added when the YTS was converted to YT in 1990. That aimed to tailor the period of government-supported training to match the training period needed for the skills which are currently in demand. This may be seen as an advance on the standard two-year YTS which could be either too short or too long for the skills required in some occupations. Further progress in this direction and in the policy-learning process is shown by the planned government support, via Youth Credits for the Modern Apprenticeships which start in September 1995.

The policy-learning process which has been detected has been far from a smooth and continuous one of development planned in the light of research and experience. It began as abrupt responses to sudden, large increases in youth unemployment. From 1983 it was much more thoroughly thought out and planned, but not all the changes which were made in the late 1980s have advanced the vocational education and training process.

Further development of the government's interventionist policy may be seen to be needed, and the results from this study suggest that they should be on the following lines:

1 Changes to make the policy more adaptable to movements in the economic cycle. This involves a better integration than exists at present between training and manpower policies in the youth labour market. A 'bridging mode' of intervention to support jobs for newly qualified young people in a recession is needed if the government-supported training processes are to operate with the degree of confidence needed for long-term stability.

2 Large demographic changes and sharp movements in the rate of economic activity have led in the past to labour market conditions which are much to the disadvantage of young people seeking training and enployment. That has induced short termism in interventionist policy. These changes and movements can be foreseen and future policy should be sufficiently adaptable to deal with the resulting 'generational' and 'age crowding' effects, and their opposites, without disturbing long-term policy.

3 Some progress has been made in the process of integrating the general education and the vocational education and training systems and in extending the reach of interventionist policies from middle school age through to qualifications at technician levels. But past policies have suffered from taking too short a view, and only recently, with the advent of Modern Apprenticeships, have the later phases of the whole educa-

tional and training process been adequately supported by government. The longer-reach policy now in place needs consolidation.

4 Further research is needed to establish the appropriate cost/benefit position of employers who participate in the training process now that government support has been extended via Youth Credits and Modern Apprenticeships, and in the light of the large proportion of all of ex-trainees who have been moving into the occupational (external) labour market (OLM) (Chapter 13). That is in line with one of the main aims of the YTS/YT ('to provide experience and skills which are transferable between employments'), but the extension forward of the interventionist policy to support training for higher skills may alter that aspect of youth labour market behaviour.

There remains the even more vital need to improve both the rate of attainment and the levels of qualification achieved by young people. It is clear from this study that much more needs to be done to achieve a higher quality of vocational education and training as a means to these much desired ends.

The *form* of the vocational education and training process has been established and integrated in the sequence TVEI, Compacts, YT, Youth Credits and Modern Apprenticeships - with courses aimed at the attainment of GNVQs for those continuing after age 16 in full-time vocational education, and the NVQ system for those moving from school directly into occupational training positions. But the *content* of courses, the quality of teaching and training and of assessment have been shown to be far too low, with consequently low rates of attainment of qualifications which are themselves of too low a standard.

One pervasive cause of the failure to achieve good yields from the process of government-financed investment in vocational education and training has been and is currently the poor educational quality of many school leavers, who in far too many cases suffer from illiteracy and innumeracy. That has much handicapped the vocational teaching and training processes. Major reforms are needed in general school education, particularly in basic literacy and numeracy but not only in that area. Improvements are also needed in the teaching of mathematics and technology and of vocational subjects at schools and at Colleges of Further Education.

On the evidence presented in earlier chapters, very large tasks are involved in achieving the necessary improvements, but if they can be done successfully, the freer, devolved *quasi*-market context for post-school vocational education and training services seems capable, if efficiently organised, of providing a favourable climate in which the quality and scope of these services could be further improved to the benefit of youth employment, the realisation of the potential talents of all young people, and the better performance of the whole economy through the increased productivity which would arise from successful investment in vocational education and training.

Appendix: Resource endowment

The purpose of this appendix is to provide a view of the relative importance of labour, and hence youth labour, as a contributor to economic growth and wealth in relation to other resource endowments. To obtain such a view a number of international comparisons are made.

A further aspect concerning the relative importance of labour is the extent to which a country engages in export trade. In the highly competitive climate of international markets the relative importance of skilled labour in particular is likely to be great. That dimension is also measured in relative terms by a comparative economic analysis.

In the comparative analyses which follow the countries involved are the Group of Seven: the United States, Canada, Japan, West Germany (statistics for the whole of Germany are given where they are available), the United Kingdom, France and Italy. Comparisons are made between each of these countries, and between them and the average for the Group of Seven and that for the twelve countries of the European Economic Community (now the European Union).

In addition to the factor labour, the factor land and the other natural resources of a country, particularly energy resources, are important sources of economic wealth and are essential means of enhancing economic growth and welfare. Capital in the form of fixed assets is also of great significance in this process, but it is man-made and therefore its contribution is originally due to labour.

Land

In the United Kingdom, the factor land, which should be seen in relation to climate, land types and location, is a natural resource which is in short supply in relation to population size. On an international comparison of population 'density', measured by inhabitants per square kilometre of agricultural land in use in 1990 (Table A.1), the UK ranks fourth out of the

Table A.1 *Agricultural land in use: area and population densities, 1990, Group of Seven countries and the EEC(12) as a whole*

Rank order of countries by 'density'	Land area in agricultural use (square kilometres)	Population at 1 January 1990 (000s)	'Density' (inhabitants per square kilometre of agricultural land)
Japan	52,430 (1990)	123,537[a]	2342
West Germany	118,680 (1990)	62,679	528
(Germany)	(169,100) (1991)	(79,753)	(472)
Italy	173,400 (1988)	57,576	322
UK	**184,470 (1990)**	**57,323**	**311**
France	305,810 (1990)	56,577	185
USA	4,312,890 (1990)	249,975[a]	59
Canada	740,500 (1990)	26,522[a]	36
Group of Seven	5,888,180 (1990)[b]	634,189	108
EEC (12)	1,280,750 (1988)	343,300	268

Notes:
[a]Average 1990 population.
[b]Includes Italy (1988), excludes Germany (1991).
Source: Basic Statistics of the Community 1992 and 1993, Tables 3.1 and 5.1.

Group of Seven countries, behind Japan, West Germany (and Germany) and Italy. In relation to the average of the twelve members of the EEC (in 1988) the UK's 'density' on this measure is 16% higher.

So the United Kingdom is not well-endowed with land as a factor of agricultural production, when that endowment is related to population and, in the same terms, to other countries of major economic importance, although it should be noted that the undoubted economic success of Japan has not been hampered by lack of endowment in agricultural land.

The same point is shown by the relative degrees of self-sufficiency in agricultural produce (Table A.2) for major European countries and for the EEC as a whole. The United Kingdom is self-sufficient only in grain, and is well below the degree of self-sufficiency of the EEC (12) as a whole in all the product groups considered here. In comparison with the other major European countries, for which data are given in Table A.2, the UK is equal to Germany (1990 only) and is more self-sufficient than West Germany and Italy in respect of total grain, and than Italy in respect of total meat. But in all other comparisons which can be made from these data the UK is less self-sufficient than any of these countries.

Table A.2 *Degrees of self-sufficiency in main types of staple agricultural produce. Averages of data for the years, 1988, 1989 and 1990,[a] major European countries and the EEC(12) as a whole (% home production of home consumption)*

	Total grain[b]	Total meat	Butter	Sugar[c]	Total oils and fats
UK	**114**	**82**	**61**	**55**	**35***
West Germany	104	89	82	137	57
(Germany 1990)	(114)	(89)	(96)	(151)	(65)
France	221*	100	108	221*	82*[d]
Italy	79	73	67	97	55
EEC (12)[e]	120*	102	109*	130*	73*[d]

Notes:
[a]Averages are made to reduce the influence of crop variations due to seasonal factors.
[b]Average of crop years 1988/89, 1989/90 and 1990/91.
[c]Includes overseas departments.
[d]1988 and 1989 only, 1990 not available.
[e]The EEC (12) averages include West German figures for 1988 and 1989 and German figures for 1990, subject to Note (d).
*Estimates made by Eurostat.
Source: Basic Statistics of the Community 1991, 1992 and 1993, Table 5.14.

Energy

For modern economic production techniques and for modern standards of living for the population of developed economies, the natural resource endowment in terms of basic fuels for the production of all forms of energy is clearly important. In absolute and comparative terms the UK is at present relatively well placed in respect of energy resource endowment. This is shown by the analysis set out in Table A.3, where account is taken of size of population. In rank order of self-sufficiency in total primary energy per head of population, the UK is in second place, after Canada, in the Group of Seven, and was well above the Group of Seven average and the EEC (12) average in 1990.

In 1989 the UK had, for the first time since 1980, a deficit of energy production in relation to domestic consumption. The deficit was small, being 0.09 of a metric tonne of oil equivalent per inhabitant per annum. This increased to 0.14 in 1990. This is still a favourable position in relative terms, but it is transitory. It is to quite a large extent based on North Sea oil which began significant production in 1975 and reached a peak in 1986. It is not

Table A.3 Energy balance: primary energy production and inland energy consumption in total and per head of population, 1990, Group of Seven countries and the EEC(12) as a whole

(1) Countries of the Group of 7 in rank order of self-sufficiency (col. 7)	(2) Total primary energy production,[a] million tons of oil equivalent (TOE)	(3) Total population, millions (at 1 Jan. 1990)	(4) Total inland energy consumption,[b] million TOE	(5) Primary energy production per head of population, TOE	(6) Inland energy consumption per head of population, TOE	(7) Per capita production minus per capita consumption, TOE
Canada	274.7	26.5[c]	210.3	10.37	7.94	+2.43
UK	**203.2**	**57.3**	**211.6**	**3.55**	**3.69**	**−0.14**
USA	1630.8	250.0[c]	1905.8	6.52	7.62	−1.10
France	97.3	56.6	212.6	1.72	3.76	−2.04
Italy	23.9	57.6	151.2	0.41	2.63	−2.22
West Germany	125.9	62.7[d]	272.8	2.01	4.35	−2.34
(Germany 1991)	(161.6)	(79.8)	(341.2)	(2.03)	(4.28)	(−2.25)
Japan	69.0	123.5[c]	428.2	0.56	3.47	−2.91
Group of 7	2424.8	634.2	3392.5	3.82	5.35	−1.53
EEC (12)	572.9	343.3	1115.3	1.67	3.25	−1.58

Notes:
[a]Coal, lignite, crude oil, natural gas, nuclear energy, and primary electricity. All converted into tonnes of oil equivalent (TOE).
[b]Production of primary energy *plus* net trade and changes in stocks of primary and derived energy sources.
[c]Average 1990 population.
[d]1989.

Source: *Basic Statistics of the Community* 1992 and 1993, Tables 3.1, 4.15 and 4.19.

intended to attempt here a forecast of North Sea oil production, but it is widely agreed that production and reserves of both oil and natural gas in this area will decline in future. This currently favourable resource endowment is not expected to endure on a large scale for many years into the next century.

Other natural resources

The UK has virtually no other natural resources. Of the main competitor countries, the USA and Canada are relatively well-endowed with mineral resources in addition to energy resources. The other main competitor countries in the Group of Seven and the EEC (12) are in much the same position as the UK, with the exception of West Germany, which has significant resources of potash.

Engagement in export trade

The United Kingdom trades widely and in substantial volume in international markets for both goods and services. That fact reflects, among other factors, historical trading links with other countries, the lack of self-sufficiency in agricultural and other natural products, and the country's comparative cost advantages. The country's economic prosperity depends in large measure upon the maintenance and further development of its export trade; and competitive factors, including particularly the efficient employment of skilled labour, are essential for the attainment of that objective.

In relative terms the UK's exports as a percentage of its total final expenditure (defined in note (a) to Table A.4) was 19.4% in 1990. That figure ranked the UK third among the Group of Seven countries. The UK's percentage is 9.3 percentage points above the corresponding figure for Japan, and 5.7 percentage points higher than the average for the Group of Seven countries.

This broad survey of relative factor endowments in land and in energy resources across the Group of Seven countries individually and as a group, and the EEC (12) as a group, shows that the UK is relatively poorly endowed in agricultural land. It is at present relatively well endowed with energy resources, but that advantageous position is likely to be short term.

As an international trader and world exporter the UK is relatively large. It also has a relatively high standard of living to maintain and improve. So for future economic growth and national prosperity it must depend largely, in the absence of other resource endowments, upon the factor labour. That dependence is even greater for Japan and West Germany, whose peoples

Table A.4 *Exports of goods and services, valued at current prices and current purchasing power parities, related to total final expenditure (TFE), 1990, Group of Seven countries ($USbn)*

(1) Rank order of countries of Group of Seven by exports as % of TFE (col. 4)	(2) Value of exports of of goods and services	(3) Total final expenditure (TFE)[a]	(4) Value of exports as % share of total final expenditure
West Germany	369.9	1,462.5	25.3
Canada	129.2	636.7	20.3
UK	**221.7**	**1,145.7**	**19.4**
France	222.5	1,206.4	18.4
Italy	194.0	1,117.4	17.4
Japan	242.5	2,406.1	10.1
USA	528.4	6,000.5	8.8
Group of Seven	1,908.2	13,975.3	13.7

Note: [a]This comprises government final consumption expenditure, private final consumption expenditure, gross fixed capital formation, increase in value of physical stocks and work-in-progress, exports of goods and services.
Source: Historical Statistics 1960–90 1992, Part I, Table C.

have shown, particularly over the past two decades, that a relative lack of natural resource endowment has not hampered their economic growth at home nor their substantial progress in selling in world markets. So it can be done by labour alone, and that must imply that skilled labour is all-important in the creation of economic wealth and in economic growth.

Bibliography

A New Training Initiative: A Programme for Action, 1981. Government White Paper, Cmnd. 8455, London: HMSO

Adult Literacy and Basic Skills Unit (ALBSU), 1992. *A Survey of Literacy and Numeracy Students*, London: ALBSU

Ainley, P. and Corney, M., 1990. *Training for the Future: the Rise and Fall of the Manpower Services Commission*, London: Cassell

Annual Abstract of Statistics, various dates. London: HMSO

Argles, M., 1964. *South Kensington to Robbins*, London: Longman, Green

Aukrust, O., 1959. 'Investment and economic growth', *Productivity Measurement Review* 16, 35–53

Barker, T. S., Borooah, V., van der Ploeg, F. and Winters, A., 1980. 'The Cambridge Multisectoral Dynamic Model: An instrument for national economic policy analysis', *Journal of Policy Modelling* 2(3), 319–44

Basic Statistics of the Community, 1991. 28th Edition, Luxembourg: Eurostat

1992. 29th Edition, Luxembourg: Eurostat

1993. 30th Edition, Luxembourg: Eurostat

Becker, G. S., 1962. 'Investment in human capital: a theoretical analysis', *Journal of Political Economy* 70, Supplement, 9–49

1964. *Human Capital: A Theoretical and Empirical Analysis, with Special Reference to Education*, First Edition, New York: National Bureau of Economic Research

1975. *Human Capital: A Theoretical and Empirical Analysis, with Special Reference to Education*, Second Edition, New York: National Bureau of Economic Research

Bedeman, T. and Courtney, G., 1982. 'Taking the opportunity', *Employment Gazette* October, 440–3

Begg, I. G., Blake, A. P. and Deakin, B. M., 1990. 'YTS and the Labour Market: Part I', mimeo (in collaboration with Pratten, C. F.), Department of Applied Economics, University of Cambridge

1991. 'YTS and the labour market', *British Journal of Industrial Relations* 29(2), 223–36

Begg, I. G., Deakin, B. M. and Pratten, C. F., 1988. 'A Survey of the Net Costs of

Training to Employers Participating in YTS', mimeo, Department of Applied Economics, University of Cambridge

Bennett, R. J., Wicks, P. and McCoshan, A., 1994. *Local Empowerment and Business Services: Britain's Experiment with TECs*, London: University College of London Press

Bierhoff, H. and Prais, S. J., 1993. 'Britain's Industrial Skills and the School Teaching of Practical Subjects', NIESR Discussion Paper No. 33, March

Bilsborough, M. and Ross, N., 1993. *Employment Gazette* August, 357–60

Bridges, J., 1991. 'Youth Training – now we are one', *Employment Gazette* July, 397–400

CBI, 1989. *Quarterly Industrial Trends Survey*, London: CBI Publications, Centre Point

1992. *Education–Business Partnerships: The Learning So Far*, London: CBI Publications, Centre Point

Chapman, P. G., 1993. *The Economics of Training*, LSE Handbooks in Economics Series, London: Harvester Wheatsheaf

Chapman, P. G. and Tooze, M. J., 1987. *The Youth Training Scheme in the United Kingdom*, Aldershot: Avebury Press

Clark, C., 1961. *Growthmanship*, Hobart Paper No. 10, London: Institute of Economic Affairs

Davison, R. C., 1938. *British Employment Policy Since 1930*, London: Longman, Green

Deakin, B. M., 1962. 'Forecasting the gross domestic product of the United Kingdom', in Geary, R. C. (ed.), *Europe's Future in Figures*, Amsterdam: North Holland

1990. 'Survey of the Wiltshire Labour Market', mimeo, Department of Applied Economics, University of Cambridge

Deakin, B. M. and Pratten, C. F., 1982. *Effects of the Temporary Employment Subsidy*, Cambridge: Cambridge University Press

1987a. 'Economic effects of YTS', *Employment Gazette* October, 491–7

1987b. 'Final Report of a Survey of the Wider Economic Effects of YTS and YWS', mimeo (in collaboration with Dunne, J. P.), Department of Applied Economics, University of Cambridge

Deane, P. M., 1967. *British Economic Growth, 1688–1959*, Second Edition, Cambridge: Cambridge University Press

Demographic Statistics 1990, 1990. Luxembourg: Eurostat

Denison, E. F., 1967. *Why Growth Rates Differ*, Washington DC: Brookings Institution

1974. *Accounting for United States Economic Growth, 1929–69*, Washington DC: Brookings Institution

1985. *Trends in American Economic Growth*, Washington DC: Brookings Institution

Department of Education Statistical Bulletin, 1993. Issue No. 16/93

Department of Employment Gazette, various dates.

Dilution of Labour Bulletin, 1918. Ministry of Munitions, March

Dornbusch, R. and Fischer, S., 1990. *Macroeconomics*, Fifth Edition, New York and London: McGraw Hill

Education and Training for the 21st Century, 1991. Government White Paper Cmnd. 1536, London: HMSO

Education Statistics for the United Kingdom, various dates. Government Statistical Service, London: HMSO

Elias, P., 1991. 'Methodological, statistical and practical issues arising from the collection and analysis of work history information by survey techniques', *Bulletin de Methodologie Sociologique* 31, 3–31

Employment Department, 1992. Data reference SSD E4/E5

Employment Gazette, various dates.

Engel, E., 1883. *Der Werth des Menschen*, Berlin: Leonhard Simion

Feinstein, C. H., 1972. *Statistical Tables of National Income, Expenditure and Output, 1855–1965*, Cambridge: Cambridge University Press

Finegold, D. and Soskice, D., 1988. 'The failure of training in Britain: analysis and prescription', *Oxford Review of Economic Policy* 4(3), 21–53

Fisher, I., 1906. *The Nature of Capital and Income*, New York: Macmillan

Fourth Report from the Committee of Public Accounts, 1983/84. House of Commons 104, London: HMSO

Freeman, R. B. and Bloom, D., 1985. 'The Youth Problem: Age or Generation Crowding', mimeo, paper prepared for the OECD, University of Harvard

Freeman, R. B. and Wise, D. A., 1982. *The Youth Labour Market Problem: Its Nature, Causes, and Consequences*, Chicago: University of Chicago Press

Garonna, P. and Ryan, P., 1991. 'The problems facing youth', and 'The regulation and deregulation of youth economic activity', Chapters 1 and 2 in Ryan, Garonna and Edwards (eds) 1991

Geddes Report, 1922. 'Interim Report of Committee on National Expenditure', in *Reports from Commissioners, Inspectors and Others*, Volume 3, National Expenditure; National Insurance, Session 7; February 1922–4 August 1922, London: HMSO

Glennerster, H., 1991. 'Quasi-markets for education', *Economic Journal* September, 1268–76

Gray, D. and King, S., 1986. 'The Youth Training Scheme: the First Three Years', Research and Development No. 35, Manpower Services Commission, Moorfoot, Sheffield

Hart, P. E., 1988. *Youth Unemployment in Great Britain*, The National Institute of Economic and Social Research Occasional Paper 43, Cambridge: Cambridge University Press

Health Services, various dates. Journal of the Confederation of Health Service Employees (COHSE), various issues

Helsby, G., 1989. 'Central control and grassroots creativity: The paradox at the heart of TVEI', in Harrison, A. and Gretton, J. (eds), *Education and Training UK 1989: An Economic, Social and Policy Audit*, Newbury: Policy Journals

Higher Technological Education: Report of a Special Committee (Percy Committee Report), 1945. London: HMSO

Historical Statistics 1960–90, 1992. OECD Economic Outlook, Paris: OECD

HMI, 1991. *Technical and Vocational Educational Initiative* (TVEI), England and Wales 1983–90, London: HMSO

1992a. *Technology - Key Stages 1, 2, and 3*, June, London: HMSO

1992b. *Technology for Ages 5 to 16*, London: Department of Education

Industrial Training: Government Proposals, 1962. Government White Paper, Cmnd. 1892, London: HMSO

Jones, I., 1988. 'An evaluation of YTS', *Oxford Review of Economic Policy* 4(3), 54–71

Junankar, P. N. (ed.), 1987. *From School to Unemployment? The Labour Market for Young People*, London: Macmillan

Katz, E. and Ziderman, A., 1990. 'Investment in general training: the role of information and labour mobility', *Economic Journal* December, 1147–58

Kiker, B. F., 1966. 'The historical roots of the concept of human capital', *Journal of Political Economy* 74, 481–99

(ed.), 1971. *Investment in Human Capital*, Columbia, South Carolina: South Carolina Press

Labour Force Quarterly Bulletin, 1992. Employment Department, September

Labour Force Survey, various dates. Employment Department

Labour Force Survey, Historical Supplement, 1993. London: Government Statistical Service

Labour Market Quarterly Report, various dates. Sheffield: Employment Department

Lalonde, R. J., 1986. 'Evaluating the econometric evaluations of training programs with experimental data', *American Economic Review* 76, 604–20

Lasko, R., 1978. 'The work experience programme', *Department of Employment Gazette* March, 294-7

Le Grand, J., 1989. 'Markets, welfare and equality', in Le Grand, J. and Estrin, S. (eds), *Market Socialism*, Oxford: Clarendon Press

1991. 'Quasi-markets and social policy', *Economic Journal* September, 1256–67

Lee, D., Marsden, D., Rickman, P. and Duncombe, J., 1990. *Scheming for Youth: A Study of YTS in the Enterprise Culture*, Milton Keynes: Open University Press

Lees, D. and Chiplin, B., 1970. 'The economics of industrial training', *Lloyds Bank Review* April, 29–41

Liesner, T., 1985. *Economic Statistics 1900–1983*, London: Economist Publications

Lindley, R., 1986. 'Labour demand: micro-economic aspects of state intervention', in Hart, P. E. (ed.), *Unemployment and Labour Market Policies*, London: Gower

Luck, A., 1991. 'The TVEI revolution' *Employment Gazette* October, 543–8

Maddison, A., 1972. 'Explaining economic growth', *Banca Nazionale del Lavoro Quarterly Review* 102, September, 3–54

Main, B. G. M. and Shelly, M. A., 1990. 'The effectiveness of the Youth Training Scheme as a manpower policy', *Economica* 57, November, 495–514

Manpower Services Commission, 1981. *A New Training Initiative*, Sheffield: MSC

Manpower Services Commission Report for 1982/83, 1983. Sheffield: MSC

Marsden, D. W., 1990. 'Institutions and labour mobility: occupational and internal labour markets in Britain, France, Italy and West Germany', in Brunetta, R.

and Dell' Arringa, C. (eds), *Markets, Institutions and Cooperation: Labour relations and economic performance*, London: Macmillan

Marsden, D. and Ryan, P., 1988. 'Apprenticeship and Labour Market Structure: UK Youth Unemployment and Training in Comparative Context', paper presented to OECD Symposium on Innovations in Apprenticeship and Training, Paris, November

1989. 'Employment and training of young people: have the government misunderstood the labour market?', in Harrison, A. and Gretton, J. (eds), *Education and Training UK 1989: An Economic, Social and Policy Audit*, Newbury, Berkshire: Policy Journals

Marshall, A., 1920. *Principles of Economics*, Eighth Edition, [first published 1890], London: Macmillan

Mason, G., Prais, S. J., and van Ark, B., 1992. 'Vocational education and productivity in the Netherlands and Britain', *National Institute Economic Review* 140, May, 45–63

Metcalf, D., 1982a. *Alternatives to Unemployment: Special Employment Measures in Britain*, London: Policy Studies Institute

1982b. 'Special employment measures: an analysis of wage subsidies, youth schemes and worksharing', *Midland Bank Review* Autumn/Winter, 9–21

Mincer, J., 1962. 'On-the-job training: costs, returns and some implications', *Journal of Political Economy* 70, Supplement, 50–79

Ministry of Labour Gazette, various dates.

Ministry of Labour Report, 1923. Ministry of Labour, London: HMSO

1924. Ministry of Labour, London: HMSO

1925. Ministry of Labour, London: HMSO

More, C., 1980. *Skill and the English Working Class*, London: Croom Helm

NATFHE Journal, various dates. Journal of the National Association of Teachers in Further and Higher Education, various issues

National Foundation for Educational Research (NFER), 1992. *The Impact of Compact 1990–91*, Nottingham: TVEI Enquiry Point

National Population Projections 1991-based, 1993. Series PP2, No. 18, London: Office of Population Census and Surveys

Nicholson, J. S., 1891. 'The living capital of the United Kingdom', *Economic Journal* March, 95–107

NUPE, 1981. *Report of the National Conference*, London: National Union of Public Employees

1983. *Report of the National Conference*, London: National Union of Public Employees

NUPE Journal, various dates. Journal of the National Union of Public Employees, various issues

Oatey, M., 1970. 'The economics of training with respect to the firm', *British Journal of Industrial Relations* 8(1), 1–21

OECD, 1980. *Youth Unemployment: The Causes and Consequences*, Paris: OECD

1986. 'The youth problem: age or generation crowding', *Employment Outlook*, 106–27

OPCS Monitor PP1 and PP2, 94/1. London: Office of Population Censuses and Survey

Opie, A., 1991. 'Compact storms the inner cities', *Employment Gazette* November, 597

Orchard, D. W. J., 1970. 'DEP direct training services', *Employment and Productivity Gazette* October, 856–61

Oulton, N. and O'Mahony, M., 1994. *Productivity and Growth. A Study of British Industry 1954–86*, NIESR Occasional Papers 46, Cambridge: Cambridge University Press

Parker, H. M. D., 1957. *Manpower: A Study of Wartime Policy and Administration*, London: HMSO

Perry, P. J. C., 1976. *The Evolution of British Manpower Policy*, London: British Association for Commercial and Industrial Education

Petty, W., 1899. *The Economic Writings of Sir William Petty*, [first published 1691], edited by Hull, C. R., Cambridge: Cambridge University Press

Prais, S. J., 1993. 'Economic Performance and Education: The Nature of Britain's Deficiencies', Keynes Lecture on Economics, The British Academy

Prais, S. J. and Beadle, E., 1991. *Pre-vocational Schooling in Europe Today*, NIESR Report, New Series No. 1, October, London: National Institute for Economic and Social Research

Prest, A. R., 1976. 'The economic rationale of subsidies to industry', in Whiting, A. (ed.), *The Economics of Industrial Subsidies*, London: HMSO

Raffe, D., 1987. 'Small expectations: the first year of the youth training scheme', in Junankar, P. N. (ed.), *From School to Unemployment*, London: Macmillan

　1988. 'Going with the grain: youth training in transition', in Brown, S. (ed.), *Education in Transition*, Edinburgh: Scottish Council for Research in Education

　1989. 'The Transition from YTS to Work: Content, Context and the External Labour Market', paper presented to the Annual Conference of the British Sociological Association, Plymouth, March

Rainbird, H., 1990. *Training Matters: Union Perspectives on Industrial Restructuring and Training*, Oxford: Blackwell

Red Tape, various dates. Journal of the Civil and Public Services Association, various issues

Report of the Central Advisory Council for Education, 15–18. England (Crowther Report), 1959-60. London: HMSO

Report of the Commissioners Appointed to Inquire into the State of Popular Education in England (Newcastle Report), 1861. London: Eyre and Spottiswoode

Report of the Committee on Education and Industry (England and Wales) (Malcolm Report), 1928. London: HMSO

Report of the Committee on Industry and Trade (Balfour Report), 1928–1929. Cmnd. 3282, Parliamentary Papers, London: HMSO

Report of the Committee on the Juvenile Employment Service (Ince Committee Report), 1945. London: HMSO

Report of the Committee on Manpower Needs (Wolfe Report), 1940. Ministry of

Labour, London, unpublished

Report of an Enquiry into Apprenticeship and Training for Skilled Occupations in Great Britain and Northern Ireland, 1925–26, 1928. London: Ministry of Labour, HMSO

Report of HM Commissioners Appointed to Inquire into the Revenues and Management of Certain Colleges and Schools (Clarendon Report), 1864. London: Eyre and Spottiswoode

Reports of the Royal Commission Appointed to Inquire into the Depression of Trade and Industry, 1886. Parliamentary Papers XXI–XXIII, London: HMSO and Eyre and Spottiswoode

Report of the Royal Commission on Scientific Instruction and the Advancement of Science (Devonshire Report), 1875. Parliamentary Papers XXVIII, London: HMSO and Eyre and Spottiswoode

Reports of the Royal Commission on Secondary Education (Bryce Commission), 1894–5. London: HMSO

Reports of the Royal Commission on Technical Instruction (Samuelson Reports), 1882–1884. London: HMSO

Review of Services for the Unemployed, 1981. Sheffield: Manpower Services Commission

'Review of training levy and grant schemes', 1969. *Department of Employment Gazette* March, 208–10

Ryan, P., 1984. 'The New Training Initiative after two years', *Lloyds Bank Review* April, 31–45

1991. 'Trade union policies towards the Youth Training Scheme in Great Britain', in Ryan, Garonna and Edwards (eds) 1991

1993. 'Trade Union Policies Towards the Youth Training Scheme: Patterns and Causes', mimeo, University of Cambridge, August

Ryan, P., Garonna, P. and Edwards, R. C. (eds), 1991. *The Problem of Youth: The Regulation of Youth Employment and Training in Advanced Economies*, Basingstoke: Macmillan

Sako, M. and Dore, R., 1986. 'How the Youth Training Scheme helps employers', *Employment Gazette* June, 195–204

Say, J. B., 1821. *Trait d'Economie Politique*, [first published 1803], translated by Princep, C. R., Boston: Wells and Lilly

Schools Enquiry Commission (Taunton Report), 1970. [First published 1867], Shannon, Ireland: Irish University Press

Scientific Manpower (Barlow Report), 1946. Cmnd. 6824, Parliamentary Papers XIV, London: HMSO

Secretary of State for Employment, 1990. Answer to Parliamentary Question on youth training put 20 February, *Employment Gazette* April, 227

Senior, N. W., 1939. *An Outline of the Science of Political Economy*, [first published 1836], New York: Fanan and Rinehart

Sheldrake, J. and Vickerstaff, S., 1987. *The History of Industrial Training in Britain*, Aldershot: Avebury

Sime, N., 1991. *Youth Cohort Study*, Sheffield University Research and Development No. 67, Youth Cohort Series No. 18, Sheffield: Employment Department

Skills and Enterprise Network, 1994. *Labour Market and Skills Trends, 1994/95,* Nottingham

Sly, F., 1993. *Employment Gazette* July, 307–312

Smith, A., 1976. *An Inquiry into the Nature and Causes of the Wealth of Nations,* [first published 1776], Cannan, E. (ed.), Chicago: University of Chicago Press

Smith, E., 1986. 'A fair deal for all – the New Workers Scheme', *Employment Gazette* November, 449-51

Smithers, A. G., 1993. *All our Futures: Britain's Education Revolution,* London: Broadcasting Support Services

Smithers, A. and Robinson, P., 1992. *Technology in the National Curriculum: Getting it Right,* London: Engineering Council

   1993. *Changing Colleges: Further Education in the Market Place,* London: The Council for Industry and Higher Education

Solow, R. M., 1957. 'Technical changes and the aggregate production function', *Review of Economics and Statistics* 39, 312–20

   1959. 'Investment and economic growth: some comments', *Productivity Measurement Review* 19, 62–8

Stevens, M., 1994a. 'Labour contracts and efficiency in on-the-job training', *Economic Journal* March, 408–419

   1994b. 'An investment model for the supply of training by employers', *Economic Journal* May, 556–70

Swann, B. and Turnbull, M., 1978. *Records of Interest to Social Scientists, 1919–39: Employment and Unemployment,* London: HMSO

Tavernier, G., 1968. 'Small firms versus the Industrial Training Act', *Personnel and Training Management* January, 18

Technical Education, 1956. Government White Paper, Cmnd. 9703, London: HMSO

Training and Education Bulletin, 1968. Supplement, London: CBI

Training for the Future – A Plan for Discussion, 1972. London: HMSO

Training for Jobs, 1984. Government White Paper, Cmnd. 9135, London: HMSO

Training for Skill: Recruitment and Training of Young Workers in Industry (Carr Report), 1958. Report by a sub-committee of the National Joint Advisory Council, London: HMSO

Training Service Agency: A Five-year Plan, 1974. Sheffield: Manpower Services Agency

Training Statistics, 1994 and earlier years. Employment Department, London: HMSO

Trevelyan, G. M., 1948. *English Social History,* London: Longman, Green

TUC, 1977. *Report of the 109th Annual Trades Union Congress,* London: TUC

   1978. *Report of the 110th Annual Trades Union Congress,* London: TUC

   1981. *Report of the 113th Annual Trades Union Congress,* London: TUC

   1982. *Report of the 114th Annual Trades Union Congress,* London: TUC

   1983. *TUC Handbook on the MSC's Youth Training Scheme,* London: TUC

   1984. *Report of the 116th Annual Trades Union Congress,* London: TUC

1985. *Report of the 117th Annual Trades Union Congress*, London: TUC

1986. *Report of the 118th Annual Trades Union Congress*, London: TUC

1987. *Report of the 119th Annual Trades Union Congress*, London: TUC

1989. *Report of the 121st Annual Trades Union Congress*, London: TUC

1991. *Report of the 123rd Annual Trades Union Congress*, London: TUC

1992. *Report of the 124th Annual Trades Union Congress*, London: TUC

Under-Secretary of State for Employment, 1981. Answer to Parliamentary Question on short time working, *Employment Gazette* December, 536

United Kingdom National Accounts, 1992. The CSO Blue Book, 1992 Edition, London: HMSO

von Thünen, J. H., 1875. *Der Isolierte Staat*, translated by Hoselitz, B. F., Chicago: University of Chicago Press

Walras, L., 1954. *Elements of Pure Economics*, [first published in two parts in 1874 and 1877], translated by Jaffé, W., London: Allen and Unwin

Wells, W., 1983. *The Relative Pay and Employment of Young People*, Research Paper 42, London: Department of Employment

Whitley, J. D. and Wilson, R. A., 1983 'The macroeconomic merits of a marginal wage subsidy', *Economic Journal* December, 862–80

Wilson, R. A., 1993. *Review of the Economy and Employment: Occupational Assessment*, 1992/93, Institute for Employment Research, University of Warwick

Working Together – Education and Training, 1986. Government White Paper, Cmnd. 9823, London: HMSO

YT Follow-up Survey, various dates. Sheffield: Employment Department

YTS Leaver Survey, various dates. Sheffield: MSC and Employment Department

YTS Management Information System, various dates. London: Department of Employment

Index